The Neighborhood Bakeshop

Also by Jill Van Cleave

Icing the Cake

Big, Soft, Chewy Cookies

The Neighborhood Bakeshop

Recipes and Reminiscences of
America's Favorite Bakery Treats

Jill Van Cleave

William Morrow and Company, Inc.
New York

It is the policy of William Morrow and Company, Inc., and its imprints and affiliates, recognizing the importance of preserving what has been written, to print the books we publish on acid-free paper, and we exert our best efforts to that end.

Library of Congress Cataloging-in-Publication Data

Van Cleave, Jill.
    The neighborhood bakeshop : recipes and reminiscences of
America's favorite bakery treats / by Jill Van Cleave.
        p.   cm.
    Includes index.
    ISBN 0-688-14893-X
    1. Baking. 2. Desserts. I. Title.
TX765.V36 1997
641.8' 15—dc21

                                                                97-11145
                                                                CIP

Printed in the United States of America

First Edition

    2   3   4   5   6   7   8   9   10

BOOK DESIGN BY RACHAEL MCBREARTY—MADHOUSE PRODUCTIONS

www.williammorrow.com

For Janet and Nicole foremost,
and to all the bakers mentioned within these pages,
who are dedicated to their life's work
without thought of compromise

Acknowledgments

A mixing bowl of thanks goes to:

My colleagues Barry Bluestein and Kevin Morrissey for their superb conceptual and editorial guidance and constant support.

My editor Naomi Glikman for her enthusiastic work and eye for detail, as well as Pam Hoenig and her colleagues at William Morrow who labored behind-the-scenes to produce this book.

Kathleen Hackett for believing in the project from the beginning.

Friends, family, and professional acquaintances who assisted with bakery contacts, city tours, personal stories, obtaining samples or tasting my work-in-progress, such as Jean Anderson, Betsey and Johnny Apple, Bernie Arnold, Archie Arpiarian, Julie and Tubby Bacon, Fran Bigelow, Liz Clark, Grace Colucci, Elaine Corn, Heidi Haughy Cusick, Cate Erickson, Judy and Joe Fell, the Georgulas family, Maida Heatter, Jean Joho, Joy Keefer, Barbara Kuck, Emeril Lagasse, Donna Lee, Chris Lindsay, Mario Martinoli, Esther Moore, Neil O'Donnell, Gail Perrin, Ina Pinkney, Rhonda Purwin, Steven Raichlen, Jon Rowley, Suzanne and Stuart Sanders, David SooHoo, Terry Steeves, Jo Terlato, James Verville, my mother and the Van Cleave clan, my loving husband and his family.

Contents

Introduction

Food memories are powerful ones that evoke strong responses years later. Few of these recollections make us feel as good as those associated with the bakeshops that dotted the neighborhoods of our youth.

Our favorite bakery remembrance may be of a cakelike cookie topped with cool white fondant on one half and rich chocolate icing on the other. Maybe it's the mouth-watering taste of a frosted seven-layer cake filled with creamy lemon curd. Perhaps it's a far-from-ordinary chocolate cake filled and frosted with dark chocolate pudding and decorated with cake crumbs. Whether the pastry was a flaky turnover encasing a soft filling of apples and raisins or an Italian bun bursting with custard, the first bite was a defining moment of pleasure.

Many of these bakeries proudly proclaimed the ethnic origins of their founders and most were family affairs; those still on the scene often are run by third- and fourth-generation owners. They were a staple in the social life of the community—serving up treats that marked special occasions and often were ritual parts of celebratory meals. Holidays at the corner bakery were a heavenly time filled with everything from egg-enriched yeast breads loaded with fruit and nuts to elaborately decorated cakes and cookies.

Local bakeries shared in the daily lives of their customers. Staff remembered babies' names and birthdays, they asked about your parents, they recalled the water damage you had during the big rains last spring, and they always gave your child a cookie.

The best of the bakeshops have always mirrored the personalities of their passionate and oftentimes colorful owners. Defying normal conventions, Ciro Pasciuto, a Seattle bakeshop owner, interviews his wholesale clients before deciding whether or not to sell them his breads. He asks chefs how they cut bread, where they store it, and what they serve it in—besides, he "only bakes for nice people."

And then there's Aldo Maiorana, a baker, cook, and philosopher who insists that visitors to his Long Island "salon" smell and feel, as well as taste, his food. Aldo is more than a baker to his customers; he is a friend who teaches them about life.

Sadly, storefront bakeries are disappearing from the landscape of late twentieth-century America, their wonderful bounty but a passionate memory in many communities. The craftsmen who toiled all night, lovingly turning and twisting dough into fragrant, personalized creations, are a dying breed, their large and careworn hands replaced by machines.

Constantly rising costs of premium ingredients, packaging, skilled labor, and facility maintenance have led to closure of many independent operations no longer able to compete with high-volume commercial operations. Once-thriving urban bakeshops have watched the children and grandchildren of their loyal clientele migrate to the suburbs. Their rural counterparts confront a dwindling small-town customer base, difficulties in recruiting bakers, and the economic realities of staffing in an age when the labor pool is no longer made up of farm wives looking for pin money.

The survivors among the bakeshops of our youth, to say nothing of the courageous newcomers, have carved out niches for themselves. Some offer specialty items and ethnic delicacies not readily available elsewhere; others sell intricate handmade pastries that just can't be duplicated in an automated setting. They pursue the tourist trade, offer their goods by mail order, and open cafes.

Sometimes these independents benefit from the idiosyncrasies of the local market. Accustomed to the diminishing bakery scene in the Midwest and Northeast, I was astounded by the number of thriving bakeshops in the Pacific Northwest. Supermarkets in the Northwest are customers rather than competitors, using prominently labeled goods from neighborhood bakeshops to lure savvy shoppers.

This book celebrates the legacy of the neighborhood bakeshop, which I had the privilege of being a part of during the years I managed a dessert bakery in Chicago. It is a tribute to those shops whose goods we so enjoy today and an homage to those who made the treats of our childhood. (See the Mail Order Source Guide regarding bakeries profiled in the book that ship their products.)

Developing the recipes in this collection was a joyful if at times painstaking act of re-creating. Many were constructed from the recollections of family and friends of bakeries now long gone.

Others are my attempts to replicate current bakery offerings. (Professional bakers often are reluctant to divulge their recipes, a position I can understand and respect.) Indeed, one of my greatest pleasures was trying to duplicate other bakers' concepts. I often came very close to the original and sometimes even improved on taste or texture a bit, since I was striving to perfect a single item rather than to produce a commercial yield. In other instances, I intentionally took a concept in my own interpretive direction. Even in those cases where bakers graciously shared their recipes, considerable tinkering in formula or methodology was necessary to convert the recipe for the home baker. For instance, I needed to create a yield of a loaf or two to replace the 100-loaf yield with which I invariably started.

In re-creating neighborhood bakeshop specialties, my goal has been to enable you to bake at home the goods that have provided many people with so much joy for so long!

The Neighborhood Bakeshop

ONE

Yeast-Raised Breads and Rolls

The story of the hardworking professionals who bake our bread is one of long hours and physical toil. Bakers work when the rest of us sleep. They tend to fiercely hot ovens that require skillful maneuvering and precise timing. At home, we have the luxury of making just a loaf or two when the urge strikes and we can do so in a relatively leisurely fashion. Nonetheless, we can share in the satisfaction of producing the most basic and nourishing of foodstuffs from scratch.

Tips and Techniques

Ingredients

- Most of my bread doughs are made with unbleached all-purpose flour or with bread flour when a higher gluten content is required. In a few recipes, I use a rye or whole wheat flour. In cases where a more exotic flour is called for, such as clear flour or baker's patent flour (see Mail Order Source Guide), I have tried to suggest acceptable substitutions that are more readily available.

- Active dry yeast can be purchased in bulk or in $^1/_4$-ounce ($2^1/_2$-teaspoon) envelopes. Know that if you use only a portion of an envelope, the remainder can be stored in the refrigerator for future use. Cake yeast, also called compressed yeast, is another option; a $^1/_2$-ounce yeast cake is equivalent to one $^1/_4$-ounce envelope of granules. Although quick-rising yeast can be substituted, it offers no advantage; the longer the dough ferments, the more flavorful the bread will be.

- Use vegetable oil cooking sprays to grease the bowls in which you place dough to rise, the plastic wrap with which you cover loaves and rolls during the last rise prior to baking, and the pans for baking.

Preparation and Baking

To proof the yeast, dissolve active dry granules in lukewarm water. The water liquefies the dry yeast, which activates the dormant yeast culture. As the yeast "wakes up," you will see signs of activity in the bowl and tiny bubbles will begin to break the surface of the mixture. If you suspect the yeast is not bubbling sufficiently, sprinkle a little sugar into the water and wait a few extra minutes. Never add salt when proofing yeast—it simply won't work.

To mix the dough, I recommend using a stationary electric mixer fitted with the flat paddle attachment. You can also mix dough in an oversize bowl by stirring vigorously with a long wooden spoon.

To knead the dough, you will have much more control if you take a hands-on approach. The exception is sourdough, which is very wet and difficult to handle, and is best kneaded in a stationary mixer fitted with the dough hook. The visual cues in other recipes, written for kneading by hand, will help you determine when just enough flour has been added and when the dough has been kneaded to the desired texture. Don't worry about kneading too much—it's virtually impossible to do so by hand.

Sometimes it is desirable to interrupt the rising process (a technique bakers refer to as "retarding the dough") to accommodate your schedule. This is accomplished by chilling a dough or a sponge starter (a fermented flour, water, and yeast mixture that adds character to the bread) in the refrigerator, which significantly slows down the rise. You could, for example, make a sponge starter, refrigerate it overnight, and resume the recipe the next day after allowing the sponge to come back to room temperature.

It is best to bake only one pan of bread at a time. For recipes that yield multiple loaves too large to fit on a single baking sheet, you will need to bake the loaves sequentially or use two ovens. To bake only one loaf at a time, place half of the dough back into the bowl after dividing it, cover again, and refrigerate. If you wish to bake the second loaf the same day, prepare it for the oven when the first loaf is baking, extending the second rise by fifteen minutes so that the dough can return to room temperature. You can also leave the dough in the refrigerator overnight, allowing two to three hours for it to come back to room temperature before proceeding with the shaping and the second rise.

Always bake bread loaves in the middle of the oven. Baking stones produce crustier breads, much like those baked in brick ovens. Made of unglazed ceramic, baking stones come in a variety of sizes, some nearly as large as the oven rack upon which they are placed. They are available in cookware stores or through mail order catalogs.

Storage

Store baked breads at room temperature. Wrapped in parchment paper or aluminum foil and placed inside a brown paper bag, crusty loaves will keep for up to two days. Avoid plastic wrap, which will soften the crust.

Home-baked breads do not contain preservatives that would extend shelf life; slice loaves as needed to prevent them from turning stale prematurely. However, most breads freeze well, with the exception of Raisin Pumpernickel. Wrap in aluminum foil and place in a plastic freezer bag. Date for use within two months. Allow the bread to thaw completely at room temperature, then unwrap the bread and heat in a 325°F oven for ten to fifteen minutes.

To refresh day-old crusty loaves, sprinkle water over the top and place in a 325°F oven for ten minutes before serving.

Italian Baker's Loaf

The breads sold in an old-fashioned Italian bakery are usually baked from the same dough (made with only flour, water, yeast, and salt) formed into different shapes. The baguette is long and skinny, the Sicilian is an elongated braid, and the Italian loaf is a crusty oblong.

Italian bakers will tell you that the secret to fine taste and texture is in the fermentation, or aging, of the dough. They age their sponge starters up to 24 hours, a process that can be replicated at home in less time owing to differences in amount of yeast used, dough volume, and room temperature. Obtaining a superior crust without a professional's brick oven is a little trickier; I use a baking stone in my oven and spritz the loaves with water to boost moisture retention.

Although you can prepare this thick dough by hand, the process is more easily executed in a stationary electric mixer.

½ **teaspoon active dry yeast**

1¾ **cups lukewarm water (95° to 110°F)**

4 to 4¼ **cups unbleached all-purpose flour (preferably organic)**

½ **tablespoon salt**

Cornmeal, for sprinkling

1. Prepare the sponge starter by dissolving the yeast in ¼ cup of the lukewarm water in a large mixing bowl. Let the mixture proof until bubbly, about 5 minutes.

2. Stir in 1 additional cup of the water. Slowly add 2 cups of the flour, mixing well with each addition to form a wet, spongy dough. Cover the bowl tightly with plastic wrap and set aside at room temperature to rise for at least 8 and up to 12 hours. The starter will triple in volume, bubble, and recede slightly.

3. Transfer the starter to the bowl of a stationary electric mixer fitted with the flat paddle attachment. Turn on the mixer. Add the remaining ½ cup lukewarm water and the salt. Slowly add 2 cups more of the flour to form a soft dough.

4. Turn the dough out onto a work surface. Knead until the dough feels smooth, moist, and springy but still sticky to the touch, 7 to 10 minutes, sprinkling with only as much additional flour as is needed. Resist the temptation to add flour liberally; it is better for the dough to be too wet than too dry.

5. Transfer the dough to a large greased bowl and cover with plastic wrap. Set aside at room temperature to rise until doubled, about 2 hours.

6. Return the dough to a lightly floured work surface and divide it in half. Quickly shape each half into an oblong loaf roughly 10 × 3 inches. Place on a baking sheet that has been lined with parchment paper and sprinkled with cornmeal. Space each half 4 to 5 inches apart. Cover loosely with a towel or plastic and set aside to rise at room temperature for 45 minutes.

7. Preheat the oven to 425°F. Place a baking stone in the oven to preheat, if desired.

8. Spritz the dough with water. (Do not make cuts into the top.) Set a baking sheet into the oven or slide a loaf and the parchment from a sheet onto the hot baking stone.

9. Bake for 5 minutes. Quickly open the oven door, spritz again with water, and close the oven. Continue to bake for about 30 minutes more, until golden brown and hollow sounding when tapped on the bottom. Place the bread on a wire rack to cool.

Yield: 2 loaves

The menu at La Panzanella Bakery in Seattle lists bread, rolls, and focaccia. "What kind of breads do you have?" I ask, eyeing some rustic, crusty, irregularly shaped loaves.

"Only one bread—Ciro's bread," is the direct answer. "It comes in loaves of different sizes or rolls, but it's all the same bread, sold by the pound."

Ciro Pasciuto is owner, baker, salesman, and resident philosopher of La Panzanella. Friends meet at his bakeshop, which looks like an indoor street scene from Gaeta—the neighborhood Ciro grew up in near Naples, Italy—complete with quarry tile floors and two large wooden farm tables with country kitchen chairs. Neighbors come regularly to sip espresso, lunch on *panini* (sandwiches) or *tiella* (stuffed bread), read the newspaper, and converse with Ciro in their native tongue. "In Italy, the home is for sleeping, but the neighborhood is where life is lived," he tells me.

Ciro does not follow recipes; and other than his baker's oven and a floor mixer, there is no equipment in sight. Fermentation is done in a separate room. "I add just a little yeast, and give the wild yeast that comes out in this humidity a chance to act upon the dough," he explains.

When I leave, Ciro hands me a plain brown bag filled with his bread, adding "Take this home and allow it to age for at least twelve hours. It will have more character after it gets used to the new surroundings."

Potato Bread

For a very long time, potato bread loaves have been staple items in neighbor-hood and small-town bakeries that cater largely to a blue-collar customer base.

Why? Potato bread is a mild-tasting, all-purpose loaf with a long shelf life. It is also quite tender, with a fine-grained texture that retains moisture. Consequently, it makes just about perfect lunchbox sandwiches. (The dough also makes lovely, light dinner rolls.)

This recipe uses potato flour—not to be confused with potato starch—instead of cooked potatoes. Potato flour is easy to use and produces a wonder-ful bread. For a boost in flavor, substitute a cup of water reserved from boil-ing potatoes for the water used to proof the yeast and make the dough. Look for the barley malt syrup in your local health food store.

1 tablespoon active dry yeast

1 cup lukewarm water (95° to 110°F)

½ cup lukewarm milk (95° to 110°F)

2 tablespoons sugar

2 teaspoons salt

2 teaspoons barley malt syrup or honey

⅓ cup potato flour

2 tablespoons unsalted butter or lard, at room temperature

¼ cup rye flour

2¾ to 3 cups bread flour (preferably high-gluten)

1 egg white, mixed with 1 tablespoon water

1. Dissolve the yeast in ½ cup of the luke-warm water in a small bowl. Let proof until bubbly, about 5 minutes.

2. Meanwhile, combine the heated milk, sugar, salt, barley malt syrup or honey, potato flour, butter, and the remaining ½ cup water in a large mixing bowl. Whisk until the ingredients are dissolved and smoothly blended. Add the yeast mixture, the rye flour, and 1 cup of the bread flour, whisking until smooth. Using a wooden spoon, stir in an additional 1½ cups bread flour, a little at a time.

3. Turn the dough out onto a lightly floured work surface and knead in as much of the remaining flour as is necessary to keep the dough from sticking to the surface. Continue to knead until the dough feels smooth and elastic but still a little tacky to the touch, 7 to 10 minutes. Transfer to a greased bowl, cover with plastic wrap, and set aside at room tem-perature until doubled, about 1 hour.

4. Punch the dough down to deflate it, cover the bowl again, and let the dough rise a second time, for 30 minutes.

5. Return the dough to a work surface. Shape it into 1 large oval loaf, or divide the dough and shape into 2 round loaves or 16 round rolls. Place on a baking sheet that has been greased or lined with parchment paper. Cover loosely with plastic wrap and set aside at room temperature for 30 minutes.

6. Preheat the oven to 400°F if baking dinner rolls or 2 rounds, or to 375°F for the single large loaf.

7. Brush the dough with the egg white and water wash. Cut shallow slashes in the dough with the tip of a sharp knife or a razor (1 slash across the top of each roll, 1 or 2 slashes across each round, or 2 to 3 slashes in the top of a large loaf).

8. Bake until well browned and hollow sounding when tapped on the bottom, about 20 minutes for rolls, 30 minutes for 2 small rounds, or 40 to 45 minutes for a single large loaf. Remove the bread to wire racks to cool.

Yield: 1 large oval loaf, 2 small round loaves, or 16 dinner rolls

Kimelweck Rolls

What exactly is a Kimelweck Roll? It's a hard roll, more specifically a crusty kaiser roll, sprinkled with caraway and coarse salt instead of the more familiar poppy seed topping. Shape the dough into a loaf to bake Vienna bread or shape it into thin ropes for salt and pepper sticks, a great snack in lieu of pretzels.

2¹/₂ teaspoons (1 envelope) active dry yeast

1 cup lukewarm water (95° to 110°F)

2 tablespoons vegetable oil

1 tablespoon sugar

¹/₂ tablespoon salt

1 teaspoon barley malt syrup or honey

2 large egg whites

3 to 3¹/₄ cups bread flour (preferably high-gluten)

1 tablespoon water

Coarse sea salt crystals and caraway seeds, for sprinkling

1. Sprinkle the yeast over ¹/₄ cup of the lukewarm water in a small bowl. Set aside to proof until bubbly, about 5 minutes.

2. Combine the remaining ³/₄ cup lukewarm water, the oil, sugar, salt, barley malt syrup or honey, and 1 egg white in a large mixing bowl. Stir to dissolve the sugar. Add 1¹/₂ cups of the flour and mix until smooth. Add the yeast solution and slowly stir in an additional 1¹/₂ cups of the flour.

3. Turn the dough out onto a lightly floured work surface. Knead the dough for 5 to 7 minutes, until smooth and elastic but still slightly tacky to the touch, adding only as much additional flour as necessary to keep the dough from sticking. Transfer to a large greased bowl, cover with plastic wrap, and set aside at room temperature to rise until doubled, about 1 hour.

4. Punch the dough down, cover the bowl again, and let the dough rise a second time, for about 30 minutes.

5. Return the dough to the work surface and divide it into 8 equal pieces. Shape each piece into a smooth round, then flatten the rounds slightly. Place on a parchment-lined or greased baking sheet, well spaced to allow spreading. Cover loosely with a towel and set aside at room temperature for 30 minutes.

6. Preheat the oven to 425°F.

7. Combine the remaining egg white and the 1 tablespoon water in a small dish and blend.

8. Brush the rolls lightly with the egg white wash. Using the tip of a sharp knife or a razor, cut 4 crescent-shaped slits into each roll, radiating out from the center. Sprinkle the rolls with the coarse salt and caraway seeds and spritz with water.

9. Bake for 5 minutes. Quickly open the oven door, spritz the rolls again with water, and close the oven. Bake the rolls for about 20 minutes more, until browned and crisp. Cool the rolls on wire racks.

Yield: 8 sandwich rolls

For a Vienna Loaf, follow the recipe directions for Kimelweck Rolls with the following exceptions: After the second rise, divide the dough in half and shape each half into an oval with tapered ends. After the final rise, apply the egg wash and cut a 1/2-inch-deep slit down the top of each loaf; omit the salt and caraway sprinkle, if desired. Bake in a 400°F oven, baking for about 30 minutes more after the second spritz with water (for a total of 35 minutes).

For Salt and Pepper Sticks, follow the recipe directions with the following exceptions: Omit the second rise. Divide the dough into 13 equal pieces, roll each piece out into a 12-inch rope of even thickness, and space the ropes 1 1/2 inches apart on the prepared baking sheet. After the final rise, apply the egg wash, but do not make any cuts into the dough; sprinkle with coarse sea salt crystals and coarsely ground or cracked black pepper, instead of with salt crystals and caraway seeds. (I like to vary the topping by sprinkling some with salt, some with pepper, and some with a little of both.) Do not spritz with water. Bake for about 18 minutes.

---

still remember my first taste of "beef on weck." It was lunchtime in a very crowded Buffalo, New York, tavern. As instructed by a local, I ordered the specialty of the house: a stein of beer on tap and beef on weck with hot horseradish. I watched the carver shave fine slices of rare roasted beef from an enormous steamship round, pile it onto the bottom of a kimelweck roll, and spoon with beef juices that soaked into the soft insides of the roll. At the table, I applied horseradish and covered my sandwich with the top of the hard-crusted roll, which was amply sprinkled with coarse salt and caraway seeds. It was love at first bite.

Kaufman's is the biggest of the bakeries in Buffalo that still make kimelweck rolls. The owner, Jay Freedman, can personally recall at least forty years of baking "wecks" for the hardy beef on weck lunch so favored by generations of the town's German and Polish communities. It's never faded as a lunchtime tradition.

Onion Pletzel

Pletzel is not a funny way of saying pretzel—it's a term used to refer to onion board, a type of flatbread. I think of Pletzel as a superior pizza, one with a consistency more like that of a bagel. Pletzel dough obtains its characteristic chew from the same bread flour used for bagel and bialy dough. Onions and poppy seeds are the classic Pletzel topping.

^{1}/3 cup minced dried onions

^{1}/3 cup cool water

2 teaspoons vegetable oil

2 teaspoons poppy seeds

2^1/2 teaspoons sea salt

1 tablespoon active dry yeast

^{1}/3 cup plus ^{3}/4 cup lukewarm water
   (95° to 110°F)

2^1/2 teaspoons sugar

2^1/2 cups plus 2 tablespoons bread flour
   (preferably high-gluten)

Starch Wash

^{1}/2 cup water

^{1}/2 teaspoon cornstarch

1. Combine the onions and cool water in a small bowl. Let the onions rehydrate for about 1 hour.

2. Once the onions have absorbed all the water, stir in the oil, poppy seeds, and ^{1}/2 teaspoon of the salt. Cover the topping and set aside until needed.

3. In another small bowl, dissolve the yeast in ^{1}/3 cup of the lukewarm water. Let the mixture proof until bubbly, about 5 minutes.

4. Meanwhile, combine the sugar and the remaining 2 teaspoons salt in a medium-size mixing bowl. Stir in the remaining ^{3}/4 cup lukewarm water to dissolve the sugar and salt. Add 1^1/2 cups of the flour, a little at a time. Mix in the yeast mixture, then continue to add 1 cup more of the flour in increments.

5. Sprinkle the remaining 2 tablespoons flour onto a work surface. Turn the dough out onto the work surface and knead the flour into the dough. Continue to knead for about 10 minutes, until the dough feels as smooth to the touch as well-worn saddle leather.

6. Transfer the dough to a greased bowl, cover with plastic wrap, and set aside at room temperature to rise until doubled, about 1 hour. Meanwhile, prepare the starch wash. Combine the water and cornstarch in a small saucepan. Bring to a boil, stirring to dissolve the cornstarch, and boil for 30 to 45 seconds. Remove from the heat and cool to room temperature.

7. Return the dough to a work surface. For 1 large Pletzel, leave it intact. For 4 small Pletzel, quarter the dough. Shape the dough, or each of the 4 pieces of dough, into a ball. Cover the dough loosely with plastic wrap and let it rest for 10 minutes.

8. Roll the large dough ball out into a 15 × 11-inch rectangle, 1/4 inch thick, or roll each of the 4 small dough balls into an 8-inch oval. (If the dough becomes too elastic to roll properly, let it rest for 5 minutes before continuing.) Transfer the large rectangle of dough to a single greased baking sheet, or 2 of the small ovals of dough to each of 2 greased sheets. Press the dough down gently onto the sheet to help maintain shape and prevent shrinkage owing to elasticity.

9. With your fingertips, make evenly spaced indentations over the surface (bakers call this "docking the dough"). Brush the dough with the starch wash, then sprinkle evenly with the onion topping, using one-fourth of the topping for each if making small oval Pletzel. Cover loosely with plastic wrap and set aside at room temperature for 30 minutes.

10. Preheat the oven to 425°F.

11. Bake for 15 to 17 minutes, until the Pletzel are browned and crisp.

12. Transfer the Pletzel to a wire rack to cool. Pletzel should be served warm or at room temperature.

Yield: 1 large or 4 small Pletzel

alking into the Flakowitz Bakeshop in Boca Raton, Florida, with its intoxicating aromas, is like walking into bakery heaven. Almost immediately, I was captivated by the sight of a huge stack of flatbreads.

"Pletzel," the saleswoman replied to my wide-eyed stare.

At Flakowitz, the Pletzel are baked in large sheet pans, stacked one atop the other for display, and then cut into more manageable quarters when purchased. I didn't even make it out of the store before consuming half of one.

Sour Rye Starter

(For Corn Rye or Marble Rye, and Raisin Pumpernickel)

A sour starter is the necessary first step in making any real rye bread, includ-ing the old-fashioned Corn Rye (page 16), Raisin Pumpernickel (page 18), and Marble Rye (page 20). The yeast mixture for the starter is set aside for 24 hours, then "fed" additional flour and water three times over the next day or two. This aging process results in a fermented dough that lends the loaves their distinctive sour taste. Cut the starter quantities in half, if desired.

For all 3 breads

2 tablespoons active dry yeast

²/₃ cup water, at room temperature

1 medium onion, peeled and quartered

1¹/₂ cups lukewarm water (95° to 110°F)

For Corn Rye or Marble Rye

4 cups light or white rye flour (see box)

1 tablespoon caraway seeds, finely ground

For Raisin Pumpernickel

4 cups medium rye flour

1. Combine the yeast and room temperature water in a medium-size bowl.

2. For the Corn Rye or Marble Rye, stir 1 cup of the light rye flour and the ground caraway seeds into the yeast mixture. For the Raisin Pumpernickel, stir in 1 cup of the medium rye flour. Blend the mixture to a thick paste.

3. Push the onion quarters into the paste. Cover with plastic wrap and poke several small holes into the plastic with the tip of a knife. Set the bowl aside at room temperature for 24 hours.

4. Remove and discard the pieces of onion and begin to feed the starter. For the first feeding, stir in ¹/₂ cup lukewarm water, then stir in 1 cup more of the light rye flour for Corn Rye or Marble Rye, or the medium rye flour for Raisin Pumpernickel. Stir the mix-ture until well blended. Cover the bowl again with the pierced plastic wrap and set aside at room temperature for at least 4 hours and as long as 12 hours.

5. For the second feeding, stir in ¹/₂ luke-warm water, then add 1 additional cup of the light rye flour or medium rye flour, depend-ing on the bread to be made, blending well. Cover the bowl as before and set aside again at room temperature for from 4 to 12 hours.

6. For the final feeding, add ¹/₂ cup luke-warm water and the remaining 1 cup light or medium rye flour. Mix until well blended, cover, and set aside at room temperature for 4 to 12 hours. The starter is now ready to use.

7. To store the starter for up to 3 days, after which it will become dormant, cover the bowl with a clean sheet of plastic wrap and refrigerate until ready to use. Allow the starter to warm to room temperature before mixing it into bread dough.

Yield: 2½ to 3 cups

This basic starter recipe has two versions. For Corn Rye (page 16), or Marble Rye (page 20), use light rye flour, sometimes called white rye flour. See the Mail Order Source Guide for specialty suppliers if you can't find it in your supermarket. For Raisin Pumpernickel (page 18), use medium rye flour or rye flour, as it is often labeled in health food stores.

At Alter's Bakery in North Tarrytown, New York, the bakers make their rye doughs using a sour starter that has been kept alive since 1929. The breads are then baked in a century-old coal-fired brick oven. Martin Schwartz, master baker and son of the bakery's founder, says his father didn't retire from baking until the age of seventy-eight. Now, at eighty-four, he still keeps busy with odd jobs around the bakery—and holds watch over his starter.

Corn Rye

Also called New York Rye, Corn Rye is the prized product of neighborhood bakeries in New York City and a few other cities with a sizable Eastern European Jewish population. It's not made from cornmeal. Rather, the name refers to the process of fermenting, or "corning," the sour starter, which provides the bread's telltale flavor and chewy texture.

1½ cups Sour Rye Starter (page 14)

1 cup lukewarm water (95° to 110°F)

1 tablespoon active dry yeast

1 tablespoon salt (preferably sea salt)

2 tablespoons caraway seeds

3 cups clear flour (see box)

Starch Wash

½ cup water

½ teaspoon cornstarch

1. Prepare the starter about 3 days in advance.

2. Pour ¼ cup of the lukewarm water into a large mixing bowl and sprinkle the yeast on top. Let proof until bubbly, about 5 minutes. Dissolve the salt in the remaining ¾ cup lukewarm water in a small bowl.

3. Blend the starter into the proofed yeast mixture. Add the salted water and caraway seeds. Add 2¾ cups of the flour, a little at a time, to produce a stiff dough.

4. Turn the dough out onto a lightly floured work surface and begin to knead in the remaining ¼ cup flour. Continue to knead

for 5 to 7 minutes, until the dough is elastic but still tacky to the touch, using only as much of the flour as needed.

5. Transfer the dough to a large greased bowl, cover with plastic wrap, and set aside at room temperature for 45 minutes. The dough will rise but not necessarily double in volume.

6. Line a baking sheet with parchment paper.

7. Return the dough to a work surface. Shape it into a smooth oval loaf and place seam side down on the prepared sheet. Cover loosely with plastic wrap and set aside at room temperature for 30 minutes.

8. Meanwhile, preheat the oven to 425°F. Place a baking stone into the oven to preheat, if desired.

9. Using a fork, poke numerous holes in the top of the dough (a procedure called stippling) or lightly slash the top in 3 places with the tip of a sharp knife. Spritz the dough with water. Set the sheet into the oven or slide the loaf and parchment from the sheet onto the hot baking stone.

10. Bake for 5 minutes. Quickly open the oven door, spritz the loaf again with water,

and close the oven. Continue to bake for about 35 minutes, until the loaf is browned and sounds hollow when tapped on the bottom.

11. While the bread is baking, prepare the starch wash. Combine the water and cornstarch in a small saucepan. Bring to a boil, stirring to dissolve the cornstarch, and boil for 30 to 45 seconds. Remove from the heat and cool to room temperature.

12. Brush the hot loaf with starch wash, then cool on a wire rack.

Yield: 1 loaf

Although light, or white, rye flour is used in the starter, clear flour is used to make the bread dough. A traditional rye bread ingredient, clear flour is a wheat flour with a high protein and ash content that lends a grainy consistency and grayish appearance. It can be obtained from specialty baking suppliers (see Mail Order Source Guide). You can substitute bread flour if necessary.

*A*corn rye is one of at least a dozen types of loaves baked daily for more than eighty years at Orwasher's on East 78th Street in Manhattan. Inside the bakery, a continuous rye starter is fed a diet of flour and water. The hand-shaped loaves are baked in the original hearth oven, rotated periodically from hot to cool spots to equalize the baking.

Raisin Pumpernickel

The bread is accurately named—it's not pumpernickel with raisins but, rather, raisins with pumpernickel! In some bakeries where this type of bread is sold by the pound, the heft of raisins per square inch is such that buying a pound yields about four slices. Raisin Pumpernickel is heavenly when toasted and spread with cream cheese.

¹/₂ cup Sour Rye Starter (page 14)

3 cups (about 1 pound) seedless raisins

2 cups hot tap water

¹/₂ cup plus 2 tablespoons lukewarm
   water (95° to 110°F)

1 tablespoon blackstrap molasses

1¹/₄ teaspoons salt

³/₄ teaspoon active dry yeast

¹/₄ cup pumpernickel flour
   (see Mail Order Source Guide)

¹/₄ cup stone-ground whole wheat flour

1¹/₄ cups clear flour (see page 17)

Yellow cornmeal, for sprinkling
   (optional)

Starch Wash

¹/₂ cup water

¹/₂ teaspoon cornstarch

1. Prepare the starter about 3 days in advance. In a medium-size bowl, soak the raisins in the hot water for 30 minutes. Drain the raisins; reserve the soaking liquid, if desired.

2. Place the starter in a large mixing bowl and set aside. In a measuring cup, combine ¹/₂ cup of the lukewarm water (or substitute ¹/₂ cup of the raisin soaking liquid), the molasses, and the salt. Stir to blend well. In a small dish, combine the remaining 2 tablespoons water with the yeast.

3. Add the molasses mixture to the starter in the mixing bowl. Stir to mix, then add the yeast mixture and blend. Add the pumpernickel flour and the whole wheat flour, blending well. Add 1 cup of the clear flour, a little at a time.

4. Turn the dough out onto a lightly floured work surface. Knead for about 5 minutes, until the dough feels elastic but still tacky to the touch, adding only as much of the remaining ¹/₄ cup clear flour as needed to keep the dough from sticking to the surface. Transfer the dough to a greased bowl, cover with plastic wrap, and set aside at room temperature to rise for 45 minutes.

5. While the dough rises, prepare the starch wash. Combine the water and cornstarch in a small saucepan. Bring to a boil, stirring to dissolve the cornstarch. Boil for 30 to 45 seconds, then remove from the heat and let cool to room temperature.

6. Line a baking sheet with parchment paper or grease it and sprinkle with yellow cornmeal.

7. Return the dough to a lightly floured work surface. Roll it out into a 10 × 18-inch rectangle. Brush with some of the starch wash. Cover the dough evenly and completely with the raisins. Starting with a short side, roll the dough up tightly around the raisins to form a log. Pinch the ends closed to seal and place the loaf onto the prepared sheet seam side down. Cover loosely with plastic wrap and set aside at room temperature for 30 minutes.

8. Preheat the oven to 400°F.

9. Spritz the dough with water. Bake for about 50 minutes, until very dark brown. Brush the hot loaf with starch wash, then cool the bread on a wire rack.

10. Use a serrated knife to cut slices.

Yield: 1 loaf

My colleague Barry Bluestein samples raisin pumpernickels from local bakeries in every city he visits. His favorite is made by the Diamond Bakery in Los Angeles. Barry describes it as a mass of plump dark raisins suspended in a thin web of good pumpernickel bread.

This recipe is the result of my efforts to make a similar loaf. How does it compare? A little too picture-perfect, with its neatly spiraled raisin filling, according to Barry, but the taste is right on target. He wants to make the recipe, which is the highest compliment I could receive.

Marble Rye

Unlike many earthy rye breads that can be as rustic in form as in texture, this loaf is a beautifully finished, swirled combination of rye and pumpernickel doughs.

Another specialty of Jewish bakeries, Marble Rye is my idea of a party bread. I like to cut thin slices into small pieces, smear them with crème frâiche, and add a layer of smoked salmon, a tiny dollop of caviar, snipped chives, then top with a grinding of coarse black pepper. And serve with iced vodka—straight up, please.

¾ **cup Sour Rye Starter (page 14)**

⅔ **cup lukewarm water (95° to 110°F)**

2 teaspoons salt

1 teaspoon honey

2 cups clear flour (see page 17)

Ingredients for pumpernickel dough (page 18), omitting the raisins and their soaking liquid

Starch Wash

½ **cup water**

½ **teaspoon cornstarch**

1. Prepare the starter about 3 days in advance.

2. Place the starter in a medium-size mixing bowl. In a measuring cup, combine the lukewarm water, salt, and honey, stirring to dissolve the salt. Add the mixture to the starter. Mix in 1¾ cups of the flour, a little at a time, to form a stiff dough.

3. Turn the dough out onto a lightly floured work surface. Knead for about 5 minutes, adding only as much of the remaining ¼ cup flour as necessary to produce an elastic dough still tacky to the touch.

4. Transfer the dough to a greased bowl, cover with plastic wrap, and set aside at room temperature to rise until doubled, about 1¼ hours.

5. Meanwhile, prepare the pumpernickel dough to the first rise and set it aside at room temperature to rise for 45 minutes.

6. Line a baking sheet with parchment paper.

7. Return both risen doughs to a work surface. Push each dough out into an 8-inch square. Place the pumpernickel dough on top of the rye dough and roll up the doughs together, tucking the ends underneath and shaping the combination into a round. With both hands, roll the round back and forth, flattening and shaping it into a smooth oval loaf. Place the loaf seam side down onto the prepared sheet, cover loosely with plastic wrap, and set aside at room temperature for 30 minutes.

8. Meanwhile, preheat the oven to 425°F. Place a baking stone into the oven to preheat, if desired.

9. Using the tip of a sharp knife, lightly slash the top of the dough in 3 places. Spritz the dough with water. Set the sheet into the oven or slide the loaf and parchment from the sheet onto the hot baking stone.

10. Bake for 5 minutes. Quickly open the oven door, spritz the loaf again with water, and close the oven. Continue to bake for about 40 minutes, until the loaf is browned and sounds hollow when tapped on the bottom.

11. While the bread is baking, prepare the starch wash. Combine the water and cornstarch in a small saucepan. Bring to a boil, stirring to dissolve the cornstarch, and boil for 30 to 45 seconds. Remove from the heat and cool to room temperature.

12. Brush the hot loaf with starch wash, then cool on a wire rack.

Yield: 1 large loaf

Marble Rye is the combination of two doughs. First prepare the longer-rising rye dough following the directions on these pages. Prepare the pumpernickel dough following the directions for Raisin Pumpernickel, omitting the raisins. (Remember that you will need a separate starter for each dough.) Return to this recipe for directions on combining and baking the loaf.

Buttercrust Bread

Buttercrust Bread is an extremely tender, very basic white bread. It makes a perfect accompaniment to the simple pot roast and meat loaf dinners that so many of us Heartlanders grew up on. After rising in the pan, the loaf is given a deep slash down the center to cradle the melted butter poured over the top before baking, lending a golden hue.

2 teaspoons active dry yeast

¼ cup lukewarm water (95° to 110°F)

1¼ cups buttermilk, at room temperature

3 tablespoons sugar

½ tablespoon salt

6 tablespoons unsalted butter, at room temperature

3½ cups unbleached all-purpose flour

1. In a small bowl, sprinkle the yeast over the water. Set aside to proof until bubbly, about 5 minutes.

2. In a large mixing bowl, combine the buttermilk, sugar, salt, and 3 tablespoons of the butter. Stir in the yeast mixture. Add 3¼ cups of the flour, a little at a time.

3. Turn the dough out onto a work surface and knead in the remaining ¼ cup flour, continuing to knead for 5 to 7 minutes, until the dough feels smooth and elastic. Transfer to a greased bowl, cover with plastic wrap, and set aside at room temperature to rise until doubled, 1 to 1½ hours.

4. Return the dough to a work surface. Push the dough out into a rectangle, roll it up, and pinch the ends to seal. Place the roll seam side down in a greased 9 × 5-inch loaf pan. Flatten the dough in the pan to fill it evenly. Cover loosely with plastic wrap and set aside at room temperature to rise until dough reaches the top of the pan, about 45 minutes.

5. Preheat the oven to 375°F.

6. Meanwhile, melt the remaining 3 tablespoons butter. Allow to cool a bit, but not to solidify. Cut a ½-inch-deep slash down the center of the risen loaf with the tip of a sharp knife or a razor blade. Drizzle the remaining melted butter into the crevice and over the top of the dough.

7. Bake for 35 to 40 minutes, until deep golden brown. (When unmolded, the loaf should sound hollow when tapped on the bottom.) Remove the bread to a wire rack to cool.

8. Cut thick slices to serve.

Yield: 1 large loaf

hicago chef John Hogan grew up in Lombard, Illinois, a quiet suburban community transformed into a garden spectacle of blooming lilac bushes every spring. Even the town's water tower is painted lavender in honor of its annual lilac festival and garden walk tours. John claims that, to this day, whenever he thinks of bread this buttercrust loaf from a local Lombard bakery comes instantly to mind—not surprisingly, it's made at the Lilac Pastry Shop on Main Street.

Wheat Walnut Bread

Stone-ground whole wheat flour, bread flour, toasted walnuts, honey, and sea salt are some of the quality ingredients that lend this hardy bread its character, while the slow-rising sponge starter is an important step in achieving the distinctive taste. I add a small amount of semolina for a slightly chewier than typical texture. This bread is a perfect match for any kind of cheese.

1 teaspoon active dry yeast

2 cups lukewarm water (95° to 110°F)

3 cups bread flour

1 tablespoon honey

1 tablespoon olive or walnut oil

1$^1/2$ cups stone-ground whole wheat flour

$^1/4$ cup semolina flour

2 teaspoons sea salt

1$^1/2$ cups coarsely chopped walnuts, toasted

$^1/2$ tablespoon butter

1. To prepare the sponge starter, dissolve $^1/2$ teaspoon of the yeast in 1 cup of the lukewarm water in a medium-size mixing bowl. Let proof until bubbly, about 5 minutes.

2. Mix in 1$^1/2$ cups of the bread flour until a smooth, thick batter forms. Cover the bowl with plastic wrap and set aside at room temperature to rise and bubble for 6 to 8 hours. The starter is now ready to use or can be refrigerated overnight.

3. Dissolve the remaining $^1/2$ teaspoon yeast in the remaining 1 cup lukewarm water in a

large mixing bowl. Set aside to proof for 5 minutes.

4. Add the sponge starter (brought back to room temperature, if refrigerated) to the proofed yeast. Stir in the honey and oil, then the whole wheat and semolina flours. Mix in the salt. Slowly add 1$^1/4$ cups of the remaining bread flour to form a stiff dough. Mix in the walnuts.

5. Turn the dough out onto a lightly floured work surface and knead in as much of the remaining $^1/4$ cup bread flour as necessary to keep the dough from sticking. Continue to knead until the dough feels smooth and elastic but still tacky to the touch, about 10 minutes. Transfer to a greased bowl, cover with plastic wrap, and set aside at room temperature to rise until doubled, about 2 hours.

6. Return the dough to a work surface and divide it in half. Shape each half into a round or oblong loaf and place on a greased or parchment-lined baking sheet spaced 4$^1/2$ inches apart. Cover loosely with plastic wrap and set aside to rise at room temperature until doubled, about 45 minutes.

7. Preheat the oven to 400°F.

8. Cut an X on the top of the round loaf or 3 slashes into the oblong loaf with the tip of a sharp knife or a razor blade. Spritz the dough with water.

9. Bake for 5 minutes. Quickly open the oven door, spritz again with water, and close the oven. Bake for 30 to 35 minutes more, until well browned and hollow sounding when tapped on the bottom.

10. While still hot, rub the bread with the butter to glaze the top and transfer to a wire rack to cool.

Yield: 2 loaves

Traveling on the "wine train"—the line that runs through the picturesque vineyards of the Napa Valley—one can see the shop-lined Main Street of St. Helena, site of the Model Bakery. You can return by car or bicycle for a visit, although in autumn (high tourist season for California's wine country), parking is hard to find and bicycles are lined up outside the windows of the welcoming bakery storefront.

The Model Bakery's brick ovens were built by Italian stonemasons in the early 1920s. Karen Mitchell purchased the bakery in 1984, refurbished the ovens, and rebuilt the business into a thriving neighborhood spot. Wheat walnut loaves are one of the eight daily hearth-baked breads at the Model Bakery.

Challah Turban

A traditional Jewish egg bread, challah is often braided. To celebrate Rosh Hashanah and other holidays, it is often formed into such fanciful shapes as a turban, which symbolizes the promise of the full year. It's best served within two days of baking; freeze half if you don't expect to finish it within that time. Challah also makes wonderful toast, French toast, and croutons.

2 teaspoons active dry yeast

³/₄ cup lukewarm water (95° to 110°F)

1 tablespoon plus ¹/₄ teaspoon sugar

¹/₂ tablespoon salt

4 tablespoons (¹/₂ stick) unsalted butter, at room temperature

3¹/₄ cups unbleached all-purpose flour

2 large eggs, plus 1 egg yolk

1 tablespoon milk

1. In a small bowl, dissolve the yeast in the lukewarm water. Set aside to proof until bubbly, about 5 minutes.

2. In a large mixing bowl, combine 1 tablespoon of the sugar, the salt, butter, and ¹/₂ cup of the flour. Mix to a paste. Stir in the yeast mixture, then 1¹/₂ cups more of the flour, mixing until smooth. Add the 2 whole eggs, one at a time, blending well with each addition. Slowly mix in the remaining 1¹/₄ cups flour to form a dough.

3. Turn the dough out onto a lightly floured surface and knead until it feels smooth, elastic, but still slightly tacky to the touch, about 5 minutes. Transfer to a greased bowl, cover with plastic wrap, and set aside at room temperature to rise until doubled, 1¹/₄ to 1¹/₂ hours.

4. Return the dough to a work surface. Push it into a 1-inch-thick rectangle, positioned with the long side facing you. Roll the dough into a cylinder, pinching the seam and the ends closed. Roll and stretch the cylinder into a smooth 18-inch rope with tapered ends. Loop 1 end to the center of the rope to form a circle and tuck the tip underneath. Continue to coil the dough upward in a beehive shape to fill in the circle, creating a domed spiral. Tuck the exposed end beneath the top coil and set the loaf on a greased baking sheet. Cover with a towel and set the pan aside at room temperature to rise for 45 minutes.

5. Preheat the oven to 375°F.

6. In a small dish, beat the egg yolk with the milk and the remaining ¹/₄ teaspoon sugar. Brush the loaf evenly with the egg yolk wash. Bake for about 35 minutes, until deep golden brown. Place the bread on a wire rack to cool.

Yield: 1 large loaf

At the dessert bakery I ran in Chicago, we made everything ourselves—except breads, which we purchased from specialty bakers. We tested many challahs from all the bread bakeries recommended to us, only to determine that no one else in town baked challah like Nicole Bergere of Nicole's Bakeshop. Each of her loaves came to us looking like a work of art—a perfectly shaped, towering, domed turban that simply sold itself. But the best part was the taste. Nicole's challah, crafted lovingly by hand, is undeniably the lightest, airiest challah ever to come out of a bakery. I've adapted her recipe for the home baker.

Orbit White Rye

Bohemian and Polish ryes are most often light in color, a hue derived from light, or white, rye flour, which is available in specialty stores or by mail (see Mail Order Source Guide). You will need to plan ahead when making this bread, as its sponge starter needs up to 24 hours to develop before you can begin to prepare the dough.

2^1/$_2$ teaspoons (1 envelope) active dry yeast

2 cups lukewarm water (95° to 110°F)

2^1/$_2$ cups light, or white, rye flour

2 teaspoons salt

2^1/$_4$ cups unbleached all-purpose flour

1. Prepare the sour sponge starter by combining 1 teaspoon of the yeast, 1 cup of the lukewarm water, and 1 cup of the light rye flour in a medium-size mixing bowl. Whisk until smoothly blended. Cover with plastic wrap and set aside at room temperature for at least 12 and up to 24 hours. The sponge will rise, bubble, and recede. When ready to use, it should smell pleasantly sour.

2. In a large mixing bowl, dissolve the remaining 1^1/$_2$ teaspoons yeast in the remaining 1 cup lukewarm water. Mix in the starter and the remaining 1^1/$_2$ cups light rye flour. Stir in the salt and slowly add 2 cups of the all-purpose flour to form a dough.

3. Turn the dough out onto a lightly floured surface and knead for 5 to 7 minutes, adding only as much of the remaining ^{1}/$_4$ cup all-purpose flour, a little at a time, as needed to achieve a smooth and elastic but still sticky dough. Transfer to a greased bowl, cover with plastic wrap, and set aside at room temperature to rise until doubled, about 1^1/$_2$ hours.

4. Return the dough to a lightly floured work surface and divide it in half. Shape each half into a smooth round and place the loaves 4 to 5 inches apart on a baking sheet that has been greased or lined with parchment paper. Cover with a towel and set aside to rise at room temperature for 45 minutes.

5. Preheat the oven to 425°F.

6. Cut an X in the top of each loaf with the tip of a sharp knife or a razor blade. Spritz with water. Bake for 5 minutes. Quickly open the oven door, spritz the loaves again with water, and close the oven. Continue to bake for about 35 minutes, until well browned and crusty. Place the loaves on wire racks to cool.

Yield: 2 loaves

Light rye bread is favored in Chicago's ethnic bakeries for its subtle taste and fine, soft texture. In the Pasieka Bakery, which specializes in baked goods of Polish origin, it is simply called rye bread. At others, such as Vesecky's, a Bohemian bakery in suburban Berwyn, customers request their ryes by shape. There's long rye, square rye, bucket rye, and round rye—referred to as the orbit rye.

Armenian Flathread

Pamela, my sister-in-law, is a New York Armenian transplanted to the Midwest. Although she now cooks with a slight Heartland accent, care is taken to pass the Armenian culinary heritage of her parents on to her children.

This Armenian Flatbread passed muster with Pamela, as well as with the kids, at a recent family gathering. Reminiscent of focaccia without the oil and herbs, it's soft and pillowy, yet has a beautiful golden crust. It proved to be just the right scoop for our dips, spreads, and relishes.

¹/₂ tablespoon active dry yeast

1 teaspoon sugar

¹/₄ cup lukewarm water (95° to 110°F)

¹/₂ cup water

¹/₂ cup milk

6 tablespoons unsalted butter

2³/₄ cups bread flour

1 teaspoon sea salt

1. In a small bowl, sprinkle the yeast and sugar over the lukewarm water. Set aside to proof until bubbly, about 5 minutes.

2. Combine the ¹/₂ cup water, milk, and 4 tablespoons of butter in a small saucepan. Heat to 95° to 110°F, or until lukewarm, stirring to dissolve the butter.

3. Pour the warm liquid into a large mixing bowl. Stir in the yeast mixture. Add 2 cups of the flour, a little at a time. Stir in the salt and ¹/₂ cup more of the flour to form a soft dough.

4. Turn the dough out onto a work surface. Gently knead in the remaining ¹/₄ cup flour,

continuing to knead until the dough feels smooth and elastic, about 5 minutes. Transfer to a greased bowl, cover with plastic wrap, and set aside at room temperature to rise until doubled, about 1¹/₂ hours.

5. Remove the dough, knead once or twice to deflate, and return it to the bowl. Cover again and set aside to rise a second time, for 1 hour.

6. Return the dough to a work surface and divide it in half.

7. To bake only 1 bread at a time, place half of the dough back into the bowl, cover again, and refrigerate. Roll the other half out into a 10-inch circle, rolling outward from the center of the dough to form an even circle. Transfer to an ungreased baking sheet. Cover and set aside to rise for 30 minutes. (When the first bread is baking, prepare the second piece of dough for the oven in the same way, allowing the dough to come to room temperature before rolling it out.)

8. To bake 2 breads simultaneously, immediately after dividing the dough, roll each out into a 10-inch circle and transfer to separate ungreased baking sheets. Cover and allow to rise for 30 minutes.

9. Preheat the oven to 375°F. (You will need 2 ovens if baking both breads simultaneously.)

10. Melt the additional 2 tablespoons butter.

11. With a fingertip, make an indentation in the center of each round and 4 more indentations around the center. Brush the dough with the melted butter. Bake for about 35 minutes, until golden brown all over.

12. Place on a wire rack to cool. Serve at room temperature.

Yield: 2 flatbreads

reater Boston is made up of dozens of neighborhoods settled by waves of immigrants over the years. In Belmont and nearby Watertown, one finds markets that reflect the Greek, Indian, Middle Eastern, and Armenian roots of the people who live and shop there.

Like most of the markets in this area, Eastern Lamejun Bakers, which specializes in Middle Eastern delicacies, is actually a combination bakery and grocery store. Their namesake, *lamejun* (considered the best by local aficionados), is a paper-thin bread crust with a smear of ground spiced lamb. Other specialties of the house include tahini bread, cheese turnovers, Armenian cracker bread, and terrific homemade baklava. Massis Bakery offers a wide assortment of breads along with an intriguing selection of cookies filled with exotic blends of dates, figs, walnuts, and honey. At Sevan Bakery, breads are primarily a mix of fresh-baked Armenian varieties, such as *simit* (a bread ring with sesame seeds), tahini (made with sesame paste), *choreg* (a sweet bread), and wonderful soft rounds of 1-inch-thick *pideh*, their Armenian flatbread.

Natural Sourdough Starter
(For Sourdough French Baguettes and Sourdough Biscuits)

A "natural" starter is made without the addition of commercial yeast. The first step is a fermentation process that traps airborne wild yeasts. It takes about ten days of periodic feeding to prepare a natural starter, but it is an extremely gratifying project that results in a product that is uniquely yours. Use this starter for Sourdough French Baguettes (page 34) and Sourdough Biscuits (page 36).

To keep your starter alive, feed it 1/2 cup lukewarm water and 1 cup organic unbleached all-purpose flour weekly. Stir, cover with plastic wrap, and set aside at room temperature for about four hours, or until doubled in size, before returning it to the refrigerator. The taste of your starter may change over time—a natural process that makes it all the more interesting.

Natural cane sugar, or turbinado sugar, is a coarse, unrefined, raw sugar. It's beige in color and has a molasses flavor derived from cane syrup. The sugar is available in health food stores.

3/4 cup (4 ounces) seedless organic raisins

2 teaspoons natural cane sugar or turbinado sugar

1 cup filtered water (or tap water brought to a boil and then cooled to room temperature)

4 cups organic unbleached all-purpose flour

1 1/2 cups lukewarm water (95° to 110°F)

1. Combine the raisins, sugar, and filtered water in a clean glass or ceramic bowl. Stir with a clean spoon to dissolve the sugar. Cover the bowl tightly with plastic wrap and set it aside in a warm spot (75° to 78°F), undisturbed, for 7 days. Air is trapped in the water and inside the bowl to ferment the natural sugars. At the end of the week, the fermented mixture should have the faint smell of fruity wine. You will also notice sediment on the bottom of the bowl; do not discard it.

2. Set a fine-mesh strainer over a clean glass or ceramic bowl and line it with a damp piece of cheesecloth. Strain the fermented raisins and soaking liquid through the lined strainer into the bowl below. Fold the cloth up around the raisins to squeeze out the juices, then discard the raisins.

3. You should have about 2/3 cup liquid. Put it in a large, clean glass or ceramic bowl. With a clean spoon, stir in 1 cup of the flour to form a loose dough. Cover the bowl tightly with plastic wrap and set aside in a warm spot for 10 to 12 hours. The mixture should rise and bubble.

4. Add ½ cup lukewarm water to the starter. Stir in 1 cup more of the flour, mixing to a soft dough. Cover as before and return the bowl to the warm spot for another 10 to 12 hours, where it should again rise and bubble.

5. Add ½ cup lukewarm water and stir in another 1 cup flour. Cover and set the bowl aside again for 8 hours.

6. Add a final ½ cup lukewarm water and stir in the remaining 1 cup flour. Cover and set aside for only 4 hours this time. The completed sourdough starter should have a faint, pleasantly sour smell and many large bubbles.

Yield: About 4 cups

Plan ahead, taking care to observe "feeding time." The starter should have a pleasantly sour aroma as it strengthens, but it could weaken and develop an unpleasant acidic smell if allowed to ferment too long without the addition of water and flour. My suggestion is to begin the week-long fermentation process on a Friday night. The following Friday night, just before midnight, begin feeding. The next feeding is midday on Saturday, followed by a midnight feeding the same day. The final feeding is then Sunday morning, and by Sunday afternoon your starter is done. Cover and refrigerate the starter until ready to use.

San Francisco's bakery sourdoughs are legendary, most likely owing to the quality of their natural starters. In this temperate city, bakery doors are swung open year-round, allowing free circulation of the wild yeast spores to be carried along on the Bay breezes.

For years, San Francisco sourdoughs were made exclusively from natural starters. Bakers had to order only two ingredients: flour and salt. Today, some sourdough bakeries add commercial yeast to their starters, which cuts the rising time and makes quality control easier, since there is unpredictability in working with a natural starter.

Sourdough French Baguettes

For most home bakers, achieving a rustic, crusty baguette of bakery quality can be an elusive goal. But it is possible to recreate bakery-style French bread using a very slow-rising, natural sourdough starter. The reward for patience is a crusty, chewy, singularly full-flavored loaf. If you don't make your own natural starter from scratch, see the Mail Order Source Guide for sources of pre-made commercial sourdough starters.

Baker's patent flour is milled from a blend of hard wheats with a protein content of 11 to 13 percent. Unbleached bread flour can also be used as a substitute; see Mail Order Source Guide.

½ cup Natural Sourdough Starter
(page 32)

1 cup lukewarm water (95° to 110°F)

2¼ cups unbleached all-purpose flour or
unbleached baker's patent flour

½ tablespoon salt (preferably sea salt)

1. In the bowl of a stationary electric mixer fitted with the flat paddle attachment, combine the starter and lukewarm water and begin to mix at low speed. Slowly add 1 cup of the flour and blend. Add the salt. Continue to add the remaining 1¼ cups flour slowly until a soft, sticky dough forms.

2. Remove the paddle and attach a dough hook. Knead at low speed for 5 minutes. The dough should still feel wet and sticky, with a soft, loose consistency.

3. Transfer the dough to a greased bowl. Cover with plastic wrap and set aside at room temperature to rise for at least 5 and up to 6 hours.

4. Spray a double-well baguette pan with vegetable oil cooking spray, line each well with silicone-treated parchment paper, and sprinkle with a little flour. Set aside.

5. Return the dough to a floured work surface and cut it in half. With floured hands, transfer 1 piece of dough to a well of the prepared baguette pan. Quickly pull it into a 14-inch rope to fill the well. Do not be overly concerned with shape. Sprinkle with flour. Repeat the procedure with the second piece of dough. Cover the pan loosely with a towel and set aside at room temperature to rise for 2 hours.

6. Preheat the oven to 450°F. Arrange a rack in the middle of the oven, with a second rack below it. Place a 9 × 13-inch baking pan half filled with water on the lower rack to create moisture.

7. Lift the dough from each well of the pan by the parchment liner and set aside. Place the empty pan into the hot oven for about 5 minutes.

8. Slide each piece of dough from the parchment into a well of the heated pan. (If you used untreated parchment and the dough has stuck, bake on the parchment.) Plunge 4 ice cubes into the pan of water on the lower rack and place the baguette pan on the rack above.

9. Bake for 30 to 32 minutes, until browned and crusty. Place the loaves on wire racks to cool.

10. Cut thick diagonal slices to serve.

Yield: 2 baguettes

Follow timing rather than visual guidelines in this recipe. The dough may or may not double in volume, but 6 hours is sufficient for the first rise and 2 hours is needed for the second.

The dough should be too wet to knead by hand; a loose dough is essential to achieving the weblike interior characteristic of sourdough French bread.

American sourdough can be traced back to the Gold Rush era in San Francisco, where the first sourdough bakeries were founded in 1849. The phenomenon was so successful that only six years later there were sixty-three bakeries and eleven flour mills in business in the city. It took the ruinous 1906 earthquake to thin their ranks.

When the Italian French Baking Company was built in 1911 on Grant Avenue in North Beach, it was situated among a string of brick-oven bakeries. Today, it houses the last brick oven still in use in San Francisco. The popular bakery, Larraburu Brothers, was in operation from 1896 until 1976. Many San Franciscans still lament its closing and the loss of their favorite "French bread," as sourdough loaves are called locally.

Sourdough Biscuits

These biscuits were most likely invented by frontier cooks in the Pacific Northwest and Alaska as the sourdough culture spread north from San Francisco. A sourdough biscuit could be baked in reasonably short order, or could even be cooked on a griddle over an open fire.

These versatile buns have a great texture—a combination of flaky biscuit and soft bread rolled into one. They are wonderful for breakfast, split and spread with sweet butter and honey, but can just as easily serve as the base for appetizer-size sandwiches or a bread pudding with berries.

1 1/2 cups unbleached all-purpose flour

1/2 tablespoon baking powder

1/2 teaspoon baking soda

1/2 teaspoon salt

4 tablespoons unsalted butter, chilled, cut into small pieces, plus 2 tablespoons butter

1/3 cup cold water

1 cup Natural Sourdough Starter (page 32)

1. Sift the flour, baking powder, baking soda, and salt together into a medium mixing bowl. Add the pieces of chilled butter and mix with a pastry blender until finely crumbled. (You can also use a stationary electric mixer fitted with the flat paddle attachment.) Add the cold water and the starter, and mix into a dough with a wooden spoon (or with the paddle of the mixer).

2. Turn the dough out onto a work surface and knead until it feels smooth and elastic, and moist but not sticky, about 2 minutes.

Cover the dough with a towel or plastic wrap and let it rest for 15 minutes.

3. Sprinkle a work surface lightly with flour and roll or push the dough out into a 1/2-inch-thick circle. Cut out biscuits using a 2-inch round cutter dipped into flour before each cut. Arrange the biscuits 1 inch apart on a greased baking sheet. Reroll the dough scraps for additional biscuits. Cover the pan loosely with plastic wrap and set aside at room temperature for 1 hour. (The dough will not necessarily rise much.)

4. Preheat the oven to 425°F.

5. Meanwhile, melt the additional 2 tablespoons butter. Allow to cool a bit, but not to solidify. Brush the tops of the biscuits with the melted butter. Bake for about 15 minutes, until lightly browned.

6. Serve the biscuits hot.

Yield: About 20 biscuits

Old-Fashioned Southern Dinner Rolls

"The South loves hot breads and rolls," Betsey Apple recalls from childhood remembrances of Virginia and her family's favorite dinner rolls from their neighborhood bakery. Popped into the oven before serving and eaten warm, the rich, buttery rolls were a dinnertime must for any special occasion.

In this recipe, rolled dough that is already enriched with milk, butter, and egg is given a final gilding of melted butter before baking. The result is a roll ever so soft and delicious! Be sure to serve them piping hot from the oven.

$^1/_2$ **cup lukewarm milk (95° to 110°F)**

$^1/_2$ **cup lukewarm water (95° to 110°F)**

$^1/_4$ **cup sugar**

1 teaspoon salt

1 teaspoon active dry yeast

$^1/_2$ **cup (1 stick) unsalted butter, at room temperature**

1 large egg

$3^1/_4$ **cups unbleached all-purpose flour**

1. In a large mixing bowl, combine the milk, water, sugar, salt, yeast, and 5 tablespoons of the butter. Stir the mixture to blend well. Set the bowl aside for 5 minutes.

2. Stir in the egg. Add the flour, $^1/_2$ cup at a time, stirring to incorporate. Turn the soft dough out onto a lightly floured work surface and gently knead until smooth and elastic, about 5 minutes. Transfer to a large greased bowl, cover with plastic wrap, and set aside at room temperature to rise until doubled, about $1^1/_2$ hours.

3. Melt the remaining 3 tablespoons butter and allow it to cool a bit, but not to solidify.

4. Return the dough to a lightly floured work surface and cut it in half. Roll each piece out into a 12-inch circle about $^1/_8$ inch thick. Brush the surface of the dough lightly with melted butter. Cut 12 wedges, as you would cut a pie. Starting at the wide end, roll each wedge up, tucking the tip underneath, and place 1 inch apart on a greased baking sheet. Cover loosely with plastic wrap and let rise at room temperature until doubled, about 45 minutes.

5. Preheat the oven to 400°F.

6. Brush the rolls with the remaining melted butter. Bake for 12 to 15 minutes, until lightly golden.

Yield: 24 rolls

Pepperoni Rolls

Though essentially a soft white bun on the outside, the meaty texture and spicy kick of the pepperoni inside make these rolls so unusual and tasty. Serve them with soup or salad, or simply tucked into a lunch bag. Sometimes I slice the rolls and serve them with a tray of crudités as an appetizer.

2 1/2 teaspoons (1 envelope) active dry yeast

1 cup lukewarm water (95° to 110°F)

1 tablespoon sugar

2 tablespoons olive oil

1/2 teaspoon salt

2 3/4 cups unbleached all-purpose flour

9 ounces pepperoni, casing removed, cut into 36 sticks, 3 inches long and 1/2 inch thick

1. Sprinkle the yeast over the water in a large mixing bowl. Let proof until bubbly, about 5 minutes.

2. Add the sugar, oil, and salt to the yeast mixture. Add 2 1/2 cups of the flour, a little at a time, to form a stiff dough.

3. Turn the dough out onto a lightly floured surface. Knead until the dough feels smooth and elastic, about 5 minutes, adding only as much of the remaining 1/4 cup flour as is necessary to prevent the dough from sticking. Transfer to a greased bowl, cover with plastic wrap, and set aside at room temperature to rise until doubled, about 1 hour.

4. Return the dough to a lightly floured work surface and shape it into a log of even width. Cut crosswise into 12 equal pieces. Roll out each piece into a 5 × 3 1/2-inch rectangle. Arrange 3 sticks of pepperoni lengthwise on each piece of dough, equally spaced. Fold the short ends of the dough in toward the center, then fold the long ends up to enclose the meat, pinching the edges together to close. Place the rolls seam side down on a greased baking sheet, spaced 2 inches apart. Cover loosely with plastic wrap and set aside at room temperature to rise for 30 minutes.

5. Preheat the oven to 400°F.

6. Spritz the rolls with water. Bake for 18 to 20 minutes, until browned. Transfer the rolls to wire racks to cool. They are best eaten warm or at room temperature the same day made; freeze the extras.

Yield: 12 rolls

Grandfather Tomaro opened a tiny bakery with a single basement brick oven in Clarksburg, West Virginia, in 1914. By the 1930s, Clarksburg's industry was largely coal mining, and the area known as Glen Elk, where Tomaro's Bakery is located, was the Little Italy of Clarksburg. Miners regularly purchased a pepperoni stick and a loaf of Italian bread from the bakery for an easy-to-carry lunch. Putting two and two together, Tomaro began making pepperoni rolls in 1939. This was the same year his grandson, whose widow now runs the bakery, was born.

Tomaro's Bakery still makes their pepperoni rolls by hand, even though the bakery was long ago automated. They give reason to heed the bakery's slogan: "Eat Tomaro's Bread Today!"

English Muffin Loaf

Although this bread does not require kneading, substantial mixing is necessary. It's well worth the effort. The texture of the baked loaf is coarse with large holes in the grain, yet very airy and light. It tastes the way an English muffin is supposed to taste, with a slightly sour tang, easily achieved in this recipe by adding buttermilk.

This loaf is meant to be thickly sliced and toasted for complete eating enjoyment. Butter and preserves are optional, but encouraged.

½ tablespoon active dry yeast

1 teaspoon sugar

1 cup lukewarm water (95° to 110°F)

1 cup buttermilk, at room temperature

3 tablespoons unsalted butter, melted and cooled

3 cups unbleached all-purpose flour or bread flour

2 teaspoons salt

Yellow cornmeal, for sprinkling

1. In a large mixing bowl, dissolve the yeast and sugar in ½ cup of the lukewarm water. Set aside to proof until bubbly, about 5 minutes.

2. Stir in the remaining ½ cup water, the buttermilk, and butter. Add the flour, ½ cup at a time, blending into a smooth batter. Stir in the salt. Beat the mixture vigorously by hand for about 5 minutes, or 3 minutes if using an electric mixer. The batter should be wet, soft, and sticky. Scrape down the sides of the bowl, cover with plastic wrap, and set aside at room temperature to rise until doubled, about 1½ hours.

3. Preheat the oven to 375°F. Grease a 9 × 5-inch loaf pan and sprinkle with cornmeal. Tilt the pan to coat the bottom and sides evenly, tapping out excess cornmeal.

4. Stir the batter down and pour evenly into the prepared loaf pan. Cover the pan completely with a large bowl and set aside at room temperature until the batter has risen to the top of the pan, 35 to 45 minutes.

5. Bake for 40 to 45 minutes, until nicely golden. Remove the bread from the pan and place on a wire rack to cool.

Yield: 1 large loaf

A home-style English muffin loaf, as distinguished from the packaged super-market staple, is a typical bakery product of the rural Midwest. It's a huge seller for the Amish women who bake the loaves daily at the Bread Box Bakeshop in Shipshewana, Indiana. While their English muffin loaf is wonderful, the success of the Bread Box Bakeshop might have something to do with the other items sold there as well. Numerous varieties of preserves, honey, and fruit butter are on display, along with a dairy case filled with logs of fresh Amish butter.

Sally Lunn Muffins

A colonial-style yeast dough that dates back to the eighteenth century, Sally Lunn is moist enough to be called a batter. Originally formed into large buns, it bakes into golden puffs. I am particularly fond of making muffin-size Sally Lunns because it allows me to serve some now and freeze the extras for another occasion.

2 teaspoons active dry yeast

¼ cup sugar

¼ cup lukewarm water (95° to 110°F)

⅔ cup lukewarm milk (95° to 110°F)

6 tablespoons unsalted butter, at room temperature

1 teaspoon salt

3 cups unbleached all-purpose flour

2 large eggs

1. In a small bowl, dissolve the yeast and 1 tablespoon of the sugar in the lukewarm water. Let proof until bubbly, about 5 minutes.

2. In the bowl of a stationary electric mixer fitted with the flat paddle attachment, combine the lukewarm milk, butter, salt, and remaining 3 tablespoons sugar. Mix at low speed to dissolve the sugar and salt. Add 1 cup of the flour and mix until smooth. Add the yeast mixture and the eggs, and blend thoroughly. Slowly add the remaining 2 cups flour and mix into a soft, wet dough.

3. Remove the flat paddle and attach a dough hook. Knead at low speed for 3 to 5 minutes to develop elasticity in the dough. Transfer to a large greased bowl, cover with plastic wrap, and set aside at room temperature to rise until doubled, about 1 hour.

4. Stir the batter down and spoon into the wells of a greased 12-cup muffin tin. Press the dough evenly into the wells, filling each about two-thirds full. Cover the tin with a towel and set aside at room temperature to rise to just above the tops of the wells, about 30 minutes.

5. Preheat the oven to 375°F.

6. Bake muffins until puffed and brown, about 25 minutes. Remove the muffins from the tin. Place them on wire racks to cool. Serve warm or at room temperature.

Yield: 12 muffins

ight and airy but rich in butter and eggs, Sally Lunn muffins make a smashing accompaniment to tea or a simple meal. They've been a featured item at Sally Bell's Bakery in Richmond, Virginia, since its inception in 1926. Fortunately, some things never change—at Sally Bell's, you can still order a vegetable or tomato aspic and a deviled egg to accompany your Sally Lunn.

TWO

Yeast-Raised Holiday Breads, Coffee Cakes, and Sweet Rolls

Holidays and baking just seem to go hand in hand, and these are surely the busiest times of year for any bakery. Bakers yearn for a holiday in every month of the year, knowing that these celebratory occasions bring in customers clamoring for special baked treats. Coffee cakes and sweet rolls are such festive foods. As I talked to folks about their favorite baked goods, the sudden remembrance of a cardamom-scented ring or a sweet, sticky pecan roll would invariably inspire an animated and loving description.

Tips and Techniques

- Recipes for sweet doughs generally call for more yeast than do other yeast-raised recipes. The volume of butter, sugar, milk, and eggs typically used in these doughs makes them heavier, necessitating a little more yeast to facilitate rising. Unlike other yeast-raised doughs, sweet doughs do not benefit from prolonged fermentation.

- Sweet doughs are soft and should be kneaded in gentle pushes and turns, using a lighter touch than you would for other yeast-raised doughs. Vigorous hand kneading can tear soft doughs.

- Bake these recipes in the middle of the oven, one loaf at a time when specified.

- Sweet breads, coffee cakes, and sweet rolls will remain reasonably fresh for two to three days if wrapped in plastic and stored at room temperature. Unlike other yeast-raised breads, they are better on the second or third day if briefly warmed in a microwave oven. Set the pastry on a paper towel and heat for 15 seconds at 50 percent power.

- Most sweet breads freeze well. Wrap in plastic and place in a plastic freezer bag. Date for use within two months. Allow the bread to thaw completely at room temperature before unwrapping.

Panettone

(Italian Holiday Bread)

You will love this rich Milanese egg bread, brimming with raisins and can-died citron. In Milan at Christmastime, some bakers dress their panettone in fanciful garb—frosted to resemble an alpine slope and topped with marzipan skiers or benches and miniature Christmas trees—but I prefer my panettone unadulterated, finished with a simple drizzle of melted butter.

2 tablespoons active dry yeast

¹/₂ cup lukewarm water (95° to 110°F)

³/₄ cup bread flour

1 cup seedless raisins

¹/₂ cup lukewarm milk (95° to 110°F)

¹/₂ cup (1 stick) plus 1 tablespoon unsalt-ed butter, at room temperature

¹/₂ cup sugar

3³/₄ to 4 cups unbleached all-purpose flour

3 large eggs, plus 2 egg yolks

1 teaspoon salt

¹/₂ tablespoon grated lemon zest

¹/₂ tablespoon grated orange zest

2 teaspoons vanilla extract

¹/₈ teaspoon anise oil (optional)

1 cup chopped candied citron

1. Prepare the sponge starter by dissolving 1 tablespoon of the yeast in the water in a small bowl. Stir in the bread flour to form a thick, pasty dough. Cover with plastic wrap and set aside at room temperature to rise until dou-bled, about 45 minutes.

2. Meanwhile, place the raisins in another small bowl and cover with hot tap water. Soak for 30 minutes. Drain and set aside.

3. Dissolve the remaining 1 tablespoon yeast in the milk in a small dish. Let proof until bubbly, about 5 minutes.

4. In the bowl of a stationary electric mixer fit-ted with the flat paddle attachment, combine ½ cup of butter and the sugar. Beat at low speed until smoothly blended. Add ½ cup of the all-purpose flour. Add the whole eggs and the additional yolks, one at a time. Add the salt, lemon zest, orange zest, vanilla, and anise oil, if desired. Mix in ½ cup more of the all-purpose flour. Add the yeast mixture. Add the sponge starter and blend well at low speed. Slowly add an additional 2½ cups all-purpose flour. Mix in the raisins and citron.

5. Turn the dough out onto a lightly floured work surface. Gently knead the soft dough for 7 to 10 minutes, adding ¼ to ½ cup more of the remaining flour as necessary to obtain a soft, elastic dough, still moist and slightly sticky to the touch. Transfer to a large greased bowl, cover with plastic wrap, and set aside at room temperature to rise until doubled, about 1 hour.

6. Return the dough to a work surface and divide it in half. Shape each piece into a smooth round. Place each flat in the bottom of a greased 1½-quart (7-inch round by 3½-inch deep) soufflé mold. Cover the molds loosely with plastic wrap and set aside to rise for 1 hour.

7. Preheat the oven to 375°F.

8. Bake for about 40 minutes, until the bread is well browned on top and a tester inserted into the center comes out clean.

9. While the bread is baking, melt the remaining 1 tablespoon butter. Allow to cool a bit, but not to solidify.

10. Transfer the molds to a wire rack and brush the tops of the loaves with the melted butter to glaze while still hot. Let the bread cool until warm, then unmold and cool completely on the racks.

Yield: 2 loaves

Specially designed panettone molds can be purchased from cookware stores or catalogs (see Mail Order Source Guide), but any cylindrical baking pan with high, straight sides can be used. For this recipe, which yields two light-textured loaves, I use two 1½-quart soufflé molds.

*A*lthough most of us associate panettone with the Christmas holidays, Joe Mallozzi, owner of the Villa Italia Pasticceria in Rotterdam, New York, calls his panettone Easter bread. (Joe assures me the bakery also offers the bread at Christmas.) The Mallozzis have been baking panettone commercially for three decades in the little town outside of Schenectady, following a recipe developed by Joe's grandmother more than sixty years ago in Minturno, Italy, to celebrate Easter.

I discovered the Villa Italia while searching for a bakery-fresh panettone. After dozens of telephone calls to Italian bakeries across the country, I was left with a single option—an imported panettone packed in a factory box shipped from Italy.

Surely there must be a source in the United States, I queried the Retail Bakers Association. Director Eric Deising replied, "I know of only one—Joe Mallozzi." Joe sent me a panettone that was consumed, some would say inhaled, in a single day. He included a recipe along with his delicious bread, which I've modified somewhat for the home kitchen. (I had to scale it down from a 113-pound yield!)

Christmas Stollen

Stollen is the hallmark Christmas treat of German and Swiss bakeries across the country. This long crescent loaf is a fragrant, rich yeast bread perfectly suited for breakfast, tea, or dessert. It's studded with blanched almonds and candied citron and has a subtle touch of spice.

1 cup mixed seedless dark and golden raisins

¼ cup dark rum

2 tablespoons almond paste

1½ tablespoons water

¼ cup confectioners' sugar, plus additional for dusting

1 tablespoon active dry yeast

1 tablespoon plus ¼ cup granulated sugar

⅔ cup lukewarm milk (95° to 110°F)

2¾ to 3 cups unbleached all-purpose flour

½ cup plus 2 tablespoons unsalted butter, at room temperature

2 large eggs, 1 separated

1 teaspoon salt

¾ teaspoon grated lemon zest

½ teaspoon vanilla extract

¼ teaspoon ground cardamom

¼ teaspoon ground nutmeg

½ cup chopped candied citron

½ cup blanched slivered almonds

1. Combine the raisins and rum in a small bowl. Cover and set aside at room temperature for at least 4 and up to 12 hours, stirring from time to time.

2. Combine the almond paste and ½ tablespoon water in another small bowl. Mix thoroughly. Add ¼ cup confectioners' sugar; cream with the back of a spoon to a smooth paste. Using ¼ teaspoon of the mixture for each, shape almond-sugar into nuggets and drop onto a plate lined with waxed paper. Set the plate in the refrigerator, uncovered, for at least 2 hours.

3. Prepare the sponge starter by combining the yeast, 1 tablespoon of the granulated sugar, and the milk in a small mixing bowl. Stir to dissolve the yeast. Add ½ cup of the flour and stir until smoothly blended. Cover with plastic wrap and set aside at room temperature until the sponge has bubbled up and fallen back slightly, 30 to 45 minutes.

4. Cream ½ cup of the butter and the remaining ¼ cup sugar in a large mixing bowl. Add 1 whole egg and the yolk of the second, reserving the egg white. Add the salt, lemon zest, vanilla, and spices, stirring until smoothly blended. Add the sponge starter. Slowly add 1¾ cups more flour. Mix in the candied citron and almonds. Drain and add the raisins.

5. Turn the dough out onto a lightly floured work surface and knead in $1/4$ cup of the remaining flour. Continue to knead the soft dough gently for 5 to 7 minutes, adding more flour as necessary, until the dough feels smooth and moist but not sticky, and holds its shape when pushed. Transfer to a greased large bowl, cover with plastic wrap, and set aside at room temperature to rise until doubled, about 1 hour.

6. Return the dough to a work surface. Push or roll it out into a 15×9-inch oval, about $1/2$ inch thick. Arrange the chilled almond nuggets in 2 rows parallel to a long side of dough, covering about a third of the surface. Beat the reserved egg white and the remaining 1 tablespoon water in a small dish. Brush the exposed two-thirds of the surface of the dough with the egg white and water wash and fold the dough over the nuggets, leaving a scant $1/2$-inch border.

7. Transfer the loaf to a nonstick baking sheet or one that has been lined with parchment paper. Shape it into a crescent with the fold facing out. Cover loosely with plastic wrap and set aside at room temperature to rise for 30 minutes.

8. Preheat the oven to 350°F.

9. Bake stollen for about 35 minutes, until golden brown.

10. Melt the remaining 2 tablespoons butter. Remove the pan from the oven and brush the hot stollen with the melted butter. Cool on a wire rack, then dust liberally with confectioners' sugar.

11. Cut the stollen into diagonal slices and serve warm. The stollen is best freshly baked; I freeze half if I don't expect the whole loaf to be consumed in a day or two.

Yield: 1 large loaf

The town of New Glarus sits in the lush farmlands of Green County, Wisconsin. Known as America's Little Switzerland, New Glarus is the home of one of Wisconsin's oldest continuously operating bakeries, the New Glarus Bakery, in existence since 1915. The Webers, who purchased the bakery in 1978, opened a tea room in an upstairs loft of the building in 1987 to accommodate the by-the-slice tourist trade. Along with a hot cup of tea or coffee, visitors can sample the bakery's European-style breads and Swiss pastries, such as a slice of stollen warm from the oven. I loved their use of marzipan nuggets to flavor the stollen so I incorporated a similar flavor element in this version.

Lucia Buns

A pre-Christmas tradition in Sweden, Lucia Buns are baked only from the first of December until the feast of St. Lucia on December 13, which commemorates the start of the holiday season. According to custom, the youngest member of the household, preferably female, serves the family Lucia Buns and coffee in bed on the morning of December 13.

Some refer to these as saffron buns, in recognition of the exotic spice eventually used to lend the buns their strongly aromatic character. I replicate that effect with the crushed seeds of less costly cardamom pods. The addition of saffron is optional.

2¹/₂ teaspoons (1 envelope) active dry yeast

²/₃ cup milk

¹/₄ cup plus 1 tablespoon sugar

4 tablespoons (¹/₂ stick) unsalted butter, at room temperature

Seeds from 5 or 6 cardamom pods (see Mail Order Source Guide), crushed (¹/₄ teaspoon)

¹/₄ teaspoon saffron (optional)

2 large eggs

¹/₂ teaspoon salt

2³/₄ cups unbleached all-purpose flour

24 seedless raisins

1 tablespoon water

1. Place the yeast in a large mixing bowl.

2. Heat the milk in a small saucepan on top of the stove or in a medium-size bowl in a microwave oven until hot but not yet sim-

mering. Remove from the heat and add ¹/₄ cup sugar, the butter, cardamom, and saffron, if desired. Stir to dissolve the butter and let cool to 95° to 110°F, until lukewarm. Add the cooled mixture to the yeast and let proof until bubbly, about 5 minutes.

3. Beat 1 egg and the salt into the yeast mixture. Add 2¹/₂ cups of the flour, ¹/₂ cup at a time, to form a dough.

4. Turn the dough out onto a work surface. Knead until the dough feels smooth and elastic, about 5 minutes, adding only as much of the remaining ¹/₄ cup flour as necessary to keep the dough from sticking. Transfer to a greased bowl, cover with plastic wrap, and set aside at room temperature to rise until doubled, about 1¹/₂ hours.

5. Return the dough to a work surface and divide it into 12 equal pieces. Roll each piece into an 8- to 9-inch rope. Shape each rope into a figure eight and place on a greased baking sheet, equally spaced to allow for spreading. Position a raisin in the center of the top and bottom loops of each bun. Cover loosely with plastic wrap and set aside to rise at room temperature for 30 minutes.

6. Preheat the oven to 350°F.

7. Beat the remaining egg and the 1 tablespoon water in a small dish. Brush the buns with the egg and water wash and sprinkle evenly with the remaining 1 tablespoon sugar.

8. Bake for about 20 minutes, until golden brown. Transfer the buns to a wire rack to cool.

9. Serve warm or at room temperature. Freeze any buns not eaten on the first day.

Yield: 12 buns

*S*t. Lucia lived in Sicily around the year 300. According to legend, Lucia was so obsessed with charitable work that she gave all her personal belongings to the poor, leading her nobleman husband to have her imprisoned. Lucia was tortured and ultimately killed following several miraculous interventions, which included the restoration of sight after her eyes had been pierced with hot spears.

Years later, Lucia was declared a saint. She came to be revered in Sweden, most likely owing to the influence of early Christian missionaries. On December 13, the Swedes celebrate the feast of St. Lucia. This marked the winter solstice on the old Swedish calendar as the day of light ("Lucia" means light). Each Lucia bun bears two raisins, symbolizing eyes that let in the light.

Yulekage
(Scandinavian Christmas Bread)

This Christmas loaf appears in Danish, Swedish, and Norwegian bakeries all over the country during the month of December. Scented with cardamom, threaded with candied fruit, and topped with a vanilla glaze, Yulekage is a treat served on any occasion. It also makes excellent toast.

2¹/₂ teaspoons (1 envelope) active dry yeast

¹/₂ cup lukewarm water (95° to 110°F)

¹/₂ cup lukewarm milk (95° to 110°F)

¹/₄ cup sugar

¹/₄ teaspoon ground cardamom, or more to taste

1 large egg

¹/₂ teaspoon salt

¹/₂ teaspoon grated lemon zest

4 tablespoons (¹/₂ stick) unsalted butter, at room temperature

3 to 3¹/₄ cups unbleached all-purpose flour

¹/₂ cup mixed chopped candied citron and candied orange peel

¹/₄ cup walnut pieces

Glaze

1 large egg white

1 tablespoon sugar

1 teaspoon vanilla extract

1. Sprinkle the yeast over the lukewarm water in a large mixing bowl. Let proof until bubbly, about 5 minutes.

2. Combine the milk, sugar, and cardamom in a small bowl. Stir to dissolve the sugar, then stir the combination into the proofed yeast mixture. Beat in the egg, salt, lemon zest, and butter. Add 2¹/₂ cups of the flour, ¹/₂ cup at a time. Stir in the candied fruit and walnuts. Add ¹/₂ cup more of the flour.

3. Turn the dough out onto a lightly floured work surface. Gently knead the soft dough until it feels smooth and elastic, about 5 minutes, adding only as much of the remaining ¹/₄ cup flour as necessary to keep the dough from sticking. Transfer to a large greased bowl, cover with plastic wrap, and set aside at room temperature to rise until doubled, about 1 hour.

4. Return the dough to the work surface and roll it out into a 10-inch square. Fold one side of the dough a third of the way over the square, then fold the opposite side over on top to cover completely. Place seam side down, with the short ends tucked underneath, into a greased 9 × 5-inch loaf pan and

gently press the dough down to fill the pan evenly. Cover loosely with plastic wrap and set aside at room temperature to rise until the dough almost reaches the top of the pan, about 45 minutes.

5. Preheat the oven to 350°F.

6. Bake loaf for about 45 minutes, until golden brown. Unmold the loaf and cool on a wire rack.

7. For the glaze, combine the egg white, sugar, and vanilla in a small dish. Beat with a fork to blend. Brush generously over the top of the loaf while still warm. Allow the bread to cool completely before slicing.

Yield: 1 loaf

The best Yulekage I've tasted comes from the historic Lehmann's Bakery in Racine, Wisconsin, from whom I borrowed the atypical idea of adding walnuts to this recipe. The building housing Lehmann's has been a bakery since 1884. The current owner, Judy Carlson, was a young bride when she and her husband bought the bakery from Mr. Lehmann in the 1940s. Not much has changed over the years at Lehmann's, including the recipes. Aside from their Yulekage, the bakery is known for coffee cakes and for a hand-made Danish dough that is used to make kringles and turnovers.

Mardi Gras King Cake

King Cake is an integral part of Mardi Gras festivities. The coffee cake, a carnival tradition, is served at parties late into the evening during the six weeks between Three Kings Day and Fat Tuesday. New Orleans residents wouldn't think of making their own King Cake; that's what bakeries are for. Besides, the bakeshops add paper crowns, plastic beads, toy coins, and other trinkets to the cake box, creating a ready-made Mardi Gras hostess gift.

Brioche

2¹/₂ teaspoons (1 envelope) active dry yeast

³/₄ cup lukewarm milk (95° to 110°F)

¹/₂ cup (1 stick) unsalted butter, at room temperature

¹/₃ cup granulated sugar

1 teaspoon salt

3 large eggs, plus 1 egg yolk

3¹/₂ cups bread flour

Filling

1¹/₃ cups mixed golden raisins and dried cranberries

2 cups almond paste

1 cup (2 sticks) unsalted butter, at room temperature

¹/₂ cup granulated sugar

4 large egg whites, 2 yolks reserved

Zest of 2 medium lemons

¹/₄ cup orange-flavored liqueur (preferably Cointreau)

2 tablespoons water

2 small plastic toy babies (optional)

Glaze

2 cups confectioners' sugar

2 tablespoons warm water

4 to 5 teaspoons rum

Food coloring (optional)

1. Prepare the brioche dough 1 day ahead. In a small bowl, dissolve the yeast in the milk and set aside to proof.

2. In the bowl of a stationary electric mixer fitted with the flat paddle attachment, cream the butter, sugar, and salt at medium speed until fluffy and light in color, about 2 minutes. Reduce the mixer speed to medium-low and beat in 1 of the eggs. Add 1 cup of the flour and blend until smooth. Beat in the remaining 2 eggs and additional egg yolk, then add ¹/₂ cup more flour. Blend thoroughly.

3. Reduce the speed to low and add the yeast mixture. Slowly add the remaining 2 cups flour, a little at a time, blending between additions. Continue to mix for 2 minutes after all of the flour has been added. Remove the bowl from the stand, cover with plastic wrap, and set aside to rise at room temperature for 1 hour.

4. Lightly grease a large bowl. Punch down the dough and transfer it to the bowl. Cover tightly with plastic wrap and refrigerate overnight. (The dough will double in volume.)

5. To prepare the filling, place the raisins and cranberries in a small bowl and cover with hot tap water. Set aside to soak for 30 minutes. Drain and pat the fruit dry with paper toweling.

6. Meanwhile, combine the almond paste, butter, sugar, and egg whites in a food processor. Process to a smooth paste. Add the lemon zest and liqueur and process until smoothly blended. Cover and set aside.

7. Beat the reserved egg yolks with the 2 tablespoons water in a small dish for a wash; cover and set aside.

8. For the glaze, combine the confectioners' sugar and warm water in a medium-size bowl. Stir in the rum and blend into a smooth, fairly thick icing. Mix in a drop or 2 of food coloring, if desired. Cover and set aside.

9. To assemble, place the chilled brioche dough on a lightly floured work surface. Knead the dough briefly to deflate and shape it into a ball. Divide the ball in half. Roll out 1 piece into an 18 × 6-inch rectangle. Spread half of the filling evenly down the center of the rectangle lengthwise. Scatter half the drained fruit over the filling.

Push a plastic toy baby into the filling, if desired. Brush the exposed dough with the egg yolk and water wash.

10. Fold one long side of the rectangle over the filling, then fold the opposite side two-thirds over the dough to completely enclose the filling. (The log will be very full.) Press lightly to seal the seams. Shape the log into a ring, fitting one end inside the other and pinching the seams to seal tightly. Transfer the ring to a cookie sheet that has been lightly greased or lined with parchment paper. Cover loosely with plastic wrap and set aside at room temperature to rise for 45 minutes.

11. Repeat the rolling, filling, shaping, and rising process for the second piece of dough. To bake the coffee cakes one at a time, place the second in the refrigerator until the first goes into the oven, then allow it to rise for 1 hour before baking.

12. Preheat the oven to 350°F. (You will need to heat 2 ovens to bake both coffee cakes simultaneously.)

13. Brush the rings with the egg yolk and water wash before baking. Bake for about 30 minutes, until the crust is deep golden brown. Remove to a wire rack and allow to cool for about 30 minutes. (The cake should be warm, but no longer hot.)

14. Set the rack over a baking sheet. Paint thoroughly with the glaze, which will melt slightly and adhere to the crust in a thin coating. Set aside to cool completely.

15. Cut into wedges and serve at room temperature.

Yield: 2 coffee cakes

Sometimes I make just one King Cake (cutting all filling and glaze ingredients in half) and use the remaining half of the dough for an airy loaf or dinner rolls.

For a Brioche Loaf, form the dough into a loaf and fit it into a greased 8½ × 4½-inch loaf pan. Cover and let rise for 45 minutes. Brush with the egg yolk and water wash and bake in a 350°F oven about 35 minutes, until well browned and hollow sounding when tapped on the bottom.

For Brioche Rolls, divide the dough into six equal pieces, shaping each into a smooth round. Cover and let rise for 30 minutes on a lightly greased baking sheet. Brush with the egg yolk and water wash and bake in a 400°F oven for about 15 minutes, until deep golden brown.

Louisiana bakers begin their own Mardi Gras observation on January 6, or Three Kings Day. By Fat Tuesday, which ends the festivities some six weeks later, bakers in New Orleans will have made more than 250,000 king cakes.

King cake is the traditional celebration cake of carnival. It's really a coffee cake, made from either brioche dough or puff pastry, filled with any number of sweet nut pastes, fruit, and pastry cream or cream cheese, and baked in a ring. The cake's decorative icing is often tinted in the Mardi Gras colors of purple (for justice), green (for faith), and gold (for power). Hidden inside, according to custom, is a plastic toy baby, which symbolizes the Christ child. It reputedly brings good fortune to the person in whose slice it is found.

Hot Cross Buns

Modern Hot Cross Buns are derived from an English spiced roll called a Good Friday bun. Legend has it that a disgruntled bakery customer once suggested that the Good Friday bun be renamed the "hot and cross" bun, owing to the ill temper caused by paying a hefty price for such a simple baked good. A more likely inspiration for the contemporary name is the distinctive cross painted atop the bun in white icing while it is still warm from the oven.

Over the years, American bakers have adjusted the formula to suit their customers by removing the spice and adding candied fruit. For a taste approximating that of the original, substitute an equal amount of pumpkin pie spice for the lemon zest.

Dough

$^1/_2$ cup seedless raisins

1 tablespoon active dry yeast

$^1/_2$ cup lukewarm water (95° to 110°F)

$^1/_2$ cup (1 stick) unsalted butter, at room temperature

$^1/_3$ cup granulated sugar

1 teaspoon salt

3 large eggs, 1 separated

$4^1/_4$ cups unbleached all-purpose flour

$^1/_2$ cup lukewarm milk (95° to 110°F)

1 teaspoon vanilla extract

$^1/_2$ teaspoon grated lemon zest

$^1/_2$ cup mixed chopped candied citron and candied orange peel

1 tablespoon water

Simple Syrup

$^1/_4$ cup granulated sugar

$^1/_4$ cup water

Icing

1 cup confectioners' sugar

2 tablespoons cream or half-and-half

$^1/_2$ teaspoon vanilla extract

1. To prepare the dough, place the raisins in a small bowl and cover with hot tap water. Soak for 30 minutes. Drain and set aside.

2. In a small bowl, dissolve the yeast in the lukewarm water. Let proof until bubbly, about 5 minutes.

3. In a large mixing bowl, combine the butter, granulated sugar, and salt. Mix until blended. Stir in 2 whole eggs and the yolk of the third, reserving the egg white. Stir in 1 cup of the flour. Add the milk, vanilla, and lemon zest, blending well. Add 1 cup more of the flour, then stir in the yeast mixture. Slowly add 1½ cups additional flour. Stir in the raisins and candied fruit. Add another ½ cup flour.

4. Turn the dough out onto a lightly floured work surface and gently knead in the remaining ¼ cup flour. Continue to knead the soft dough until it feels smooth and elastic, about 5 minutes. Transfer to a large greased bowl, cover with plastic wrap, and set aside at room temperature to rise until doubled, about 1 hour.

5. Return the dough to a work surface, cover loosely, and let it rest for 30 minutes.

6. Meanwhile, prepare the simple syrup by combining the granulated sugar and water in a small saucepan. Bring to a boil and continue to boil over medium heat for 1 minute. Remove from the heat and allow to cool.

7. Beat the reserved egg white and the 1 tablespoon water in a small bowl and set aside.

8. Preheat the oven to 400°F.

9. Divide the dough into 12 equal pieces and shape each into a smooth round bun. Set the buns on a baking sheet that has been greased or lined with parchment paper, spaced equally to allow for spreading. Cover loosely with plastic wrap and set aside to rise for 10 minutes.

10. Using scissors, cut an X in the top of each bun, cutting one-third of the way through the dough. Brush the buns with some of the egg white and water wash. Cover again and let the buns rise for 15 minutes more. Brush the buns again with the wash.

11. Bake for 18 to 20 minutes, until golden brown.

12. Remove the buns to a wire rack, placing a baking sheet under the rack. Brush the hot buns with the simple syrup to glaze.

13. For the icing, combine the confectioners' sugar, cream or half-and-half, and vanilla in a small bowl. Stir until completely blended. While the buns are still warm, spoon the icing into the X cuts.

14. Serve warm or at room temperature. Freeze any buns not eaten on the first day.

Yield: 12 large buns

When Ed McDonnell was growing up in New York's Washington Heights, his family frequented Cushman's Bakery at 175th Street and St. Nicholas Avenue. From Ash Wednesday until Easter, Cushman's provided their predominately Irish Catholic clientele with a steady supply of hot cross buns. Ed still remembers how much he loved biting into a Cushman's bun, savoring the gentle infusion of candied citrus and the sweet cross of icing on top.

Greek Easter Bread

The day before Easter Sunday is one of the busiest of the year for those who observe traditional Greek Orthodox holidays. Saturday, the last day of Lenten fasting, is devoted to shopping, cooking, and preparing for the big Easter feast. One visits the local butcher for lamb or goat, the green market for fruit and produce, the cheese market for feta and olives, and a favorite neighborhood bakery for cakes, pastries, and the celebratory Easter bread. At home, fresh eggs are boiled in red dye, vinegar, and water, rubbed to a brilliant sheen with olive oil, and piled in the center of the braided golden ring of Easter bread as a glorious centerpiece for the Easter Sunday breakfast table.

Tradition aside, this is a fabulous-tasting loaf with a very fine texture—perfect for breakfast or midday snacking any day of the year.

³/₄ cup milk

¹/₂ cup (1 stick) unsalted butter, at room temperature

¹/₂ cup sugar

¹/₂ teaspoon salt

¹/₄ teaspoon anise seeds, finely crushed

¹/₄ teaspoon ground cinnamon

2¹/₂ teaspoons (1 envelope) active dry yeast

3 tablespoons lukewarm water (95° to 110°F)

1 teaspoon honey

4 large eggs

4¹/₄ cups unbleached all-purpose flour

1 tablespoon water

1 tablespoon sesame seeds

1. Heat the milk in a saucepan on top of the stove or in a medium-size bowl in a microwave oven until hot, but not yet simmering. Remove from the heat and stir in the butter, sugar, salt, anise seeds, and cinnamon. Set the mixture aside and allow to cool to 95° to 110°F, until lukewarm.

2. Meanwhile, combine the yeast with the water and honey in a large mixing bowl. Let proof until bubbly, about 5 minutes.

3. When the milk mixture has cooled sufficiently, stir it into the yeast mixture. Beat 3 of the eggs lightly and add to the mixing bowl. Add 4 cups of the flour, ¹/₂ cup at a time.

4. Turn the dough out onto a lightly floured work surface and gently knead in the remaining ¹/₄ cup flour. Continue to knead the soft dough until it feels smooth and elastic, about 5 minutes. Transfer to a large greased bowl, cover with plastic wrap, and set aside at room temperature to rise until doubled, about 1½ hours.

5. Return the dough to a work surface and divide it into 3 equal pieces. Roll each piece into a 20-inch rope. Pinch 1 end of each together, braid the ropes tightly, and pinch the loose ends together. Shape the braid into a ring, tucking the ends of the braid to close the ring. Transfer to a greased or parchment-lined baking sheet. Cover loosely with plastic wrap and set aside at room temperature to rise until doubled, about 45 minutes.

6. Preheat the oven to 350°F.

7. Beat the remaining egg and the 1 tablespoon water in a small dish. Brush the braided ring evenly with the egg wash and sprinkle with the sesame seeds. Bake for about 35 minutes, until deep golden brown. Place the bread on a wire rack to cool.

8. Cut into wedges to serve.

Yield: 1 large loaf

Sweet Yeast Bun Dough

(For Judy's Cinnamon Buns and Pecan Sticky Buns)

Even in times of trimmed-down cuisine, sweet bakery buns are still the rage. Puffed up and piping hot from the oven, redolent of cinnamon or bursting with nutty goodness, they tame the ravaged spirit. One bite and the harsh realities of today melt into the innocence of yesterday.

Use this sweet bun dough to make Judy's Cinnamon Buns (page 68) and Pecan Sticky Buns (page 70).

1 tablespoon active dry yeast

¹/₃ cup lukewarm water (95° to 110°F)

¹/₂ cup (1 stick) unsalted butter, at room temperature

¹/₃ cup sugar

2 teaspoons salt

¹/₄ teaspoon ground nutmeg

2 large eggs, at room temperature

1 cup milk, at room temperature

1 cup cake flour

3¹/₄ cups bread flour

1. In a small bowl, dissolve the yeast in the water. Let proof until bubbly, about 5 minutes.

2. In a large mixing bowl, cream the butter, sugar, salt, and nutmeg to a smooth paste. Add the eggs and blend. (Do not worry if the mixture looks curdled.) Stir in the milk.

3. Into a separate bowl, sift together the cake flour and 3 cups of the bread flour. Add 2 cups of the sifted flour to the liquid ingredients in the mixing bowl, stirring to blend. Stir in the yeast mixture. Add the remaining sifted flour, a little at a time, and mix into a smooth dough.

4. Turn the dough out onto a lightly floured work surface and knead for about 7 minutes, adding as much of the remaining ¹/₄ cup bread flour as necessary to produce a smooth, springy dough still tacky to the touch. Transfer to a large greased bowl, cover with plastic wrap, and set aside at room temperature to rise until doubled, about 1¹/₂ hours.

5. The dough can be covered and stored in the refrigerator for up to 12 hours.

Yield: 2³/₄ pounds, or enough for 12 large buns

Steve Maltzman is part of a family of bakers that had been in business for sixty-eight years. Steve's father started the Station Bakery in New York City, where his sons worked by his side. It was here, according to Steve, that "frozen dough" was born. (The name alludes to the fact that bakers can freeze this extra-rich dough without any loss of quality.)

Early one morning, the father and son team was unable to distinguish between the bucket filled with rising sweet bun dough and the bucket containing the danish dough. Adopting a somewhat fatalistic attitude, the Station bakers combined the contents of both buckets. Chilled, rolled, sprinkled liberally with cinnamon and sugar, drizzled with butter, and baked until golden and flaky, the improvisation quickly became a local breakfast hit. It wasn't long before other bakeries started producing their own frozen doughs, with a variety of fillings to choose from.

Steve started the M & M Bake Shop, which closed in 1980, from his father's Station Bakery.

Judy's Cinnamon Buns

Almost every bakery sold cinnamon buns or rolls when my friend Judy Fell was growing up, and many still do. Judy can't resist them, even today, but she's a tough customer to please. Her ideal cinnamon bun has a soft, squishy texture, an intensely flavorful cinnamon filling, and some—but not too many—moist, plump raisins. And don't forget to apply the icing when the bun is hot, so that it adheres lovingly.

Here it is—developed with Judy's patient guidance and final enthusiastic approval.

1 cup seedless raisins

½ cup granulated sugar

¼ cup packed light brown sugar

2 tablespoons ground cinnamon

1 recipe Sweet Yeast Bun Dough (page 66)

½ cup (1 stick) unsalted butter, at room temperature

1 large egg, beaten with 1 tablespoon water

Icing

2 cups confectioners' sugar

¼ cup heavy cream or half-and-half

1 teaspoon vanilla extract

1. Place the raisins in a small bowl and cover with hot tap water. Soak for 30 minutes. Drain and pat dry with paper toweling. Set aside.

2. Combine the sugars and cinnamon in a small bowl, stirring to mix.

3. Place the dough on a lightly floured work surface and divide it in half. Roll one piece out into a 15 × 8-inch rectangle ¼ inch thick. Spread 4 tablespoons of the butter over the dough. Sprinkle with half of the cinnamon-sugar and half of the raisins. Starting with a long side, roll the dough up tightly around the filling and pinch along the seam to seal. Roll the cylinder back and forth to form an even 2½-inch-thick log about 14 inches long. Repeat the process for the second piece of dough. Cut each log crosswise into 6 equal pieces.

4. Place the buns, cut side up, ½ inch apart on a greased baking sheet. Flatten each slightly with your hand. Cover loosely with plastic wrap and set aside at room temperature to rise for 30 minutes.

5. Preheat the oven to 375°F.

6. Brush the exposed surface of the buns with the egg and water wash. Bake for about 20 minutes, until golden brown.

7. While the buns are baking, prepare the icing. Combine the confectioners' sugar, cream or half-and-half, and vanilla in a medium bowl. Stir until smoothly blended; the icing should be thick but spoonable.

8. Remove the buns to a wire rack set atop a baking sheet. Spoon the icing over the hot buns to glaze. The buns are best when eaten within 2 days of baking; freeze any extras.

Yield: 12 large buns

Like so many sweet rolls, coffee cakes, and holiday breads, Judy's Cinnamon Buns are best served warm. To warm in a microwave oven, set the pastry on a paper towel and heat for 15 seconds at 50 percent power.

Judy Fell's childhood was spent in Chicago Heights, Illinois, during the 1940s and 1950s. She fondly remembers the Eagle Bakery, a German bakeshop that was a neighborhood favorite. Judy's mother was a regular customer for the breads, mostly the sour rye. Judy, however, had an insatiable sweet tooth. Her big brown eyes always fixated on the Eagle's cinnamon buns, alluringly draped with white icing.

Pecan Sticky Buns

Pecan Sticky Buns are best made by hand, the old-fashioned way. With every bite, their syrupy caramelized crust gives way to a wonderfully soft interior, to say nothing of the nutty crunch on top. Use muffin tins with oversize (¾-cup) wells.

1 cup dark corn syrup

1½ cups packed light brown sugar

¾ cup (1½ sticks) unsalted butter, melted

2 cups coarsely chopped pecans

2 teaspoons ground cinnamon

1 recipe Sweet Yeast Bun Dough
(page 66)

1. Combine the corn syrup and 1 cup of the brown sugar in a medium-size bowl. Add ½ cup of the melted butter (make sure that it's still hot) and whisk to a smooth syrup. Divide the syrup among twelve ¾-cup wells of a nonstick muffin tin. Sprinkle ⅔ cup of the pecans evenly over the syrup. Set aside.

2. Combine the remaining ½ cup brown sugar, the remaining 1⅓ cups chopped pecans, and the cinnamon. Mix thoroughly.

3. Place the dough on a lightly floured work surface and divide it in half. Roll out each piece into an 18 × 6-inch rectangle ¼ inch thick. Brush lightly with melted butter. Sprinkle each with half of the sugar and nut mixture.

4. Starting with a long side, roll one piece of dough up tightly around the filling and pinch the seam to seal. Roll the cylinder back and forth into an even 3-inch-thick log about 15 inches long. Repeat the process for the second piece of dough. Cut each log crosswise into 6 equal pieces.

5. Place cut side up in the wells of the prepared muffin tin. Flatten the buns into the wells slightly with your hand. Brush with the remaining melted butter and set aside at room temperature to rise for 20 minutes.

6. Preheat the oven to 375°F.

7. Place the muffin tin on a baking sheet. Bake for about 25 minutes, until the buns are browned and the syrup is bubbling. Carefully unmold the buns while still hot by placing a flat pan over the tin and inverting to release the buns with the syrup and nuts on top. Spoon any syrup that might run off back onto the buns. Let cool a bit—but not too much—and enjoy!

8. Freeze any buns not eaten by the second day.

Yield: 12 large buns

My friend Jon Rowley lives in Seattle, Washington. He frequently travels to the Cascades to hike and forage for mushrooms in autumn, when they are plentiful. On his way down the mountain one particularly misty, chilly day, he noticed a small wooden roadside sign tacked onto the trunk of a tree. In handwritten letters the sign read "Home Fires Bakery," with an arrow pointing straight ahead. After a few more miles of twists and turns, a second "Home Fires Bakery" sign appeared, with the arrow pointing to a right turn.

Falling for the lure, Jon followed a narrow route for quite a while, wondering all along why he was bothering. Finally, a small home appeared in the distance—a home transformed into a bakery, that is. The bakery specialized in homey-looking banana bread, cinnamon rolls, and sticky buns.

Jon decided the sticky buns were worth the detour. He also concluded that anyone who stumbled upon this hidden gem simply had to buy something.

Moravian Sugar Bread

Sugar bread, a breakfast treat, is a specialty of Moravian communities. The dough is prepared with mashed potatoes, which provide a delightfully fluffy texture. Spread into a shallow pan and dimpled with the fingertips like a flatbread, the dough is then drizzled with butter and brown sugar. The result is a tender cake encased in a crunchy crust.

4 ounces red potato, peeled and coarsely chopped (1 medium-size potato)

1 cup water

½ tablespoon active dry yeast

½ cup (1 stick) unsalted butter, at room temperature

½ cup granulated sugar

½ teaspoon salt

1 large egg

2½ cups unbleached all-purpose flour

⅓ cup packed light brown sugar, sieved

1. Boil the potato in the water, uncovered, until completely soft, 12 to 15 minutes. Drain, reserve the cooking liquid (you'll need almost ½ cup; add more water, if necessary), and let the liquid cool to 95 to 110°F, until lukewarm.

2. Meanwhile, in a small bowl, mash the potato to a puree and set aside.

3. When the cooking liquid has cooled sufficiently, combine 2 tablespoons and the yeast in a small bowl. Set aside for 5 minutes to proof, until bubbly.

4. In a medium-size mixing bowl, cream 6 tablespoons of the butter with the granulated sugar until fluffy. Add the salt and egg. Stir in the mashed potato and the yeast mixture. Add ⅓ cup of the reserved cooking liquid. (Do not be concerned if the mixture looks curdled at this stage.) Add the flour, a little at a time, to form a dough.

5. Turn the soft, moist dough out onto a lightly floured work surface. Knead until the dough feels smooth and elastic, about 5 minutes. Transfer to a greased bowl, cover with plastic wrap, and set aside at room temperature to rise until doubled, about 1½ hours.

6. Preheat the oven to 350°F. Grease the bottom and sides of a 9 × 12-inch baking sheet or a jelly roll pan.

7. Return the dough to a work surface and roll or push it out into a rectangle the size of the prepared pan. Fit the dough into the pan and push it down to fill the pan completely. Cover with a towel and set aside at room temperature for 45 minutes. (The dough will rise a little, but will not double.)

8. Melt the remaining 2 tablespoons butter. Dimple the dough by making deep indentations with your fingertips at 1½-inch intervals. Drizzle with the melted butter, then push brown sugar into each dimple. Sprinkle the remaining brown sugar evenly over the top.

9. Bake for about 25 minutes, until the crust is golden brown and the sugar crunchy. Cool in the pan on a wire rack.

10. Cut into 3-inch squares and serve the coffee cake warm.

Yield: 1 coffee cake

Winston-Salem, North Carolina, was settled by Moravians in the mid-1770s. The town's church-owned bakery was built in 1800 and passed to Christian Winkler seven years later. To this day, all baking at the Winkler Bakery is done without the benefit of electricity. The domed brick oven is fired up by burning logs and the baking is done in stages. Breads are loaded into the oven first, while it is still very hot. The sugar bread, or "cake" as it is called at the bakery, is baked next, with cookies last to go in as the oven cools down. The process is a fascinating one that can be viewed by visitors, since the Winkler Bakery is part of the Historic Old Salem Museum.

Houska

A rich braided loaf, Houska is studded with golden raisins and almonds. It is most often eaten for breakfast. I love cutting it into thick slices, toasting them, and smearing each with softened sweet butter. Houska also makes divine French toast.

⅔ cup lukewarm milk (95° to 110°F)

¼ cup sugar

2½ teaspoons (1 envelope) active dry yeast

4 tablespoons (½ stick) unsalted butter, melted and cooled

1 large egg

¼ teaspoon almond extract

2¾ cups unbleached all-purpose flour

1 teaspoon salt

½ cup golden raisins

¼ cup sliced or slivered almonds

1. Combine the milk, 1 tablespoon of the sugar, and the yeast in the bowl of a stationary electric mixer fitted with the flat paddle attachment. Allow to proof until bubbly, about 5 minutes.

2. In a small bowl, combine the melted butter, egg, almond extract, and the remaining 3 tablespoons sugar. Add to the yeast mixture and begin to mix at low speed. Add 1 cup of the flour, then the salt. Continue to add the remaining 1¾ cups flour, a little at a time, until a dough forms.

3. Turn the dough out onto a lightly floured work surface and knead in the raisins and almonds. Sprinkle with additional flour as necessary to keep the dough from sticking. Continue to knead until the dough feels smooth and elastic, about 5 minutes. Transfer to a greased bowl, cover with plastic wrap, and allow to rise until doubled, about 1 hour.

4. Return the dough to a work surface and knead briefly. Push or roll the dough out into a rectangle about 14 inches long. Cut lengthwise into thirds, terminating each cut just before reaching the far side so that one short end of the rectangle remains intact. Starting there, braid the strips of dough together and fold both ends under. Place the braid into a greased 9 × 5-inch loaf pan. Cover loosely with plastic wrap and set aside until the dough rises just above the rim of the pan, about 40 minutes.

5. Preheat the oven to 375°F.

6. Bake for about 30 minutes, until the loaf is a deep golden brown.

7. Unmold the bread onto a wire rack to cool.

Yield: 1 loaf

*H*ouska is the most popular item at Vesecky's on Cermak Road in Berwyn, Illinois. Fans of the more than sixty-year-old bakery may make their own houska at home during the week, but like their parents and grandparents, they never let a Saturday go by without buying one of Vesecky's houska for Sunday morning. Defying the trends of the times, Vesecky's is a neighborhood bakeshop that still has customers taking numbers and waiting their turn.

Dutch Apple Nut Bread

This tender loaf is swirled with soft cooked apple slices, cinnamon sugar, and chunks of walnuts. It has a luxuriously moist texture with a nutty crunch. I've added raisins to the traditional ingredients to boost the bread's fruity flavor.

½ cup golden raisins

1 teaspoon active dry yeast

2 tablespoons lukewarm water (95° to 110°F)

1 cup lukewarm milk (95° to 110°F)

2 tablespoons granulated sugar

½ tablespoon salt

½ cup (1 stick) unsalted butter, at room temperature

2¾ to 3 cups unbleached all-purpose flour

2 medium apples (about 1 pound), peeled, cored, and thinly sliced

⅓ cup packed dark brown sugar

1 tablespoon ground cinnamon

1 cup coarsely chopped walnuts

1. Place the raisins in a small bowl and cover with hot tap water. Soak for 30 minutes. Drain and set aside.

2. In a second small bowl, dissolve the yeast in the water. Set aside to proof for 5 minutes, until bubbly.

3. In a large mixing bowl, combine the milk, granulated sugar, salt, and 2 tablespoons of the butter. Stir to dissolve the butter. Add 1

cup of the flour and blend until smooth. Stir in the yeast mixture. Slowly add 1¾ cups more flour to form a stiff dough.

4. Turn the dough out onto a lightly floured work surface and knead until it feels smooth and elastic, about 8 minutes, adding more flour as necessary to keep the dough from sticking. Transfer to a greased bowl, cover with plastic wrap, and set aside at room temperature to rise until doubled, 1½ to 2 hours.

5. Punch the dough down, cover again, and let it rise again for 45 minutes.

6. Meanwhile, prepare the filling. Combine the apple slices and 1½ tablespoons of the butter in a skillet. Cook over medium heat until very soft but not browned, stirring occasionally, about 12 minutes. Remove from the heat, stir in the raisins, and allow to cool.

7. In a small bowl, combine 4 tablespoons of the butter, the brown sugar, and cinnamon. Cream the mixture with a spoon until smooth.

8. Return the dough to a lightly floured work surface. Roll it out into a 12 × 8-inch rectangle and spread half of the brown sugar mixture evenly over the surface. Sprinkle with ½

cup of the walnuts. Fold one short end over to the middle of the rectangle, then fold the opposite end over on top to cover completely, forming 3 layers. Roll out a second time into a 12 × 8-inch rectangle, spread with the remaining brown sugar mixture, sprinkle with the remaining ½ cup walnuts, and fold into thirds again as before.

9. Roll the dough once more into a 12 × 8-inch rectangle. (Do not worry about nuts and cinnamon popping through the dough.) Spread with the apple and raisin mixture in an even layer. Fold into thirds as before to enclose the filling. Pinch all seams closed to seal. Place the dough in a greased 9 × 5-inch loaf pan, seam side down, and press down on the dough to fill the pan evenly. Cover with a towel and set aside at room temperature until the dough rises to the top of the pan, about 30 minutes.

10. Preheat the oven to 375°F.

11. Cut 4 slashes crosswise into the dough with the tip of a sharp knife or a razor blade. Bake for about 45 minutes, until well browned. Remove the loaf from the pan to cool on a wire rack. Rub the top of the hot loaf with the remaining ½ tablespoon butter to glaze.

12. Slice and serve the bread warm, at room temperature, or toasted.

Yield: 1 loaf

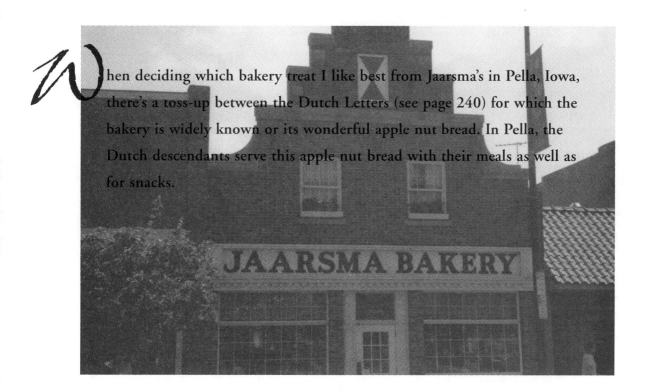

When deciding which bakery treat I like best from Jaarsma's in Pella, Iowa, there's a toss-up between the Dutch Letters (see page 240) for which the bakery is widely known or its wonderful apple nut bread. In Pella, the Dutch descendants serve this apple nut bread with their meals as well as for snacks.

Maple Bars

Maple Bars are rectangular raised doughnuts topped with maple glaze, and are a specialty item of bakeries in the Pacific Northwest. They remind me of Indian fry bread as much as of doughnuts, and are simply spectacular tasting. Homemade Maple Bars are best when eaten within a few hours of the making. Pure maple syrup can be found in health food stores or gourmet food stores.

Dough

¹⁄₂ tablespoon active dry yeast

2 tablespoons lukewarm water (95° to 110°F)

¹⁄₄ cup granulated sugar

2 tablespoons unsalted butter

¹⁄₂ teaspoon salt

³⁄₄ cup milk

1 large egg

¹⁄₄ teaspoon ground nutmeg

2¹⁄₂ cups unbleached all-purpose flour

Maple Glaze

1¹⁄₂ cups confectioners' sugar

¹⁄₃ cup pure maple syrup

1¹⁄₂ tablespoons heavy cream

Canola oil, for frying

1. Prepare the dough by dissolving the yeast in the lukewarm water in a small dish. Let proof until bubbly, about 5 minutes.

2. Combine the sugar, butter, and salt in a medium mixing bowl. Heat the milk in a saucepan on top of the stove or in a glass bowl in the microwave oven until hot but not yet simmering, and pour it over the ingredients in the mixing bowl. Stir to dissolve the sugar and melt the butter. Let cool until warm.

3. Stir the yeast mixture into the warm milk mixture. Beat in the egg and nutmeg. Add the flour, ¹⁄₂ cup at a time, to form a soft dough.

4. Turn the dough out onto a floured work surface. Gently knead until the dough feels smooth and elastic, 3 to 5 minutes. Transfer to a greased bowl, cover with plastic wrap, and set aside at room temperature to rise until doubled, about 1¹⁄₂ hours.

5. Return the dough to a work surface and roll it out into a 12 × 8-inch rectangle. Cut the rectangle into twelve 4 × 2-inch pieces and place them on a lightly floured baking sheet. Cover with a towel and let rise for 20 minutes at room temperature.

6. While the doughnuts are rising, prepare the glaze. Stir the confectioners' sugar and maple syrup together in a bowl. Add the cream and whisk until the mixture is smoothly blended, with a thick, spreadable consistency. Cover and set aside while the doughnuts fry.

7. Fill a high-sided frying pan with 2 to 2½ inches of oil and heat to 365°F as registered on a deep-frying thermometer. Fry the doughnuts, a few at a time, until well browned on each side. (Total cooking time will vary from 6 to 7 minutes. Begin to check each side for doneness after about 3 minutes.) Drain on paper toweling.

8. Glaze when the doughnuts are barely warm or at room temperature. Let the glaze set before serving.

Yield: 12 doughnuts

My favorite maple bars are made in a West Seattle bakery called Blakes. It has been in business for more than a hundred years, a full half-century in the West Seattle location. Now run by the third generation of the family, the shop is well known for its large variety of breakfast baked goods, including custard-filled bismarcks, danish rolls and twists, coffee cakes, tea cakes, and heavenly maple bars.

Sitting at a little round table in Blakes one morning I polished off my maple bar in two minutes flat, pausing only long enough to savor the glaze—a mixture of maple syrup and sugar enhanced by a touch of cream.

Cardamom Tea Ring

This tea ring derives its character from freshly ground cardamom. For the dough, use seeds from cardamom pods rather than ground cardamom for their greater aromatic intensity. The cardamom-sugar topping, for which I use pre-ground cardamom, adds visual appeal and crunch, along with a subtle boost to the ring's spice flavor.

½ tablespoon active dry yeast

¾ cup lukewarm milk (95° to 110°F)

½ cup (1 stick) unsalted butter, at room temperature

½ cup plus 2 tablespoons sugar

3½ cups plus 2 tablespoons unbleached all-purpose flour

2 large eggs, plus 1 egg white

½ teaspoon salt

½ teaspoon vanilla extract

Seeds from 18 to 20 cardamom pods, crushed (1 rounded teaspoon)

½ teaspoon ground cardamom

1 tablespoon water

1. Dissolve the yeast in ¼ cup of the milk in a small bowl. Let proof until bubbly, about 5 minutes.

2. Combine the butter and ½ cup of the sugar in the bowl of a stationary electric mixer fitted with the flat paddle attachment. Cream at medium-low speed until fluffy, about 2 minutes. Add the yeast mixture and 1 cup of the flour, beating until smoothly blended. Slowly pour in the remaining ½ cup milk. Add the whole eggs, 1 at a time, blending after each addition.

3. At low speed, add 2 cups more of the flour, a little at a time. Blend in the salt, vanilla, and crushed cardamom, then slowly add ½ cup additional flour. The dough should feel soft and pliable.

4. Turn the dough out onto a work surface sprinkled with 1 tablespoon flour. Gently knead, adding the remaining 1 tablespoon flour as necessary. Continue to knead until the dough feels smooth and elastic, about 5 minutes. Transfer to a large greased bowl, cover with plastic wrap, and set aside at room temperature to rise until doubled, about 1½ hours.

5. In a small dish, combine the remaining 2 tablespoons sugar and the ground cardamom. Stir until thoroughly mixed, and set aside.

6. Grease the bottom and sides of a 10-inch round cake pan. Grease the outside of a 2½- to 3-inch ramekin, or of a clean and dry aluminum can of similar diameter, and place it in the center of the pan.

7. Return the dough to a work surface and divide it in half. Roll each piece into a rope about 24 inches long. Sprinkle generously with about three-fourths of the cardamom-sugar, rolling the ropes in the mixture to coat thoroughly. Cross the ropes in the center to form an X. Working from the center, twist the ropes on one side of the X together, then braid the other side of the X. Transfer the woven length of dough to the prepared pan and form it into a circle, tucking the ends together to seal the ring. Cover with a towel and let rise at room temperature until doubled, about 45 minutes.

8. Preheat the oven to 350°F.

9. Beat the remaining egg white with the water in a small dish. Brush the dough evenly with the egg white and water wash and sprinkle the top with half of the remaining cardamom-sugar. Bake for 40 to 45 minutes, until golden brown.

10. Remove the tea ring from the pan to a wire rack. While still hot, brush the top of the coffee cake lightly with the wash and sprinkle with the remaining cardamom-sugar.

11. Serve warm or at room temperature.

Yield: 1 coffee cake

M y Grandmother Wilson lived on a farm in Indiana for most of her ninety-eight years. Once she reached the age when she could no longer bake several times a week, her children would bring her favorite treats when they visited. My mother made the trip from Chicago several times a year, usually preceded by a telephone call inquiring as to what she could bring that would please her mother. Most of the time the answer was the same: "Oh, just bring me a cardamom ring from Kirschbaum's, please."

On Burlington Avenue in suburban Western Springs sits a tidy brick storefront bakery that has been in the Kirschbaum family for over forty years. Three generations keep the bakery humming, with Cele and Les Kirschbaum running the shop, while son Bob and grandson Mike do the baking.

Their coffee cake ring, which my grandmother so loved, is made from a soft dough woven into a ring. It exudes the heady perfumed scent of freshly ground cardamom seeds.

Seven Sisters Almond Coffee Cake

The "sisters" are seven rolls filled with almond paste, nested to form a coffee cake and sprinkled with sliced almonds and streusel. After baking, I finish the coffee cake with a simple drizzle of white icing. I've seen the girls in other guises, sometimes topped with a variety of fruit preserves and definitely overdressed for the occasion, since this coffee cake is perfect for brunch or afternoon tea.

2 tablespoons active dry yeast

1/2 cup lukewarm water (95° to 110°F)

1/2 cup sour cream, at room temperature

3 tablespoons granulated sugar

3 cups unbleached all-purpose flour

1/2 cup (1 stick) unsalted butter, melted and cooled

2 large eggs, 1 separated

1 teaspoon salt

1/2 teaspoon ground cardamom

1 cup prepared almond cake filling

1 tablespoon water

1/2 cup sliced almonds

1/2 cup Streusel Crumb (see box)

Icing

1 cup confectioners' sugar

1 tablespoon water

1. Prepare the sponge starter by combining the yeast and lukewarm water in the bowl of a stationary electric mixer. Let proof until bubbly, about 5 minutes.

2. Using the flat paddle attachment, mix in the sour cream and 1 tablespoon of the sugar at low speed, until blended. Add 1 1/2 cups of the flour, 1/2 cup at a time, mixing into a soft dough. Cover with plastic wrap and let the starter sit at room temperature to rise, bubble, and fall back slightly, about 2 hours.

3. Uncover the bowl and fit the mixer with the dough hook. At low speed, add the remaining 2 tablespoons sugar, the melted butter, 1 whole egg and the yolk of the second egg (reserving the egg white), the salt, and cardamom. Slowly add the remaining 1 1/2 cups flour. Continue to knead at low speed until the dough is soft, smooth, and elastic, about 3 minutes. Remove the dough to a large greased bowl. Cover with plastic wrap and set aside at room temperature to rise until doubled, 1 to 1 1/2 hours.

4. Return the dough to a lightly floured work surface and divide it in half. Roll one half out into a 12 × 8-inch rectangle. Spread evenly with 1/2 cup of the almond filling. Starting with the long side, roll the dough up around the filling to form a log. Cut the log crosswise into 7 rolls of equal size. Arrange the rolls cut side down in a greased 8-inch round cake pan, with 1 roll in the center and the other 6 clustered around the first to form a coffee cake. Cover loosely with plastic wrap. Repeat the process with the second piece of dough. Set the pans aside and allow the dough to rise at room temperature for 30 minutes.

5. Preheat the oven to 350°F.

6. Beat the remaining egg white with the 1 tablespoon water in a small dish. Paint the tops of the coffee cakes with the egg white and water wash. Sprinkle ¼ cup of the almonds over each, then ¼ cup of the streusel crumb.

7. Bake for about 30 minutes, until browned.

8. While the coffee cakes bake, make the icing. Combine the confectioners' sugar and water in a medium bowl, whisking until smoothly blended.

9. Remove the pans to a wire rack. Drizzle the coffee cakes with icing while still warm. Once the icing has set, unmold.

10. Separate the coffee cakes into individual rolls to serve.

Yield: 2 coffee cakes (14 rolls)

Streusel crumb is a brown sugar and cinnamon mixture that is as versatile as it is delicious. I use it in Seven Sisters Almond Coffee Cake, Russian Coffee Cake (page 88), Chocolate Babka (page 90), and Fruit Kuchen (page 92). To make, combine ⅔ cup all-purpose flour, ⅔ cup packed dark brown sugar, and 2 teaspoons ground cinnamon in a medium bowl. Using a pastry blender, cut in 6 tablespoons softened butter until fine crumbs form. Store the streusel in a covered container in the refrigerator for up to 1 month or in the freezer for up to 3 months. Yields about 1¾ cups.

Pecan Kringle

Kringle *is the Danish word for "pretzel," the configuration in which the coffee cake of the same name was originally made, but oval has been the favored shape for about the past eighty years. It's an exceptionally fine coffee cake, made of many feathery layers of danish pastry, usually filled with choice pecans, shaped into a large, flattened oval, and baked to a flaky golden brown. The final touch is a drizzle of white icing. The result is so splendid it defies description. Danes believe good luck will come to those presented with* kringle *on their birthday breakfast tray.*

³/₄ cup (1¹/₂ sticks) unsalted butter, cut into 12 pieces

2¹/₂ teaspoons (1 envelope) active dry yeast

¹/₄ cup lukewarm water (95° to 110°F)

¹/₄ cup lukewarm milk (95° to 110°F)

¹/₄ cup granulated sugar

¹/₂ teaspoon salt

¹/₂ teaspoon lemon extract

1 large egg, lightly beaten

1²/₃ cups unbleached all-purpose flour

Filling

³/₄ cup packed dark brown sugar

¹/₃ cup unsalted butter, at room temperature

¹/₄ teaspoon ground cinnamon

¹/₈ teaspoon salt

1 tablespoon all-purpose flour

1 large egg white

2 cups coarsely chopped pecans

Icing

1 cup confectioners' sugar

1 tablespoon water

1. Mound 6 tablespoons of the butter onto each of 2 plates and set aside to soften. Shape one mound into a ball, center it on a sheet of waxed paper, and cover with a second sheet of waxed paper. Using a rolling pin, push and roll the butter out into a smooth 8 × 6-inch rectangle. Set in the refrigerator. Repeat the process with the other mound of butter. Chill until cold, about 30 minutes.

2. Dissolve the yeast in the water in a large mixing bowl. Let proof until bubbly, about 5 minutes. Add the milk. Stir in the sugar, salt, lemon extract, and egg. Add the flour, ¹/₃ cup at a time, to form a stiff dough.

3. Turn the dough out onto a lightly floured work surface and knead until it feels very smooth, about 5 minutes. Add extra flour if necessary to keep the dough from sticking.

Shape the dough into a flattened disk and wrap completely in plastic wrap. Refrigerate along with the sheets of butter until the butter is sufficiently cold.

4. On a lightly floured work surface, roll the dough out into an 8 × 12-inch rectangle. Peel the waxed paper from one of the chilled sheets of butter and center the butter lengthwise on the dough (so that the smaller rectangle of butter is centered atop the larger rectangle of dough). Fold the short end of the dough one-third of the way over the rectangle, then fold the opposite end over on top to cover completely. Starting with the short end of the folded envelope of dough, repeat the 2 folds in the opposite direction. Wrap in plastic wrap and refrigerate for 30 minutes.

5. Return the dough to a lightly floured surface and roll it again into an 8 × 12-inch rectangle. Peel the waxed paper from the remaining sheet of cold butter, center it lengthwise on the dough, and fold up in both directions exactly as before. Wrap in plastic wrap and refrigerate for at least 2 and up to 12 hours.

6. For the filling, cream the brown sugar, butter, cinnamon, and salt in a medium-size bowl. Stir in the flour and egg white, mixing into a smooth, soft paste.

7. Cut the chilled dough in half crosswise, for 2 equal pieces. On a lightly floured surface, roll 1 piece out into a 20 × 6-inch rectangle.

Spread half of the filling lengthwise down the center of the dough, leaving a 1½-inch border on each side, and sprinkle 1 cup of the pecans on top. Fold the long side of the dough over to the middle to cover half the filling. Moisten the edge of the opposite side with water and fold over the filling, overlapping the dough to seal.

8. Place the filled dough on a nonstick baking sheet, seam side up, and shape it into an oval ring. Moisten and press the ends together to seal. Flatten the dough evenly with your hand, maintaining the oval shape. Cover loosely with plastic wrap. Roll out the second piece of dough, spread with the remaining filling and pecans, fold up, shape into an oval ring on a second baking sheet, and cover. Set aside at room temperature for 1 hour.

9. Preheat the oven to 350°F.

10. Bake the coffee cakes, one at a time, for about 25 minutes, until golden brown.

11. For the icing, combine the confectioners' sugar and the water in a bowl and whisk until smooth.

12. Remove each coffee cake to a wire rack to cool. Drizzle with the icing. Serve warm or at room temperature.

Yield: 2 coffee cakes

Racine, Wisconsin, is famous for two things, neither of which is the expanse of lake on which it rests. The city is known for the rich heritage of its large Danish community, which constitutes half the population, and for their beloved coffee cake, called kringle. For the best of both, head straight to the O & H Danish Bakery, where kringle is baked by three generations of the Olesen family—Christian, the founder; his son Ray; and grandsons Eric, Michael, and Dale.

The delicate kringle dough is rolled and folded into as many as thirty-two layers at the O & H Danish Bakery, a process that can take up to three days. This kringle recipe, adapted from one provided by Mr. and Mrs. Ray Olesen, produces a coffee cake very close in taste to the bakery's with less than a day's investment of time. The recipe makes two kringles, a minimum quantity for the holiday baking season, when it's inconceivable not to share something this good.

Babka Coffee Cake Dough

(For Russian Coffee Cake and Chocolate Babka)

With its soft, rich texture, Babka Dough is the perfect host for swirled fruit or chocolate filling in loaf-style coffee cakes. The moist dough makes a coffee cake that stays fresh and flavorful for days at room temperature. Use this recipe to prepare the dough for Russian Coffee Cake (page 88) and for Chocolate Babka (page 90).

1 tablespoon active dry yeast

1 tablespoon nonfat dry milk

½ cup lukewarm water (95° to 110°F)

3¼ to 3½ cups unbleached baker's patent flour (see Mail Order Source Guide) or bread flour

⅓ cup sugar

½ tablespoon salt

½ tablespoon vanilla extract

¼ teaspoon ground cardamom

2 large eggs, plus 1 egg yolk

½ cup (1 stick) unsalted butter, melted and cooled

1. Prepare the sponge starter by dissolving the yeast and dry milk in the water in a large mixing bowl. Add ¾ cup of the flour, stirring until smoothly blended. Cover with plastic wrap and set aside at room temperature until the sponge has bubbled up and fallen back slightly, 45 minutes to 1 hour.

2. Stir the sugar, salt, vanilla, and cardamom into the starter. Mix in the eggs and egg yolk, blending well. Add 2 cups of the flour, a little at a time, mixing to incorporate completely. Pour in the melted butter in a slow, steady stream while mixing the dough. Stir in ¼ cup more of the flour to form a smooth dough.

3. Turn the dough out onto a work surface and gently knead for about 5 minutes, adding ¼ cup or more of the remaining flour as necessary to produce a dough that is smooth and elastic but not dry. Transfer to a clean bowl, cover with plastic wrap, and set aside at room temperature to rise until doubled, 50 minutes to 1 hour.

4. The dough can be covered and refrigerated for up to 24 hours.

Yield: 2 pounds, or enough for 2 coffee cakes

Russian Coffee Cake

Russian Coffee Cake is the mother lode of breakfast pastries. It's so full of good-ies that it is often sold in strips by the pound, rather than by the loaf. The but-tery dough is swirled with streusel and stuffed with fruit, raisins, and walnuts.

²/₃ cup golden raisins

³/₄ cup all-purpose flour

2 tablespoons almond paste

4 tablespoons (¹/₂ stick) unsalted butter, at room temperature

2 tablespoons plus ¹/₄ cup sugar

1 large egg white

1¹/₄ cups Streusel Crumb (see page 83)

1 recipe Babka Coffee Cake Dough (page 87)

12 ounces each of 2 flavors of prepared fruit pie filling, such as apricot or raspberry

1 cup coarsely chopped walnuts

¹/₄ cup water

1. Place the raisins in a small bowl and cover with hot tap water. Soak for 30 minutes. Drain and set aside.

2. To make the shortbread crust, combine the flour, almond paste, butter, and 2 table-spoons of the sugar in a small mixing bowl. Mix to fine crumbs. Add the egg white and mix to form a smooth dough. Divide the dough in half and press each piece evenly into the bottom of a greased 8¹/₂ × 4¹/₂-inch

loaf pan. Sprinkle 2 tablespoons of the streusel crumb over each crust and set aside.

3. On a lightly floured surface, roll out half the dough into a 14 × 10-inch rectangle. Spread one of the fruit fillings evenly over the dough, then sprinkle with ¹/₃ cup raisins, ¹/₂ cup walnuts, and ¹/₂ cup of the streusel crumb. Starting with the short end, roll the dough up as tightly as possible around the filling. (The roll will be stuffed very full.) Pinch the seam and the ends closed. Place seam side down in a prepared loaf pan and push the dough down slightly to fill the pan. Repeat the rolling and filling procedure with the remaining piece of dough, using the other fruit filling. Cover with plastic wrap and set aside at room temperature to rise for 45 minutes.

4. Preheat the oven to 350°F.

5. Make a simple syrup by combining the remaining ¹/₄ cup sugar and the ¹/₄ cup water in a small saucepan. Bring to a boil and keep over medium heat for 1 minute. Remove from the heat and allow to cool.

6. Place the loaf pans onto a baking sheet. Bake for about 40 minutes, until the crust is golden. Transfer the pans to a wire rack.

While the loaves are still hot, brush them with the simple syrup to glaze. Cool to room temperature before removing from the pan.

Yield: 2 coffee cakes

The Russian coffee cake I tasted from the Flakowitz Bakeshop in Boca Raton, Florida, was awe-inspiring. First, the box told me what to expect—plain black lettering on a simple white bakery box exclaiming "If taste is test . . . ours is the best!"

In addition to the usual excess of a Russian coffee cake, Flakowitz includes two flavors of pie fillings and an almond-scented shortbread crust. This was the coffee cake of my dreams. My husband, Bill, who normally frowns at sweet treats in the morning, quickly devoured two slices.

Here is my version of this coffee cake of coffee cakes. It is not exactly like Flakowitz's, but it is a close approximation.

Chocolate Babka

Chocolate Babka is a pretty special coffee cake by definition. Most versions have a bittersweet chocolate filling combined with crumbly streusel. Some have dried fruit, currants, or raisins as well. I decided to add an almond accent when developing this recipe—to raves from friends who tasted it.

^{1}/$_2$ cup almond paste

2 large egg whites

1^2/$_3$ cups Streusel Crumb (see page 83)

6 ounces semisweet chocolate, shredded

**1 recipe Babka Coffee Cake Dough
(page 87)**

2 tablespoons butter, melted

1. Combine the almond paste and egg whites in a small bowl and mix until smoothly blended.

2. In another bowl, combine ^{2}/$_3$ cup of the streusel crumb and about one-fourth of the shredded chocolate for a topping. Set aside.

3. Place the dough on a lightly floured work surface. Divide it in half and roll one piece out into a 14 × 10-inch rectangle. Spread evenly with half of the almond mixture. Sprinkle with ^{1}/$_2$ cup of the remaining plain streusel crumb and half of the remaining

plain shredded chocolate. Starting with the short end, roll the dough up tightly around the filling. Pinch the seam and ends closed. Place seam side down in a greased 8^1/$_2$ × 4^1/$_2$-inch loaf pan, pushing the dough down slightly to fill the pan. Repeat the process with the second piece of dough. Cover with plastic wrap and set aside at room temperature to rise for 45 minutes.

4. Preheat the oven to 350°F.

5. Place the pans on a baking sheet. Brush the dough with the melted butter and sprinkle each with half the reserved chocolate-streusel topping.

6. Bake for about 40 minutes, until crusty and browned. Set the loaf pans on a wire rack. Cool to room temperature before removing the loaves.

Yield: 2 coffee cakes

Grossinger's Bakeshop on Columbus Avenue in Manhattan has been making babkas (and much more) for at least forty years. The tiny retail storefront, hiding a gigantic bakery production kitchen, resembles an old-fashioned apothecary, with ceiling-high cabinetry behind two neat rows of glass-fronted wooden cases. Some of the saleswomen move with a slow shuffle, but they're quick to size up their customers and may respond to an inquiry with "You don't want the raspberry babka; you should take the chocolate." And you just know they're right.

Fruit Kuchen

Kuchen is a coffee cake to sink your teeth into. It's equally good for breakfast or as a dessert in the evening. The breadlike dough is filled with fruit or a combination of fruit fillings, and baked like a tart.

1 cup lukewarm milk (95° to 110°F)

¹/₂ tablespoon active dry yeast

¹/₂ cup granulated sugar

¹/₂ cup (1 stick) unsalted butter, at room temperature

¹/₂ teaspoon salt

1 teaspoon grated orange zest

1 large egg yolk

2¹/₂ cups unbleached all-purpose flour

3¹/₂ to 4 cups fresh or frozen (thawed) fruit, such as blueberries or sliced peaches

¹/₂ cup packed light brown sugar

1 teaspoon ground cinnamon

¹/₄ cup orange juice

¹/₄ cup cornstarch

¹/₂ cup Streusel Crumb (see page 83)

1. Pour ¹/₂ cup of the milk into a small bowl, and sprinkle with the yeast and 1 tablespoon of the sugar. Set aside to proof until bubbly, about 5 minutes.

2. In a large mixing bowl or in the bowl of a stationary electric mixer fitted with the flat paddle attachment, combine the remaining ¹/₂ cup milk, 4 tablespoons of the butter, 3 tablespoons of the sugar, the salt, and orange zest. Blend in the egg yolk and 1 cup of the flour, then the yeast mixture. Slowly add the remaining 1¹/₂ cups flour to form a dough.

3. Turn the soft dough out onto a lightly floured work surface and knead gently until it feels smooth and elastic, 3 to 5 minutes. Transfer to a greased bowl, cover with plastic wrap, and set aside at room temperature to rise until doubled, about 1 hour.

4. While the dough is rising, prepare the fruit filling. In a medium saucepan, combine the fruit, the remaining 4 tablespoons butter, the remaining ¹/₄ cup granulated sugar, the brown sugar, and cinnamon over medium heat. Bring to a boil, stirring constantly. Boil for 3 minutes, until the fruit begins to soften.

5. Combine the orange juice and cornstarch in a small dish and mix until smoothly blended. Stir the mixture into the fruit, bring back to a boil, and boil for 1 minute more to thicken. Transfer the hot fruit filling to a bowl (you should have about 3 cups) and refrigerate.

6. Preheat the oven to 400°F.

7. Return the dough to a lightly floured work surface and roll it out into a 13-inch circle about ¼ inch thick. Line a greased 10-inch round cake pan with the dough, which should just fit the pan. Spread the cooled fruit filling over the dough and sprinkle evenly with the streusel crumb.

8. Bake for about 25 minutes, until the crust is well browned and the fruit is bubbly. Cool in the pan on a wire rack.

9. Cut the kuchen into wedges and serve warm or at room temperature.

Yield: 1 coffee cake

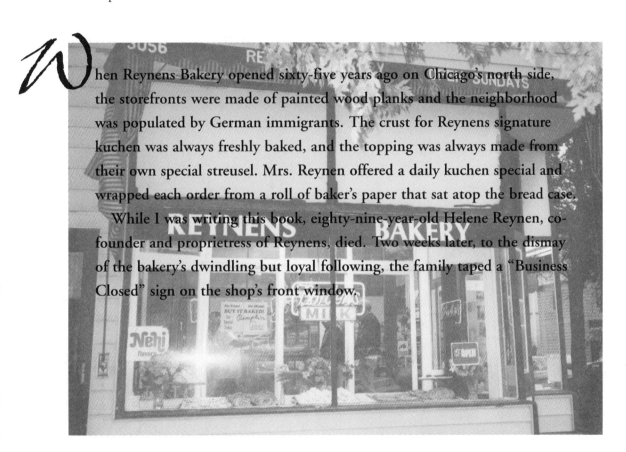

When Reynens Bakery opened sixty-five years ago on Chicago's north side, the storefronts were made of painted wood planks and the neighborhood was populated by German immigrants. The crust for Reynens signature kuchen was always freshly baked, and the topping was always made from their own special streusel. Mrs. Reynen offered a daily kuchen special and wrapped each order from a roll of baker's paper that sat atop the bread case.

While I was writing this book, eighty-nine-year-old Helene Reynen, cofounder and proprietress of Reynens, died. Two weeks later, to the dismay of the bakery's dwindling but loyal following, the family taped a "Business Closed" sign on the shop's front window.

THREE

Special Occasion Cakes

There was a time when bakery cakes were special. Layers of cake were made from scratch by creaming, blending, and beating—not by scooping out of a fifty-pound bag of cake mix. The ingredients that went into cake batters, fillings, and frostings were real eggs, sweet butter, high-butterfat cream, whole milk, pure extracts, natural fruit purees, and premium chocolates.

Have times changed? Sadly, yes. As dedicated bakers of the old school retire or pass on, their methods often go with them. Can you still find cakes made the way all once were? Yes, but you have to look harder these days—or you can bake them at home. Baking is both an art and a science, requiring patience as you perfect your skills, but it is a truly rewarding experience.

Tips and Techniques

Ingredients and Equipment

- Use cake flour in these recipes, as specified. It has a distinct texture and color and a very low protein content that provides volume and high moisture retention. In a pinch you might substitute bleached pastry flour or bleached all-purpose flour, but don't count on the same excellent results.

- Use only pure extracts and fresh citrus zest. (A zester is well worth the minimal expense.) Replace your supply of baking powder and baking soda at least once a year, and check spices periodically to ensure that they are still fresh and aromatic. Likewise, use only unsalted butter for its sweet taste and to avoid the excess moisture that would be lent by salted butter. When the addition of salt is called for in a recipe, you should not eliminate the salt and substitute salted butter.

- Some recipes require using pans of depths differing from that of standard-size cake pans. I specify the depth of pan to be used when this factor will significantly affect the outcome (see Mail Order Source Guide).

Preparation and Baking

Correct mixing of the batter is the key to a tender cake. Most of my cakes fall into one of three basic categories—creamed cakes, sponge cakes, or chiffon cakes—for which mixing tips follow. There are, of course, a few exceptions to the rules. Graham Cracker Cake combines creamed and sponge methods, Pineapple Upside-Down Cake involves a simple combination of ingredients, and Chocolate Hazelnut Meringue Torte and the cheesecakes (White Chocolate Cheesecake and the cheesecake layer of the Two-in-One Cake) defy easy categorization.

Sponge cakes (Danish Layer Cake, Cassata Cake, Fruit Basket Cake, Chocolate Roll, and Charlotte Russe) are prepared in two stages. First, beat the egg yolks to thicken and aerate (adding sugar or melted chocolate as directed) and gently fold in the sifted dry ingredients with a large rubber spatula. Second, make a meringue by beating room-temperature egg whites to stiff and shiny peaks and fold into the egg yolk mixture. Take care not to overbeat the egg whites, as dry peaks will be difficult to fold in. When sugar is added to the egg whites, pour in a slow, steady stream from the spout of a liquid measuring cup.

Chiffon cakes (Chocolate Knockout Cake) involve preparing a meringue as you would for sponge cakes. Add wet ingredients to dry ones, beat to blend thoroughly, and fold in the meringue. (This process is much like the preparation of a boxed cake mix.)

The remaining cakes in this chapter are creamed cakes, also called butter cakes. First cream room-temperature butter and sugar with an electric mixer at medium speed until fluffy. Add the eggs one at a time, or in a slow, steady stream as specified, blending fully after each addition to keep the mixture airy. Add the remaining ingredients at low speed to avoid splashing, alternating additions of dry ingredients and liquids; scrape down the bowl as necessary. Don't be concerned if the mixture at first looks curdled.

Bake all cakes in the middle of the oven.

Decorating

Use a pastry bag to pipe soft doughs or meringues onto baking sheets, pipe whipped cream or pastry cream into baked pastries as a filling, or decorate cakes. The cone-shaped bags are available in department and cookware stores, as well as in many supermarkets. They are fitted with tips that control the shapes of the item being piped. A circular "open-hole" tip is used to pipe doughs or meringues before baking.

Frost the cakes using a long, thin metal spatula. (It's easier when you elevate the cake on a stand—a turntable is particularly helpful.) If the cake is crumbly, apply a thin layer of frosting and let it set before spreading on the remaining frosting. If the frosting is too creamy to spread easily, chill the frosting to thicken or chill the cake to firm.

To garnish the sides of a frosted cake with toasted nuts or cake crumbs, hold the cake up from the bottom and press the nuts or crumbs into the frosting with the palm of your hand.

Storage

Homemade cakes are best when served fresh. Baked and cooled, they can be wrapped in plastic wrap and set aside at room temperature for a day before frosting. Preferably, wrap first in plastic wrap and then in aluminum foil and freeze (on a level surface in the freezer) for up to one month. Thaw cakes in their wrapping at room temperature.

Serve the cake on the same day as you frost it. In general, creamed cakes are best served at room temperature. I note in individual recipes when frostings or fillings require that the cake be refrigerated.

German Chocolate Cake

For a taste of real Old World German chocolate cake, try this recipe. It's not exactly what you might be expecting—no coconut or pecans—but it's pretty terrific, and authentic, I'm told. For a dramatic presentation, arrange a few fresh edible flowers in the center of the cake.

Cake

3 ounces semisweet chocolate, coarsely chopped

¹/₃ cup boiling water

1³/₄ cups cake flour

³/₄ teaspoon baking soda

¹/₂ teaspoon salt

10 tablespoons (1¹/₄ sticks) unsalted butter, at room temperature

1¹/₄ cups sugar

3 large eggs, at room temperature

¹/₂ tablespoon vanilla extract

³/₄ cup buttermilk, at room temperature

Chocolate Ganache

12 ounces semisweet chocolate, coarsely chopped

1¹/₂ cups heavy (whipping) cream

1 teaspoon vanilla extract

1. Preheat the oven to 350°F. Grease two 8-inch round cake pans, 2 inches deep. Cut and fit circles of waxed paper to line the bottom of each pan.

2. To make the cake, place the chocolate in a bowl and pour the boiling water over it. Stir until smoothly blended and set aside to cool to room temperature.

3. Sift the flour, baking soda, and salt together into a medium-size bowl.

4. Combine the butter and sugar in a large mixing bowl. Cream with an electric mixer at medium-high speed. Beat until fluffy and light in color, about 3 minutes. Reduce the speed to medium-low and add the eggs, one at a time, beating well after each addition. Pour in the chocolate mixture.

5. Stir the vanilla into the buttermilk. Reduce the mixer speed to low and slowly add the flour mixture, alternating with the buttermilk mixture and blending thoroughly after each addition.

6. Divide the batter equally between the prepared pans and smooth with a spatula. Bake for 25 to 30 minutes, until a cake tester comes out clean. Cool the cakes in the pans on wire racks for 15 minutes, then unmold the cakes onto the racks, turning them right side up to cool completely.

7. Meanwhile, prepare the ganache. Place the chocolate in a medium bowl. Bring the cream to a boil in a small saucepan. Immediately remove the cream from the heat and pour it over the chocolate. Gently whisk until smooth, adding the vanilla. Set aside to cool and thicken to a spreadable consistency. (The ganache can be made a day in advance; allow to cool completely, cover, and store at room temperature.)

8. Before assembling, even the top of each cake by cutting off a thin, horizontal slice with a long serrated knife. Peel off the waxed paper, then cut each cake in half horizontally to make 4 equal layers.

9. Place a bottom layer on a cardboard cake circle or a cake plate. Spread with a thin coating of ganache, just enough to cover evenly. Add a second and then a third layer of cake, coating each with a thin layer of ganache. Add the top layer and frost the top and sides of the cake smoothly with ganache. Serve at room temperature.

Yield: 8 to 10 servings

To trim cakes and divide them into layers before assembling, use a long serrated knife (with scalloped, rather than sawtooth serrations), such as a bread knife. This type of knife is also helpful in cutting finished cakes into serving pieces. To cut cheesecakes and mousse cakes, use a chef's knife dipped into hot water and wiped clean between each cut.

Rindelaub's Bakery has been the premiere German bakeshop in Philadelphia since 1930. The family-owned shop is known and loved for a singular legacy: German chocolate cake. I asked my husband to pick up a sample when he was in Philadelphia a few months ago.

Bill arrived home bearing a very tasty light chocolate layer cake, filled and frosted with rich dark chocolate ganache and decorated with a pretty buttercream border of piped flowers. It was delightful, but I thought he had brought home the wrong cake. Where were the coconut, pecans, and sweet cream frosting?

I called Rindelaub's the next day to clarify what exactly Bill had purchased. "Oh, but that *is* German chocolate cake," I was told by the woman who answered the phone. "You might have been expecting something off a candy bar, but we make authentic German chocolate cake."

Come to think of it, she's right. Our expectations of German chocolate cake come from the recipe printed on every bar of a popular brand of chocolate, a recipe made so often that it has taken on a life of its own and become the defining standard.

Chocolate Knockout Cake

It would take days to duplicate the knockout Balducci cake made by the Epicure Gourmet Market's bakery. I concocted a knockout of my own, just as rich and very similar tasting, without the time-consuming cheesecake layer. This is a tall two-layer chocolate cake with two fillings—one is a fluffy combination of cream cheese and white chocolate, the other is raspberry—frosted with gently whipped chocolate cream.

Cake

2 large eggs, separated, at room temperature

1¹/₂ cups granulated sugar

1³/₄ cups cake flour

³/₄ teaspoon baking soda

¹/₂ teaspoon salt

¹/₃ cup canola oil

1 cup buttermilk, at room temperature

2 ounces unsweetened chocolate, melted

1 teaspoon vanilla extract

Cream Cheese–White Chocolate Filling

2 ounces white chocolate, chopped

¹/₄ cup heavy (whipping) cream

2 tablespoons unsalted butter

4 ounces cream cheese, cut into tablespoon-size pieces

¹/₄ teaspoon almond extract

¹/₄ cup confectioners' sugar (or more, to taste)

Chocolate Whipped Cream Frosting

4 ounces sweet chocolate, chopped

1 cup heavy (whipping) cream

¹/₄ cup Raspberry Filling (see page 117), chilled

Semisweet chocolate shavings (optional, for garnish)

1. Preheat the oven to 350°F. Grease two 8-inch round cake pans, 2 inches deep.

2. To make the cake, put the egg whites into a medium-size mixing bowl. Beat until foamy with an electric mixer at medium speed. Gradually add ¹/₂ cup of the granulated sugar while beating to glossy, stiff peaks, about 3 minutes.

3. Sift the flour, the remaining 1 cup granulated sugar, the baking soda, and salt together into a large bowl. Combine the oil and ¹/₂ cup of the buttermilk and beat into the flour mixture at medium speed for 1 minute. Add the remaining ¹/₂ cup buttermilk, the egg yolks, melted chocolate, and vanilla. Beat for 1 minute more. Fold in the meringue with a rubber spatula until thoroughly blended.

4. Divide the batter equally between the prepared pans. Bake for about 30 minutes, until a cake tester comes out clean. Cool in the pans on wire racks for 10 minutes, then unmold and cool completely on the racks.

5. To prepare the cream cheese filling, place the white chocolate in a medium-size mixing bowl. Combine the cream and butter in a small saucepan over medium heat. Bring to a full boil, remove from the heat, and pour over the white chocolate. Whisk the mixture until the chocolate is completely melted. Add the cream cheese, one piece at a time, blending smoothly. Add the almond extract and confectioners' sugar, stirring until the mixture is smooth. Transfer the filling to a container, cover, and refrigerate until firm and spreadable, at least 2 hours.

6. For the frosting, melt the chocolate in a microwave oven at 50 percent power for 1 to 4 minutes, checking every 30 seconds or in a double boiler over simmering water. Stir until smooth and set aside. Whip the cream until soft peaks form, add the chocolate, and whisk just until stiffened to a fluffy, spreadable consistency. (If overbeaten, the mixture will separate.) Chill while assembling the cake.

7. Using a long serrated knife, cut a thin slice, horizontally, from the top of each cake to even. Place one cake layer on a cardboard cake circle or a cake plate and spread evenly with one half of the cream cheese filling. Spread the raspberry filling over the cream cheese. Turn the second cake layer over and spread remaining cream cheese filling onto the bottom. Fit, spread side down, atop the first cake. Frost the top and sides of the cake with the chocolate whipped cream. Garnish the top with chocolate shavings, if desired. Chill until ready to serve, at least 1 hour.

Yield: 10 to 12 servings

The bakery department of the Epicure Gourmet Market in Miami Beach operates as if it were a freestanding retail shop, with high-quality on-premise baking and personalized services. The other distinguishing feature of the bakery and of the market as a whole is the large number of offerings with a distinct New York accent.

I felt as though I were standing on Sixth Avenue when I spied a bakery counter bedecked with New York cheesecake, black-out cake, Irish Cream truffle cake, chocolate seven-layer cake, and a real knockout named Balducci for the Manhattan market that created the recipe. It's a killer combination of two layers of chocolate cake sandwiching a middle layer of cheesecake, with raspberry filling between each layer and rich chocolate ganache frosting.

Brooklyn Chocolate Decadence

This Chocolate Decadence cake is an attempt to re-create the infamous black-out cake popularized by the legendary Ebinger's Bakery in Brooklyn. Today, New York bakeries call it mud cake. My mother's neighborhood bakery, Kirschbaum's, in suburban Chicago, makes it too. They call it chocolate lovers' cake, and it happens to be their biggest seller.

Cake

2 cups cake flour

¹/₂ cup unsweetened cocoa powder

1 teaspoon baking soda

¹/₂ teaspoon salt

³/₄ cup (1¹/₂ sticks) unsalted butter, at room temperature

1¹/₂ cups sugar

2 large eggs, at room temperature

2 teaspoons vanilla extract

2 cups sour cream, at room temperature

Pudding Frosting

4 ounces unsweetened chocolate, cut into small pieces

1¹/₂ cups sugar

¹/₃ cup cornstarch

1¹/₂ cups boiling water

4 tablespoons (¹/₂ stick) unsalted butter, cut into 4 pieces, at room temperature

¹/₂ tablespoon vanilla extract

1. Preheat the oven to 350°F. Grease two 8-inch round cake pans and dust the bottoms evenly with flour, shaking out excess flour.

2. To make the cake, sift the flour, cocoa, baking soda, and salt together into a medium bowl. Set aside.

3. Cream the butter and sugar in a large bowl with an electric mixer at medium speed until light and fluffy, about 3 minutes. Reduce the speed to low and add the eggs and vanilla, blending thoroughly. Slowly add the flour mixture, alternating with the sour cream and blending well after each addition.

4. Divide the batter equally between the prepared cake pans and smooth with a spatula. Bake for 25 to 30 minutes, until a cake tester comes out clean. Cool the cakes in the pans on wire racks for 15 minutes, then unmold the cakes onto the racks to cool completely.

5. Meanwhile, prepare the pudding. Melt the chocolate in a bowl over barely simmering water or in a microwave oven at 50 percent power for 1 to 4 minutes, checking every 30 seconds. Whisk until smooth and set aside.

continued

6. Combine the sugar and cornstarch in a saucepan and whisk to mix thoroughly. While whisking, pour the boiling water over the mixture. Bring to a boil over medium heat, whisking constantly, 5 to 7 minutes. Boil for 1 minute to thicken and remove the pan from the heat. Immediately whisk in the melted chocolate. Add the butter and allow it to melt, then stir in the vanilla. Pour the pudding into a bowl, cover the top with a piece of waxed paper, and allow to cool completely at room temperature.

7. To assemble, cut each cake in half horizontally to make 4 equal layers. Reserve 1 layer for the garnish.

8. Place a layer on a cardboard cake circle or a cake plate and cover with pudding. Add a second layer and spread with another coating of pudding. Top with a third layer of cake. Frost the top and sides of the cake evenly with the pudding. (The pudding frosting will look droopy at this stage.)

9. Crumble the remaining piece of cake into crumbs. (I use a food processor for this step.) Generously sprinkle crumbs all over the cake. Serve at cool room temperature.

Yield: 8 to 10 servings

*I*na Pinkney ran a small, special-order-only bakery in Chicago for seven years before opening her popular breakfast café. As she says, both businesses are about flour, eggs, butter, sugar, and cream, just mixed up differently.

When Ina was growing up in Brooklyn, her mother always had a cake on hand "just in case" there was drop-in company, and the black-out cake from Ebinger's was her all-time favorite. The mythology surrounding this particular cake, made by Ebinger's, a Brooklyn bakery in business for almost seventy-five years, has continued to grow. Numerous bake-offs have been held over the years, with contestants striving to replicate that moist chocolate cake, filled and frosted with dark chocolate pudding and decorated with cake crumbs.

Golden Cake

(For Birthday Chocolate Cake and Burnt Almond Cake)

This is also called yellow cake or butter cake, but the word golden *best describes its rich color, moist texture, and satisfying taste. It's the primary building block for my Burnt Almond Cake (page 110) and Birthday Chocolate Cake (page 108).*

Like all layer cakes, Golden Cake is best when served freshly baked. However, it can be frozen (wrapped in plastic wrap and then in aluminum foil) as soon as it has cooled. Use it within a month of freezing. You can also bake it a day in advance—wrap the cake securely in plastic wrap, and store at room temperature.

2¹/₂ cups cake flour

¹/₂ tablespoon baking powder

¹/₂ teaspoon baking soda

¹/₂ teaspoon salt

³/₄ cup (1¹/₂ sticks) unsalted butter, at room temperature

1¹/₄ cups sugar

4 large eggs, at room temperature

1 cup buttermilk, at room temperature

¹/₂ tablespoon vanilla extract

1. Preheat the oven to 350°F. Grease two 8-inch round cake pans, 2 inches deep.

2. Sift the flour, baking powder, baking soda, and salt together into a bowl and set aside.

3. Cream the butter and sugar in a large bowl with an electric mixer at medium speed until light and fluffy, about 5 minutes. Reduce the speed to medium-low. Add the eggs, one at a time, beating for 30 seconds between additions. Add alternating increments of the flour mixture and the buttermilk and vanilla, blending well after each addition; this should take 3 to 5 minutes.

4. Divide the batter evenly between the prepared pans. Bake for about 30 minutes, until a cake tester comes out clean. Cool in the pans on wire racks for 10 minutes, then unmold the cakes and let cool completely on the racks.

Yield: Two 8-inch round cakes

Birthday Chocolate Cake

My experience in the bakery business confirms that Golden Cake frosted with chocolate is a favorite for birthday parties, especially for children. The version we made at our dessert bakery in Chicago became so popular that we referred to it simply as "birthday cake."

The cake takes on different personalities depending on the type of chocolate used in the frosting. I recommend sweet chocolate for a child's cake and semisweet for an adult's. You may have a little frosting left over after preparing this cake, and it can be chilled and rolled into balls for chocolate truffles.

1 pound sweet or semisweet chocolate

³/₄ cup heavy (whipping) cream

6 tablespoons unsalted butter

1 tablespoon vanilla extract

**1 baked 8-inch round Golden Cake
   (page 107)**

1. Cut the chocolate into small pieces and place in a medium-size mixing bowl.

2. Combine the cream and butter in a small saucepan. Bring to a full boil over medium heat. Remove the pan from the heat and pour contents over the chocolate. Beat with an electric mixer at medium-low speed until the chocolate has melted and the mixture is smooth, then blend in the vanilla.

3. Set the frosting aside at room temperature to cool and thicken to a spreadable consistency.

4. To assemble, cut the cake in half horizontally into 2 equal layers. Place a layer on a cardboard cake circle or a cake plate and spread with a thick coat of chocolate frosting. Cover with the remaining layer of cake. Spread frosting generously on the top and sides of the cake. Serve at room temperature.

Yield: 8 servings

"Dot's! Oh, boy!" was the gleeful response sounded by kids in Richmond, Virginia, when they spied a shiny white box from Dot's Bakery wrapped with white ribbon on the kitchen counter—as recognizable and every bit as dear as a blue box from Tiffany.

A long-gone but never forgotten Richmond tradition, Dot's built its reputation on terrific tasting, old-fashioned bakery goods and an army of friendly saleswomen dressed in pastel uniforms with fancy pocket hankies and name tags pinned to their lapels. The ladies were an integral part of Dot's mystique, but Virginians returned to the bakery again and again for its ever-popular yellow cake with dark chocolate fudge frosting.

Burnt Almond Cake

The original recipe for Burnt Almond Cake is a well-guarded secret of Dick's Bakery in San Jose. My version may not be Dick's, but this is truly a great-tasting cake: two layers of rich golden cake filled and frosted with custard cream and garnished with a covering of honey almond brittle.

Honey Almond Brittle

¹/₂ cup granulated sugar

3 tablespoons honey

1¹/₂ tablespoons water

2 ounces slivered almonds
   (about ¹/₂ cup), toasted

1 tablespoon unsalted butter

¹/₈ teaspoon baking soda

Custard Cream

1 cup milk

3 large egg yolks

¹/₃ cup granulated sugar

2 tablespoons cornstarch

1 tablespoon unsalted butter

¹/₂ teaspoon vanilla extract

¹/₃ cup heavy (whipping) cream

1 tablespoon confectioners' sugar

1 baked 8-inch round Golden Cake
   (page 107)

1. To make the brittle, combine the granulated sugar, honey, and water in a medium-size saucepan. Bring to a boil over medium heat, stirring to dissolve the sugar. Boil, without stirring, until the mixture turns a deep amber color, about 10 minutes. Remove the pan from the heat and immediately stir in the toasted almonds, butter, and baking soda. Mix with a wooden spoon just until the butter melts and the foaming subsides. Pour the mixture into a nonstick or lightly greased baking sheet and set aside to cool. Once the brittle has hardened, break it up and crush to fine crumbs in a food processor. Store the crumbs in a covered container in the refrigerator until ready to use.

2. Prepare the custard cream by heating the milk to a bare simmer in a heavy-bottomed saucepan over medium-low heat. Meanwhile, combine the egg yolks, granulated sugar, and cornstarch in a medium mixing bowl. Whisk to blend smoothly. Stir the heated milk into the egg mixture, then return the combination to the saucepan. Bring back to a boil over medium-low heat, whisking constantly. Still whisking, boil for 1 minute.

3. Remove the pan from the heat and add the butter and vanilla, stirring to melt the butter. Transfer the custard to a bowl, place a piece of waxed paper directly on the top to prevent a crust from forming, and refrigerate until cold.

4. Whip the cream and confectioners' sugar until stiff peaks form. Fold into the chilled custard and refrigerate until ready to use.

5. To assemble, cut the cake in half horizontally into 2 equal layers. Place one layer on a cardboard cake circle or a cake plate, spread with cold custard cream, and sprinkle with brittle crumbs. Cover with the remaining layer of cake. Spread the remaining custard cream over the cake, applying a thinner coat to the sides than the top. Chill for at least 1 hour before garnishing.

6. To garnish, press brittle crumbs onto the sides of the cake with the palm of your hand and sprinkle a layer of crumbs on the top. Refrigerate until ready to serve.

Yield: 8 servings

To toast nuts, arrange them in a single layer on a small baking pan. Bake in a 375°F oven until golden brown, 7 to 10 minutes. Remove the pan and allow the nuts to cool before using.

---

hen Rhonda Purwin was a child in San Jose, California, her favorite hometown bakery was Dick's. It was called Peter's before Dick Sota and his brother Clarence bought the establishment from their cousin Peter shortly after World War II. In 1956, the Sota brothers moved the business to their present facility on Meridian Avenue, which remains virtually unchanged— other than the recent removal of a soda fountain–like counter where coffee and pastries or cake by the slice were once dispensed.

Dick's Bakery is a full-service, made-from-scratch operation (Dick still bakes every day), defying the trends of the times and still bustling with customers. Rose, who's been the manager for at least thirty years, says you can always tell when church is out because that's when people start coming in for their cake orders.

Rhonda's personal sweet of choice was always Dick's danish, for which she has since found no equal. The bakery's claim to fame, however, is its burnt almond cake, made daily in great quantity to satisfy demand.

Two-in-One Cake

When I heard about The Sweetery's somewhat offbeat combination of yellow cake and cheesecake baked together in a single pan, I just had to come up with my own version. The result is a stunning combination of textures in one dessert. It may not be the prettiest cake in the world, but you'll forget about appearances with the first bite.

Cake Layer

1 cup all-purpose flour

1 teaspoon baking powder

1/4 teaspoon salt

6 tablespoons unsalted butter, at room temperature

1/2 cup sugar

1 large egg, plus 1 egg yolk

3/4 teaspoon vanilla extract

1/3 cup milk, at room temperature

Cheesecake Layer

8 ounces cream cheese, at room temperature

1/2 cup sugar

2 large eggs

2 tablespoons all-purpose flour

1 cup heavy (whipping) cream

1 teaspoon vanilla extract

1/2 cup chopped pecans, toasted

1. Preheat the oven to 325°F. Grease an 8 1/2-inch springform pan.

2. To make the cake layer, sift the flour, baking powder, and salt together into a medium-size bowl and set aside.

3. Using an electric mixer at medium speed, cream the butter and sugar until light and fluffy, about 3 minutes. Add the egg and the yolk and beat thoroughly. Lower the speed and add the vanilla. Spoon in the flour mixture, alternating with the milk, blending to a smooth batter. Pour into the prepared pan and spread evenly with a spatula.

4. For the cheesecake layer, beat the cream cheese with the sugar until fluffy. Add the eggs and blend well. Stir in the flour, then add the cream and vanilla. Mix until smoothly blended.

5. Sprinkle the toasted pecans over the cake batter. Pour in the cheesecake batter. Place the springform pan in the oven on top of a baking sheet and bake for 55 to 60 minutes, until the cake is golden and the center is set but jiggles slightly when the pan is shaken.

6. Cool in the pan on a wire rack until the top cheesecake layer has shrunk away from the sides of the pan. Remove the sides of the pan and let the cake cool completely. The cake is best when served at room temperature.

Yield: 8 servings

There's a bakery-café called The Sweetery in Anderson, South Carolina, which is known for Southern-style layer cakes, cheesecakes, and pound cakes made from recipes dating back a hundred years, as well as for something called "uggly cake."

The Sweetery's motto (all bakeries seem to have mottos—didn't you know?) is "We take our baking as seriously as your grandmother did," and the bakery's owner, Jane Jarahian, could be a grandmother straight out of central casting.

I called Jane to ask her what in the world was an "uggly cake." She responded, in her soft, Southern lilt, that it was a bottom layer of yellow cake and a cheesecake upper layer with pecans in between.

"Is it frosted?" I asked.

"Why no," Jane replied, "it's ugly."

Pineapple Upside-Down Cake

This is an easy, attractive, and luscious cake that is smothered in glazed fruit. Use fresh, ripe pineapple rings; I buy them peeled and cored in the produce department of my supermarket. Omit the candied red cherries, please, rather than substitute maraschino cherries. Serve the cake plain or garnish it with a dollop of whipped cream.

³/₄ cup (1¹/₂ sticks) unsalted butter, at room temperature

¹/₂ cup packed dark brown sugar

Ten ¹/₂-inch-thick rings of fresh pineapple

1¹/₂ cups cake or pastry flour

1 teaspoon baking powder

¹/₄ teaspoon baking soda

¹/₄ teaspoon salt

³/₄ cup granulated sugar

¹/₂ cup buttermilk

2 large eggs

1 teaspoon vanilla extract

Candied red cherries (optional, for garnish)

1. Preheat the oven to 350°F. Grease a 10-inch round cake pan.

2. In a large skillet, melt 4 tablespoons of the butter over medium heat. Stir in the brown sugar. When the sugar has melted and the mixture is bubbly, add a single layer of pineapple rings. Cook for about 3 minutes on each side, until soft and glazed. Cook the remaining rings in single-layer batches.

3. Arrange 6 of the rings in the bottom of the cake pan (they should fit snugly in 1 layer). Cut 4 rings in half and stand them up around the sides of the pan.

4. Sift the flour, baking powder, baking soda, and salt together in a medium mixing bowl. Add the granulated sugar and mix thoroughly with a wooden spoon. Add the remaining 8 tablespoons butter and stir until the mixture is crumbly. Stir in the buttermilk, eggs, and vanilla. Mix vigorously for about 2 minutes, until the batter is smoothly blended and fluffy. Spread evenly over the pineapple rings in the pan.

5. Bake for about 45 minutes, until browned and firm to the touch in the center. Cool in the pan on a wire rack for 10 minutes, then unmold the cake onto a serving platter.

6. Cut candied cherries in half and place cut side down in the center of each pineapple ring, if desired. Allow the cake to cool to room temperature before serving.

Yield: 10 servings

You'll love this cake! I know I might sound like your mother, but old-fashioned upside-down cake, which has suffered a lot of bad press over the years, is really terrific. It's still a favorite at old-time Midwestern bakeries, such as Dinkel's in Chicago and Tag's in suburban Evanston. Trust me; if the only pineapple upside-down cake you've ever tasted came from a box mix and involved canned fruit and maraschino cherries, you are in for a thrilling surprise.

Banana Cake

Just Desserts dropped their wonderful banana cake from the menu a decade ago, so replicating the cake of my friend's "California dreaming" was something of a challenge. She described a two-layer banana cake with raspberry filling, vanilla buttercream frosting, and a garnish of chopped toasted walnuts on the sides, all of which sounded quite wonderful to me.

Cake

2 cups cake flour

1 teaspoon baking soda

$1/2$ teaspoon salt

$1/2$ cup (1 stick) unsalted butter, at room temperature

$1/2$ cup packed light brown sugar

$1/2$ cup granulated sugar

2 large eggs, at room temperature

1 teaspoon vanilla extract

1 cup mashed ripe banana pulp (about 2 large bananas)

$2/3$ cup buttermilk, at room temperature

Buttercream Frosting

3 large egg whites, at room temperature

$1/3$ cup plus $1/2$ cup granulated sugar

$1/4$ teaspoon cream of tartar

1 tablespoon plus $1/4$ cup water

$1^1/2$ cups (3 sticks) unsalted butter, cut into 24 pieces, at room temperature

1 tablespoon vanilla extract

$1/3$ cup Raspberry Filling (see page 117), chilled

1 cup chopped walnuts, toasted

1. Preheat the oven to 350°F. Grease two 8-inch round cake pans.

2. To make the cake, sift the flour, baking soda, and salt together into a medium bowl and set aside.

3. Cream the butter and sugars in a large bowl with an electric mixer at medium speed until light and fluffy, about 3 minutes. Add the eggs, one at a time, blending until smooth after each addition. Add the vanilla. Reduce the speed to low. In a separate bowl, combine the banana and buttermilk. Add the flour mixture and the buttermilk and banana mixture in alternating increments, blending until smooth between additions.

4. Divide the batter evenly between the prepared pans. Bake for 25 to 30 minutes, until a cake tester comes out clean. Cool in the pans on wire racks for 10 minutes, then unmold and let cool completely on the racks.

5. For the frosting, combine the egg whites, $1/3$ cup of the sugar, the cream of tartar, and 1 tablespoon water in the top of a double boiler over simmering water. Whisk constantly while the mixture heats to a white, thick, foamy mass, about 2 minutes. Transfer the mixture to a mixing bowl.

6. Combine the $1/2$ cup of the granulated sugar with the $1/4$ cup water in a small saucepan. Cook over medium-high heat, stirring, to a syrupy consistency with large bubbles covering the surface, about 3 minutes. (This should be approximately when the syrup will form a "soft ball" if dropped in ice water, or will reach 240°F on a candy thermometer.) Remove the syrup from the heat.

7. Immediately begin beating the egg white mixture with an electric mixer at medium speed, while pouring in the hot sugar syrup. Beat until the mixture is thick and glossy,

about 1 minute. Add the butter, one piece at a time. By the time all of the butter has been added, the mixture should be thick, smooth, and fluffy. Mix in the vanilla and set aside at room temperature until ready to use. (The buttercream can be made a day in advance and stored in the refrigerator in a covered container. Bring back to room temperature before using.)

8. To assemble, place one cake layer on a cardboard cake circle or a cake plate. Spread with a thin coat of buttercream, then cover the buttercream with the raspberry filling. Top with the second cake layer. Frost the top and sides of the cake smoothly with buttercream. Press the chopped walnuts into the sides of the frosted cake. Serve at room temperature.

Yield: 8 to 10 servings

Raspberry Filling

Far superior to commercial jams or preserves, this Raspberry Filling is rich and intensely flavored. I use it in the Banana Cake, Chocolate Knockout Cake (page 103), Danish Layer Cake (page 122), and New York–Style Charlotte Russe (page 141).

Two 10-ounce packages frozen raspberries in syrup, thawed

$1/2$ cup sugar

1 tablespoon crème de cassis liqueur

1 teaspoon unflavored gelatin

1 tablespoon plus 1 teaspoon cold water

1. Drain the raspberries in a colander set over a medium bowl, reserving $1/4$ cup of the juice. Fit a food mill with a fine-hole screen over a medium-size bowl and work the drained raspberries through the mill. You should have about $3/4$ cup raspberry puree.

2. Combine the sugar, raspberry puree, and reserved juice in a small saucepan. Bring to a boil over medium heat. Boil, stirring occasionally, for 5 minutes, until glossy and slightly thickened. Remove the pan from the heat and stir in the liqueur.

3. Meanwhile, combine the gelatin and cold water in a small dish. Let stand 1 minute, then dissolve the gelatin by heating for 30 seconds in a microwave oven at full power, or by placing the dish into a pan of simmering water. Stir into the hot puree. Transfer to a container and allow to cool. Cover and refrigerate until gelled, at least 4 hours.

Yield: About 1 cup

My Chicago friend Rhonda, who moved from her native San Francisco thirteen years ago, still misses Just Desserts' banana cake. Before expanding into other locations and a wholesale operation, the bakery started out as a small retail shop and café on Nob Hill. It was the place to go for a slice of carrot, chocolate, or banana cake during the 1970s.

Graham Cracker Cake with Caramel Frosting

Armed with Kevin Morrissey's description of a fabulous-sounding graham cracker cake once made by a neighborhood Chicago bakery, I created this recipe. Graham cracker crumbs and finely chopped nuts replace most of the flour, resulting in a tortelike dessert—light and moist with a nutty pecan taste. The frosting is very soft and subtle, somewhat of a cross between caramel and maple. Toasted nuts are pressed onto the cake sides for a finishing touch. Kevin heartily approves!

Cake

2 cups graham cracker crumbs

³/₄ cup finely chopped pecans

¹/₂ cup cake flour

2 teaspoons baking powder

¹/₄ teaspoon salt

1 cup (2 sticks) unsalted butter, at room
    temperature

1 cup packed light brown sugar

3 large eggs, separated, at room
    temperature

¹/₂ tablespoon vanilla extract

1 cup milk, at room temperature

¹/₄ cup granulated sugar

Caramel Frosting

2 tablespoons granulated sugar

1¹/₂ cups (3 sticks) unsalted butter,
    at room temperature

¹/₂ cup packed dark brown sugar

¹/₂ cup heavy (whipping) cream

³/₄ cup confectioners' sugar

¹/₂ cup finely chopped pecans, toasted

1. Preheat the oven to 350°F. Grease two 9-inch cake pans. Cut and fit circles of waxed paper to line the bottom of each pan.

2. To make the cake, combine the graham cracker crumbs, pecans, flour, baking powder, and salt in a medium-size bowl. Stir to mix thoroughly and set aside.

3. Cream the butter and light brown sugar in a large bowl with an electric mixer at medium speed until fluffy, about 3 minutes. Reduce the mixer speed to medium-low. Slowly add the egg yolks, blending until smooth. Reduce the speed to low. Combine the vanilla and milk. Add the crumb mixture to the mixer bowl in increments, alternating with the milk mixture and blending well after each addition. *continued*

4. In a medium-size bowl, beat the egg whites at medium speed until foamy. Gradually add the granulated sugar, continuing to beat to soft peaks. Fold into the batter gently but thoroughly.

5. Divide and spread the batter evenly into the prepared pans. Bake for about 25 minutes, until a cake tester comes out clean. Cool in the pans on wire racks for 10 minutes, then unmold the cakes onto the racks right side up and let them cool completely. When cool, peel off the waxed paper.

6. Prepare the frosting by melting the granulated sugar in a heavy-bottomed medium-size saucepan over medium heat until it browns to a caramel color. Remove the pan from the heat and add 4 tablespoons of the butter, swirling the pan to melt the butter. Whisk in the dark brown sugar and return the pan to the heat. Bring to a boil, stirring constantly. Drizzle in the cream and bring back to a boil. Boil for 1 minute and remove from the heat.

7. Place the confectioners' sugar in a large mixing bowl. While beating at medium-low speed, slowly add the hot caramel. Beat the mixture until the bottom of the bowl feels barely warm, about 5 minutes. Add the remaining 1¼ cups (2½ sticks) butter, 1 tablespoon at a time, blending until smooth between additions. If the mixture looks as though it will curdle or break at any time while adding the butter, increase the speed to high for 1 minute until the consistency is creamy again, then reduce the speed and continue to add the remaining butter. Refrigerate the frosting until ready to use.

8. To assemble, place 1 cake layer on a cardboard cake circle or a cake plate. Stir the caramel frosting and then spread an even layer over the cake. Cover with the second cake layer. Frost the top and sides of the cake with caramel frosting. Press the toasted pecans into the sides. The frosting will remain soft, and it is best to keep the cake at a cool room temperature until serving.

Yield: 8 to 10 servings

One of the joys of growing up in Chicago's South Shore community at mid-century was savoring bakery treats from Burny Brothers. For younger fans, such as my colleague Kevin Morrissey, the bakery's appeal was certainly enhanced by local television ads featuring animated characters portraying the "Burny Brothers Better Bakers."

Kevin didn't consider a birthday to be a birthday without a Burny Brothers graham cracker cake, which he can describe to this day in intimate detail. He also remembers sitting on the bench seats in the shop at 71st and Jeffery, watching a crowd of people taking numbers and waiting in line for their favorite baked goods.

Sponge Cake

(For Danish Layer Cake, Cassata Cake, and Fruit Basket Cake)

This light and airy sponge cake has become a staple recipe in my cake repertoire. It's so versatile, a particularly good host for fluffy whipped cream frostings and custard fillings. I use it as the basis for my Danish Layer Cake (page 122), Cassata Cake (page 124), and Fruit Basket Cake (page 126). Sponge cake freezes beautifully; cover with an inner layer of plastic wrap and an outer layer of aluminum foil.

1¹/₂ cups cake flour

¹/₂ teaspoon baking powder

¹/₄ teaspoon salt

5 large eggs, separated, at room temperature

¹/₂ cup cold water

1¹/₄ cups sugar

¹/₂ tablespoon vanilla extract

¹/₂ teaspoon cream of tartar

1. Preheat the oven to 325°F. Grease two 9-inch round cake pans, 2 inches deep. Cut and fit a round of parchment or waxed paper to line the bottom of each pan.

2. Sift the flour, baking powder, and salt together into a medium-size bowl and set aside.

3. Place the egg yolks in a large bowl and beat with an electric mixer at medium-high speed until thick, about 4 minutes. Gradually add the cold water—the mixture will look foamy. Slowly add the sugar, beating to dissolve completely, about 3 minutes. Beat in the vanilla. Sift in the flour mixture. Fold with a large rubber spatula.

4. In a medium-size bowl with a clean beater, beat the egg whites and cream of tartar until stiff peaks form, shiny but not dry. Thoroughly fold into the yolk mixture.

5. Divide the batter equally between the prepared pans, smoothing the tops evenly with a metal spatula. Bake for about 25 minutes, until the centers are springy and a cake tester comes out clean. Cool in the pans on wire racks for 10 minutes, then unmold the cakes onto the racks, inverting so they sit on the paper pan liners. Allow to cool completely before peeling the liners.

Yield: Two 9-inch round cakes

Danish Layer Cake

For easy entertaining, I prepare this cake in stages, baking the sponge cake layers and cooking the custard filling a day in advance. The day of the party, I whip the cream for the topping and assemble the cake.

Custard Filling

1 large egg

$^1/_2$ cup granulated sugar

$^1/_3$ cup all-purpose flour

$^1/_2$ teaspoon salt

$1^1/_3$ cups half-and-half

2 tablespoons unsalted butter

1 teaspoon vanilla extract

$^1/_4$ teaspoon almond extract

Whipped Cream Topping

$1^1/_2$ cups heavy (whipping) cream, chilled

$^1/_4$ cup confectioners' sugar

2 baked 9-inch round Sponge Cake (page 121)

$^3/_4$ cup Raspberry Filling (see page 117) or raspberry spreadable fruit

1. To make the custard filling, beat the egg lightly with a fork in a small mixing bowl and set aside.

2. Combine the granulated sugar, flour, and salt in a heavy-bottomed medium-size saucepan. Whisk in the half-and-half until smoothly blended. Cook over medium-low heat, whisking constantly, until the mixture comes to a boil, about 5 minutes. Boil for 1

minute while still whisking. Remove the pan from the heat and spoon about $^1/_2$ cup of the hot mixture into the beaten egg, whisking to blend thoroughly, then add the egg mixture to the pan and return to medium-low heat. Bring back to a boil, whisking constantly. Remove the pan from the heat and add the butter and extracts, whisking until the butter melts. Transfer the custard to a bowl, cover with waxed paper or plastic wrap, and refrigerate until cold.

3. Just before assembling the cake, prepare the topping. Whip the cream with an electric mixer until thickened. Add the confectioners' sugar and continue to beat until stiff peaks form.

4. To assemble, cut each sponge cake horizontally into 2 equal layers. Place a bottom layer on a cardboard cake circle or a cake plate. Spread with half of the custard. Cover with a second layer of cake. Spread with the raspberry filling and place a third layer over the fruit. Spread with the remaining custard and cover with the top layer of cake. Frost the top and sides of the cake with the whipped cream topping. Refrigerate until ready to serve.

Yield: 10 to 12 servings

*A*sk for cake in one of Racine, Wisconsin's Danish bakeries and you will receive a classic Danish layer cake. The delicious sponge cake, filled with creamy custard and raspberry jam, and frosted with either whipped cream or buttercream, draws customers from throughout the region. The O & H Danish Bakery offers a four-layer Danish cake, while the bakers at nearby Lehmann's build to six layers and add almond paste to the fillings.

Cassata Cake

Cannoli lovers of the world unite! Cassata is essentially an abundance of cannoli filling that is spread between layers of feathery sponge cake instead of stuffed inside fried cannoli shells. My homespun rendition of this bakery treat is a rich concoction of four layers of sponge cake brushed with rum syrup. It's covered with a ricotta cheese and candied fruit filling, and topped with chocolate glaze.

Ricotta Filling

2 pounds whole-milk ricotta cheese

2¼ cups confectioners' sugar

½ teaspoon ground cinnamon

1 teaspoon vanilla extract

2 ounces semisweet chocolate

½ cup chopped candied citron or lemon peel

Rum Syrup

⅓ cup granulated sugar

¼ cup water

2 tablespoons light rum

2 baked 9-inch round Sponge Cake (page 121)

Chocolate Glaze

6 ounces bittersweet or semisweet chocolate, cut into small pieces

⅓ cup heavy (whipping) cream

3 tablespoons unsalted butter, cut into small pieces

1. To make the filling, place the ricotta in a large mixing bowl and beat until well mixed. Sift the confectioners' sugar and cinnamon together onto the cheese and blend thoroughly. Beat in the vanilla. Coarsely grate chocolate shavings over the mixture. Stir in the shavings, then stir in the candied citron or lemon peel. Cover and refrigerate until firm. (The filling can be made in advance and refrigerated overnight.)

2. Prepare the rum syrup by combining the granulated sugar and water in a small saucepan. Bring to a boil over medium heat, stirring until the sugar has dissolved, and boil for 1 minute. Remove the pan from the heat, stir in the rum, and set aside to cool to room temperature.

3. To assemble, cut each sponge cake horizontally into 2 equal layers. Place one layer on a cardboard cake circle or a cake plate and dab on rum syrup with a brush. Spread evenly with a thick coating of ricotta filling, using up to 1½ cups of the filling. Add a second and then a third layer of cake, dabbing each with syrup and spreading each with filling as before. Top with the remaining layer of cake. Refrigerate for at least 3 hours to set.

4. Meanwhile, prepare the chocolate glaze. Melt the chocolate and cream together in a medium bowl over barely simmering water or in a microwave oven at 50 percent power for 1 to 4 minutes, checking every 30 seconds. Whisk until the chocolate is smooth. Add the butter, whisking so that it melts smoothly into the chocolate mixture. Set aside to cool to a spreadable consistency.

5. Spread the chocolate glaze over the top of the chilled cake. Serve while the glaze is still soft or chill for a firmer glaze (it's very tasty either way).

Yield: 12 servings

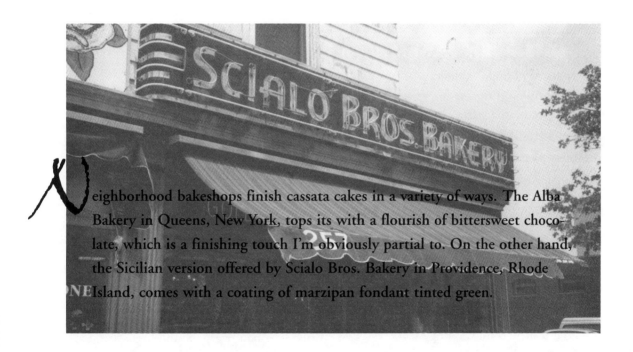

eighborhood bakeshops finish cassata cakes in a variety of ways. The Alba Bakery in Queens, New York, tops its with a flourish of bittersweet chocolate, which is a finishing touch I'm obviously partial to. On the other hand, the Sicilian version offered by Scialo Bros. Bakery in Providence, Rhode Island, comes with a coating of marzipan fondant tinted green.

Fruit Basket Cake

Frosted in white cream, this tall and elegant creation features strawberry and pineapple conserves sandwiched between layers of sponge cake. It's definitely an extravagant dessert for a special occasion. The conserves can be made a week in advance and stored in the refrigerator, and the sponge cakes can be baked up to a month in advance and frozen.

Pineapple Conserve

1 ripe pineapple, peeled, cored, and coarsely chopped (about 1¹⁄₄ pounds fruit)

¹⁄₂ cup granulated sugar

¹⁄₂ cup water

1 tablespoon fresh lemon juice

Strawberry Conserve

¹⁄₃ cup granulated sugar

¹⁄₃ cup water

1 pint strawberries, hulled (about 1 pound)

¹⁄₄ teaspoon vanilla extract

2 baked 9-inch round Sponge Cake (page 121)

2 cups heavy (whipping) cream

¹⁄₄ cup confectioners' sugar

2 ripe bananas

Orange juice, for dipping banana slices

1. To make the pineapple conserve, combine the pineapple, granulated sugar, water, and lemon juice in a saucepan. Bring to a boil over medium heat and boil until the fruit has softened, about 10 minutes.

2. Remove the pan from the heat. Fit a sieve over a medium bowl, transfer the fruit to the sieve with a slotted spoon, and strain. Add the juice from the bowl to the saucepan and return to medium heat. Bring the syrup back to a boil and reduce the volume to ¹⁄₂ cup, 8 to 10 minutes. Remove from the heat and stir in the pineapple from the sieve. Transfer the mixture to a bowl and allow to cool to room temperature. Cover and chill; store in the refrigerator until ready to use.

3. For the strawberry conserve, combine the granulated sugar and water in a shallow pan. Bring to a boil over medium-high heat, stirring to dissolve the sugar. Boil for 1 minute, add the strawberries, and bring back to a full boil. Boil for 5 minutes more. Remove the pan from the heat and coarsely crush the berries with a potato masher or a large pestle.

4. Transfer the pulp with the slotted spoon to the sieve, set over a bowl to collect the juice, and strain. Add the juice to the pan and return to medium-high heat. Bring back to a boil and boil the syrup to thicken and reduce the volume to about $\frac{1}{3}$ cup, 12 to 15 minutes. Remove the pan from the heat. Stir in the vanilla, then the strawberry pulp. Transfer to a bowl and let cool. Cover, chill, and store in the refrigerator until ready to use.

5. While assembling the cake, drain the pineapple conserve.

6. Cut each sponge cake horizontally into 2 equal layers. Place a bottom layer on a cardboard cake circle or a cake plate.

7. Whip the cream with the confectioners' sugar until stiff peaks form. Spread a thin coating of whipped cream over the bottom layer of cake and cover evenly with the drained pineapple conserve. Place a second layer of cake on top of the fruit and spread it with another thin layer of whipped cream. Cover with the strawberry conserve. Add a third layer of cake and spread it with some more whipped cream.

8. Peel the bananas and slice diagonally. Dip the slices into a shallow bowl of orange juice to prevent discoloration and arrange them on the cake. Top with the remaining cake layer. Frost the top and sides of the cake with the rest of the whipped cream. Refrigerate until ready to serve.

Yield: 12 servings

I use the versatile strawberry conserve from this recipe as an all-purpose layer cake or cake roll filling, to top shortcake or ice cream, to embellish whipped cream toppings—or simply spread on toast, waffles, or pancakes as a breakfast treat. The ingredients are easily doubled for a 2-cup yield, and the conserve will keep in the refrigerator for up to 3 weeks.

Tucked away on a residential side street in midtown Sacramento, California, is the New Roma Bakery, where a gas-fired brick oven and much of the other original 1934 baking equipment are still in use. The bakery no longer bakes pans of lasagne for church functions of its Italian clientele, many of whom have moved from the neighborhood. But New Roma customers remember the old days, and they return for the bakery's signature fruit basket cake, a favorite choice for children's birthdays.

White Chocolate Cheesecake with Raspberry Glaze

This elegant cheesecake is just right for entertaining; it looks attractive and tastes fabulous. The chocolate crumb crust and raspberry glaze set off a creamy white chocolate filling. Be sure to use a quality brand of white chocolate that contains cocoa butter.

Chocolate Crust

1 cup graham cracker crumbs

2 tablespoons sugar

2 tablespoons unsweetened cocoa powder

4 tablespoons unsalted butter, melted

White Chocolate Filling

8 ounces white chocolate, cut into small
   pieces

1 tablespoon unsalted butter

16 ounces cream cheese, at room
   temperature

^{1}/$_2$ cup sugar

1 cup heavy (whipping) cream

1 tablespoon vanilla extract

4 large eggs

Raspberry Glaze

One 10-ounce package frozen raspberries
   in syrup, thawed

2 tablespoons sugar

1 tablespoon cornstarch

^{1}/$_2$ teaspoon lemon juice

1. Preheat the oven to 300°F.

2. To make the crust, combine the graham cracker crumbs, sugar, and cocoa in a medium-size bowl. Stir to mix thoroughly. Add the melted butter and stir until the crumbs are evenly moistened. Press firmly into the bottom of a 9-inch springform pan. Set the pan into the freezer for 10 minutes for the crust to set while mixing the filling.

3. Prepare the filling by melting the white chocolate and the butter in another bowl over a pan of simmering water or in a microwave oven at 50 percent power for 1 to 4 minutes, checking every 30 seconds. Stir until smooth and set aside.

4. Beat the cream cheese in a large bowl with an electric mixer at medium-low speed until smooth. Pour in the white chocolate. Add the sugar and blend thoroughly. While mixing, slowly pour in the cream and vanilla. Add the eggs, one at a time, blending thoroughly after each addition.

5. Wrap aluminum foil around the bottom and sides of the chilled springform pan and set it on a baking sheet. Pour the filling over the crust. Fill the baking sheet with water, set it into the oven, and bake for about 1½ hours, until the top is golden and the filling will shake slightly (it will firm as it cools).

6. Cool the cheesecake to room temperature in the springform pan on a wire rack, then refrigerate overnight.

7. For the glaze, drain the raspberries over a bowl, reserving ½ cup of the juice. Combine the berries and sugar in a saucepan. Stir the cornstarch into the reserved juice and add it to the saucepan. Bring the mixture to a boil over medium heat, stirring, and boil for 1 minute to thicken. Remove from the heat and press through a fine-mesh sieve set over a bowl, discarding the seeds. Stir the lemon juice into the glaze; allow to cool. Cover and refrigerate overnight.

8. The next day, release the sides from the springform pan. Spread the glaze evenly over the top of the cheesecake. Refrigerate until ready to serve. Cut wedges with a knife wiped clean and dipped into hot water between each slice.

Yield: 12 to 16 servings

*I*n 1987, Hank Krussel opened a little store in Richmond Heights, Missouri, on the edge of St. Louis, with a handful of cheesecake recipes and a business plan. Today, Hank's Cheesecakes offers customers thirty-five different flavors of rich and creamy cheesecake, thirty sweet dessert cakes, and five savory cakes intended as appetizers. Some of Hank's techniques are a bit unorthodox, but they seem to work for him. For instance, his best seller is a white chocolate cheesecake—over which Hank squeezes a spiral design in raspberry glaze while the cake rotates on a record turntable.

Chocolate Hazelnut Meringue Torte

This recipe is a singular combination of all the features that make meringue tortes so appealing. It's a layered rectangle of crunchy, nutty meringue and soft chocolate mousse. The hazelnuts add flavor intrigue as well as texture to the meringue. Notice the absence of egg yolks and cream from the mousse filling—the result is tantalizingly light and refreshing.

Hazelnut Meringue

4 ounces hazelnuts

1 cup sugar

2 tablespoons cornstarch

6 large egg whites, at room temperature

1/4 teaspoon cream of tartar

Chocolate Mousse Filling

6 ounces semisweet chocolate, coarsely chopped

2 ounces unsweetened chocolate, coarsely chopped

1 cup sugar

1/4 cup water

6 large egg whites, at room temperature

1/4 teaspoon cream of tartar

Garnish

2 ounces hazelnuts, coarsely ground and toasted

2 tablespoons unsweetened cocoa powder

1. Line a baking sheet with parchment paper. Outline three 4 × 11-inch rectangles on the paper in pencil, spaced 1 inch apart. Spray each rectangle with vegetable oil cooking spray or grease with butter and sprinkle with flour, shaking off excess flour.

2. Preheat the oven to 300°F.

3. To make the meringue, combine the hazelnuts and 3/4 cup of the sugar in a food processor and process until finely ground. Stir in the cornstarch and set the mixture aside.

4. Beat the egg whites in a large bowl with an electric mixer at low speed until foamy. Add the cream of tartar and beat at medium-high speed to form soft peaks. Slowly add the remaining 1/4 cup sugar, continuing to beat until the meringue is stiff and glossy. Fold in the hazelnut and sugar mixture with a large rubber spatula; the egg whites will deflate somewhat.

5. Spoon the meringue into a pastry bag fitted with a 1/2-inch open tip. Pipe the mixture in a continuous stream to fill 1 rectangular outline on the parchment, beginning with the outside edge and working in to the center. Repeat the process for the 2 remaining rectangles.

6. Bake for about 1 hour, until crisp and dry. Cool in the pan on a wire rack. To dislodge, loosen with a metal spatula. (The meringue can be made up to 7 days ahead; layer with parchment paper and store at room temperature in a covered container.)

7. For the mousse, melt the chocolates together in a medium-size bowl over barely simmering water or in a microwave oven at 50 percent power for 1 to 4 minutes, checking every 30 seconds. Stir until smooth and allow to cool.

8. In a small saucepan, combine $1/2$ cup of the sugar and the water. Bring to a boil over medium heat, swirling the pan to dissolve the sugar. Boil until the mixture reaches the soft-ball stage or 240°F on a candy thermometer, about 4 minutes.

9. Meanwhile, beat the egg whites in a large clean bowl with clean beaters at low speed until foamy. Add the cream of tartar and beat at medium-high speed to form soft peaks. Slowly add the remaining $1/2$ cup sugar and beat until stiff and glossy. Pour the hot sugar syrup into the mixture, continuing to beat until cooled to room temperature, about 2 minutes. Remove the bowl from the mixer stand and fold in the chocolate with a large rubber spatula; the mixture will deflate slightly. Chill for at least 1 hour before using. (The mousse can be made 1 day in advance and stored in the refrigerator.)

10. To assemble the torte, first reserve 1 cup of the mousse. Spread half of the remainder evenly on a hazelnut meringue. Add a second meringue and cover with the rest of the mousse. Top with the last meringue. Spread the reserved mousse onto the sides of the torte. Supporting the cake securely on the bottom, gently hold it up and press the ground toasted hazelnuts evenly onto the sides. Return the cake to a work surface and sift the cocoa powder evenly over the top through a fine-mesh sieve. Refrigerate until ready to serve.

Yield: 8 servings

*M*any small bakeries prepare their own unique meringue tortes. At our Chicago bakery, we layered walnut meringue with two rich chocolate mousse fillings, one dark and one white, then dusted the top with confectioners' sugar. Called a marjolaine, it is named after a famous dessert created at La Pyramide restaurant in France and was one of our biggest sellers. The Downtown Bakery & Creamery in Healdsburg, California, prepares a similar marjolaine, as well as a popular version featuring hazelnuts. A relative newcomer on the bakery scene, the Downtown Bakery & Creamery has captured a loyal following by reviving recipes from the past that appeal to today's customers.

Boston Cream Pie

This so-called pie (perhaps so named because it's baked in a pie tin) was recently declared the official state cake of Massachusetts. It's an appealingly simple dessert concocted by filling a cake with vanilla custard and glazing it with chocolate.

Cake

1¼ cups cake flour

¾ teaspoon baking powder

¼ teaspoon baking soda

¼ teaspoon salt

6 tablespoons unsalted butter, at room temperature

⅔ cup sugar

2 large eggs, at room temperature

½ cup buttermilk, at room temperature

¾ teaspoon vanilla extract

Custard Filling

1 cup milk

3 large egg yolks

⅓ cup sugar

2 tablespoons cornstarch

1 tablespoon unsalted butter

1 teaspoon vanilla extract

Chocolate Glaze

3 ounces semisweet chocolate, cut into small pieces

3 tablespoons unsalted butter, at room temperature

1 tablespoon light corn syrup

1. Preheat the oven to 350°F. Grease a 9-inch pie pan, 1½ inches deep.

2. To make the cake, sift the flour, baking powder, baking soda, and salt together into a medium-size bowl and set aside.

3. Cream the butter and sugar in a large bowl with an electric mixer at medium speed until light and fluffy, about 5 minutes. Reduce the speed to medium-low. Add the eggs, one at a time, mixing well between additions. Add alternating increments of the flour mixture and of the buttermilk and vanilla, blending well after each addition, about 3 minutes total.

4. Pour the batter into the prepared pan and smooth the top evenly. Bake for 25 to 30 minutes, until the cake is golden brown and a cake tester comes out clean. Cool the cake in the pan on a wire rack for 10 minutes, then unmold the cake and let it cool completely on the rack.

5. For the custard filling, heat the milk to a bare simmer in a heavy-bottomed medium saucepan over medium-low heat. Meanwhile, combine the egg yolks, sugar, and cornstarch in a medium mixing bowl. Whisk until smooth. Add the heated milk to the egg mixture, stir, and return the combination to the saucepan. Whisking constantly, bring back to a boil over medium-low heat and boil for 1 minute. Remove from the heat and add the butter and vanilla, whisking until the butter has melted. Transfer the custard to a bowl, place a piece of waxed paper directly on the top to prevent a crust from forming, and chill.

6. Prepare the chocolate glaze by melting the chocolate over a pan of barely simmering water or in a microwave oven at 50 percent power for 1 to 4 minutes, checking every 30 seconds. Stir until smooth. Add the butter and corn syrup and stir again. Set aside at room temperature until the mixture has thickened to a spreadable consistency.

7. To assemble, cut the cake in half horizontally into 2 equal layers. Place the bottom layer on a cardboard cake circle or a cake plate and spread with the cold custard. Cover the custard with the top layer of cake. Spread evenly with the chocolate glaze. Refrigerate the cake until ready to serve. Before cutting, score the hardened chocolate glaze into serving wedges with a knife.

Yield: 8 servings

oston cream pie is still made in Boston—although, technically speaking, it's a cake, not a pie. Actually, it should really be called a Parker House chocolate cream pie for the hotel that created the dessert we know today. The original Boston cream pie of the mid-nineteenth century was a golden layer cake filled with custard and topped with a dusting of confectioners' sugar. The Parker House substituted a chocolate glaze for the sugar topping, and the fancier finish was an instant hit with Boston hostesses.

Silver Cake

(For Peanut Squares and Seven-Layer Lemon Cake)

A classic variety of white cake, silver cake is made similarly to golden cake, using only the whites of the eggs, some of which have been whipped to lighten the batter. It's a tender and delicious cake.

The recipe will produce sufficient batter to bake a cake in either a 9 × 13-inch baking pan for Peanut Squares (page 135), or in a 12 × 17-inch baking sheet for the Seven-Layer Lemon Cake (page 136). You could also divide the batter into three 9-inch round cake pans for a layer cake; follow baking directions for the sheet cake.

3 cups cake flour

1 tablespoon baking powder

$^{1}/_{2}$ teaspoon salt

1 cup (2 sticks) unsalted butter, at room temperature

$1^{1}/_{2}$ cups sugar

6 large egg whites, divided, at room temperature

$^{1}/_{2}$ tablespoon vanilla extract

$^{1}/_{2}$ teaspoon almond extract

$1^{1}/_{4}$ cups milk, at room temperature

1. Preheat the oven to 350°F. Grease either a 9 × 13-inch baking pan or a 12 × 17-inch baking sheet.

2. Sift the flour, baking powder, and salt together into a medium-size bowl and set aside.

3. Cream the butter and sugar in a large bowl with an electric mixer at medium speed until light and fluffy, about 5 minutes. Reduce the mixer speed to medium-low. Add 2 of the egg whites, one at a time, blending smooth between additions. Reduce the speed to low and add the extracts. Spoon in the flour mixture, alternating with the milk and blending well after each addition.

4. In a medium-size mixing bowl, beat the remaining 4 egg whites to soft peaks with clean beaters at medium speed. Fold into the cake batter gently but thoroughly. Spread the batter evenly into the prepared pan.

5. Bake until the cake is golden and a cake tester comes out clean, about 25 minutes for a 12 × 17-inch sheet cake or 35 minutes for a 9 × 13-inch cake. Cool in the pan on a wire rack for 10 minutes, then unmold the cake. Let a 9 × 13-inch cake cool completely on the rack or a sheet cake atop a clean cloth towel.

Yield: One 9 × 13-inch cake or one 12 × 17-inch sheet cake

Peanut Squares

Delicate rectangles of silver cake are dipped into fondant and then rolled in crushed peanuts. These treats are just the right size for children's party fare.

1 baked 9 × 13-inch Silver Cake (page 134)

6 cups confectioners' sugar

⅓ cup light corn syrup

⅓ cup water

2 cups finely crushed roasted unsalted peanuts

1. Trim the sides of the cake with a long serrated knife and cut it crosswise into 4 strips, each about 3 inches wide. Turn each strip on its side and cut a thin slice off the top to even, then cut each strip crosswise into 4 rectangles, each about 2 inches wide.

2. Combine the confectioners' sugar, corn syrup, and ⅓ cup water in the top of the double boiler over barely simmering water, making sure the water is not touching the bottom of the insert. Heat and stir until the sugar is completely dissolved and the mixture is smoothly blended. (It should flow off a spoon easily.) Take care all the while not to let the water in the bottom of the double boiler come to a boil. If the mixture becomes too thick, drizzle in more water or corn syrup.

3. Pierce a rectangle of cake from beneath with a fork and hold it suspended upright over the double boiler. Spread the hot icing onto the top and sides of the cake with a metal spatula, allowing excess icing to drip back into the pan. Immediately place the cake, iced side down, onto a plate of crushed peanuts and remove the fork. Push peanuts into the sides of the cake. Repeat the process for the remaining bars. (The icing will harden quickly, so coat bars one at a time, transferring each to a platter when done.)

4. Set the garnished cakes onto a platter and serve at room temperature.

Yield: 16 squares

Arlene and C. "Jake" Wautlet opened their small bakery in Algoma, Wisconsin, soon after Jake returned from World War II. The business grew steadily for thirty-five years as Jake baked from scratch daily and Arlene decorated the cakes.

Now that they've sold the bakery, Mrs. Wautlet told me, "It's not the same anymore. These days, bakers use a lot of mixes—but we never did."

Seven-Layer Lemon Cake

This is a divine dessert for a birthday or any other special occasion. There's a rich and buttery lemon curd filling between the layers, and the cake is frosted with sweetened whipped cream softly scented with lemon peel.

Separate pans for each layer of a multilayer cake such as this present no problem for professional bakers. For the home baker, I recommend baking a single sheet cake that will subsequently be cut into layers. You'll end up with one leftover piece of cake, but I'm sure that will make someone a nice snack. When finished, the cake is the shape of a rectangular loaf, easy to slice and beautiful to serve.

Lemon Curd Filling

¹/₃ cup fresh lemon juice
    (about 2 lemons)

¹/₂ cup granulated sugar

2 large egg yolks, plus 1 whole egg

¹/₂ cup (1 stick) unsalted butter, chilled,
    cut into small pieces

Lemon Cream Frosting

1¹/₄ cups heavy (whipping) cream, chilled

¹/₂ cup confectioners' sugar

¹/₂ tablespoon grated lemon zest

1 baked 12 × 17-inch Silver Cake
    (page 134)

1. To make the lemon curd, combine the lemon juice, granulated sugar, egg yolks, and whole egg in a heavy-bottomed medium-size saucepan (preferably enameled cast-iron). Cook over low heat, whisking constantly, until the mixture is very foamy and has thickened such that the whisk leaves tracks on the surface, 8 to 10 minutes. Immediately, remove the pan from the heat and add the butter, whisking until the butter is melted and smoothly blended into the mixture. Transfer the curd to a bowl and let cool to room temperature, then cover and refrigerate until cold. (The lemon curd can be made a day in advance and stored overnight in the refrigerator.)

2. For the lemon cream frosting, whip the cream with an electric mixer until thickened. Add the confectioners' sugar and lemon zest and continue to beat to stiff peaks. Refrigerate until ready to use.

3. To assemble the cake, trim the crusty edges from the cake with a long serrated knife. Cut the cake crosswise into four 4 × 11-inch strips, then cut each of the strips horizontally into equal halves. Place a bottom layer on a cake plate or platter and spread with a thin coating of chilled lemon curd. Repeat the process to add 6 more layers, stacking the pieces of cake atop each other and coating each with lemon curd between additions. Frost the top and sides of the cake with the lemon cream. Refrigerate the cake until 30 minutes before serving, then set it out at room temperature.

Yield: 12 servings

My friend Gail, who was raised in Washington, D.C., says her mouth still waters when she thinks about the lemon cake from Shupp's on Connecticut Avenue. The cake was seven layers high, filled with creamy lemon curd and frosted white. It was her birthday request year after year. She has never forgotten a tenth birthday party with a tragic climax when her mother slaved over a home-baked wonder, realizing too late that the birthday girl had visions only of Shupp's seven-layer cake.

Chocolate Roll

Made of a light sponge cake hiding a creamy filling and usually finished with a simple dusting of cocoa or confectioners' sugar, a chocolate roll is irresistible. The best, in my opinion, is flourless (or nearly so), as popularized by Alice Medrich at Cocolat, the elegant Berkeley, California, bakery that she ran for more than a decade.

Rolling a delicate flourless cake up around its filling, however, can be a tricky operation for all but the most experienced of bakers. I've added just a small amount of cake flour in this recipe to shore up the structure of the cake while retaining much of the taste and texture of the flourless version.

I fill the roll with luxurious chocolate rum mousse, which is also quite good served with fresh raspberries, spread as a filling between the layers of a sponge cake, or piped into a crisp meringue shell. For variety, I use a simple whipped cream filling instead (see page 140).

Quality ingredients, such as the finest European chocolate, Caribbean rum, Italian espresso, and Madagascar vanilla, are the secrets to a superior mousse. Whenever raw eggs are called for, be sure to use farm-fresh eggs or those from a supplier whose sources you trust.

Chocolate Rum Mousse

1 pound bittersweet or semisweet chocolate (preferably imported)

$^{1}/_{3}$ cup dark rum

$^{1}/_{4}$ cup brewed espresso coffee

3 large eggs, separated, at room temperature

$^{1}/_{4}$ cup granulated sugar

1 cup heavy (whipping) cream, chilled

$^{1}/_{2}$ teaspoon vanilla extract (preferably Madagascar)

Cake

5 large eggs, separated, at room temperature

4 ounces semisweet chocolate, coarsely chopped

2 tablespoons brewed espresso coffee

1 teaspoon vanilla extract

Pinch of salt

$^{1}/_{2}$ cup granulated sugar

$^{1}/_{3}$ cup cake flour

Confectioners' sugar or unsweetened cocoa powder, for dusting

1. To make the mousse, melt the chocolate in a medium-size bowl over barely simmering water or in a microwave oven at 50 percent power for 1 to 4 minutes, checking every 30 seconds. Whisk until smooth, then whisk in the rum and coffee. Slowly add the egg yolks, whisking until smoothly blended. Set aside.

2. Beat the egg whites in a large bowl with an electric mixer at medium speed to form soft peaks. Raise the speed to medium-high and slowly add 2 tablespoons of the granulated sugar. Beat until stiff and shiny peaks form. Fold into the chocolate mixture with a large rubber spatula.

3. In a medium-size mixing bowl, beat the cream until thick. Add the remaining 2 tablespoons granulated sugar and the vanilla. Continue to beat until stiff, then fold into the chocolate mixture. Refrigerate the mousse until set, at least 2 hours.

4. Preheat the oven to 375°F. Grease an 11 × 17-inch jelly roll pan and line it with waxed paper. Grease and flour the waxed paper, shaking out excess flour.

5. For the cake, place the egg yolks in a large mixing bowl.

6. Melt the chocolate and stir until smooth. Add the coffee and vanilla. Stir to blend, then stir the mixture into the egg yolks.

7. Combine the egg whites and salt in a large bowl and beat at medium speed to form soft peaks. At medium-high speed, gradually pour in the granulated sugar, beating until the whites are stiff and shiny, about 3 minutes. Sift in the flour and fold with the rubber spatula. Fold half of the combination into the chocolate mixture, then fold in the remainder.

8. Pour the batter into the prepared pan and spread it evenly with a metal spatula. Bake for 10 minutes, reduce the oven temperature to 350°F, and bake for about 5 minutes more. (The cake should feel springy on top.)

9. Remove the pan to a wire rack and let it cool for only 5 minutes, then invert the pan onto a clean cloth towel, lift it off the cake, and peel off the waxed paper. Immediately roll the cake up lengthwise in the towel and set aside to cool.

10. Gently unroll the cake and spread evenly with 3 cups of the mousse. Reroll the cake around the mousse and dust the top with confectioners' sugar or cocoa powder, using a sieve. Store in the refrigerator and serve chilled.

Yield: 12 servings

For a slightly less decadent chocolate roll that can be made in almost no time at all, substitute Whipped Cream Filling for the mousse. Whip 1¹/₂ cups chilled heavy (whipping) cream with an electric mixer until thick. Add ¹/₂ cup sifted confectioners' sugar and ¹/₂ teaspoon vanilla extract. Continue to beat to form stiff peaks. Refrigerate until ready to use. Makes 3 cups.

Ursula's European Pastries in Cranston, Rhode Island, is a little gem—a well-kept neighborhood secret of which even many locals aren't aware. And that's just the way Ursula wants it. After years of selling her pastries wholesale, she set up a retail operation in a quaint, inconspicuous store just outside Providence. She doesn't advertise and probably never will; her faithful following of customers keep her just as busy as she wants to be.

Ursula's pastries—faithful recreations of Austrian and Hungarian classics—are works of art. She makes her strudel dough by hand, imports ingredients whose domestic counterparts she finds lacking, and won't let the word *compromise* enter her vocabulary. She makes a chocolate rum mousse roll that is without equal, rolling a flourless chocolate cake that is as ethereal as a fallen soufflé around a silky bittersweet chocolate mousse spiked with rum.

New York–Style Charlotte Russe

Made of a layer of light sponge cake smeared with raspberry filling and topped with a big mound of stiffened whipped cream, Charlotte Russe is kid bliss! But this dessert is simply too good for kids of any age to pass up. Grown-ups will appreciate a drizzle of fruit liqueur.

Cake

¾ cup cake flour

¼ teaspoon baking powder

⅛ teaspoon salt

3 large eggs, separated, at room temperature

¼ cup cold water

⅔ cup granulated sugar

½ teaspoon vanilla extract

¼ teaspoon lemon extract (optional)

¼ teaspoon cream of tartar

Lemon Syrup

¼ cup granulated sugar

2 tablespoons fresh lemon juice (about 1 lemon)

2 tablespoons water

About ¼ cup Raspberry Filling (see page 117), seedless raspberry jam, or sieved raspberry preserves

Whipped Cream Topping

2 teaspoons unflavored gelatin

2 tablespoons water

2 teaspoons vanilla extract

3 cups heavy (whipping) cream

⅓ cup superfine sugar

6 maraschino cherries (optional, for garnish)

1. Preheat the oven to 325°F. Lightly grease six 10-ounce custard cups or ramekins and place them on a baking sheet.

2. Prepare the cakes by sifting the flour, baking powder, and salt together into a medium-size bowl. Set aside.

3. Beat the egg yolks in a bowl with an electric mixer at medium-high speed until thick, about 3 minutes. Gradually pour in the cold water, then slowly add the granulated sugar, mixing until completely dissolved, about 2 minutes. Beat in the vanilla and lemon extract, if desired. Remove the bowl from the mixer stand and sift in the flour mixture. Fold with a rubber spatula.

continued

4. In a medium-size mixing bowl, beat the egg whites and cream of tartar with clean beaters until stiff and shiny peaks form. Thoroughly fold into the yolk mixture.

5. Divide the batter equally among the cups and smooth the tops evenly. Place the cups into the oven on the baking sheet and bake for about 20 minutes, until the centers are springy to the touch and a cake tester comes out clean. Cool the cakes to room temperature in their cups on a wire rack.

6. Meanwhile, prepare the lemon syrup. Combine the granulated sugar, lemon juice, and water in a small saucepan. Bring to a boil over medium heat, stirring until the sugar dissolves. Boil for 1 minute and remove from the heat. Allow to cool to room temperature.

7. When both have cooled sufficiently, brush the cakes with the syrup to glaze and spread a thin layer of raspberry filling over each.

8. For the topping, combine the gelatin and water in a heat-resistant dish. Set aside for 5 minutes, then heat in a microwave oven at full power for 30 seconds to liquefy. Set aside until cooled to room temperature but not yet set, about 5 minutes. Stir in the vanilla.

9. Whip the cream using an electric mixer at medium speed, gradually adding the superfine sugar. When thickened, scrape in the gelatin mixture. Continue to beat to form stiff peaks.

10. Spoon the cream equally over the cakes, shaping the top of each charlotte into a peaked cone with a metal spatula. Refrigerate until ready to serve.

11. Garnish with a maraschino cherry perched on the tip of each cone, if desired.

Yield: 6 servings

For generations of New York City children, the dessert of choice from a neighborhood bakeshop was a pint-size charlotte russe. New York native Elaine Barlas's grandmother bought it as a treat for Elaine's mother, who in turn bought it for Elaine from the family's favorite bakery, Richer's, on Horace Harding Boulevard in Queens. The charlotte russe from Richer's Bakery came in a white cardboard container with a scalloped top edge that made it look like a crown. The box had a false bottom, similar to a spring-form pan, that Elaine used to push up the dessert with her thumbs as she devoured it.

FOUR

Quick Breads,
Cakes, and
Biscuits

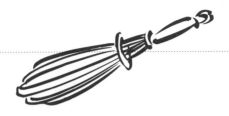

Quick breads and biscuits (and scones and muffins) are increasingly the choice of harried urban dwellers to finish a meal on the run. Professional bakers love these baking powder and soda-leavened goods for precisely the same reason home bakers do—they're easy and fast to prepare. For the baking novice, this is the place to start.

Tips and Techniques

- For best results, use uncoated shiny aluminum pans.

- I call for use of a stationary electric mixer in many quick cake recipes for ease of preparation, but you can prepare the batters by hand as well. Use two bowls, one for sifting the dry ingredients and one for creaming, a long wooden spoon, and a little elbow grease.

- Quick bread and biscuit batters are prepared by hand. Once the wet and dry ingredients have been combined, mix gently, just to moisten.

- Once prepared, quick bread, muffin, and scone batters can be refrigerated for three to four hours. Bring back to room temperature before baking.

- Biscuits, scones, and muffins freeze well for up to three months. Store loosely in a plastic freezer bag for easy individual retrieval.

Prune Loaf

Mr. Lynn Craig of the Dutch Maid Bakery in Tracy City, Tennessee, sent me this recipe for Prune Loaf, which is similar to the bakery's popular sugar plum cake. It's wonderfully moist and soft and slightly spicy, with an occasional crunch of pecan. The prune butter lends plenty of fruit flavor and also provides a silky texture. I think it's ideal with tea or coffee—and it even improves in taste the second day.

1 cup cake flour

1/2 teaspoon baking powder

1/2 teaspoon ground cinnamon

1/4 teaspoon ground nutmeg

1/4 teaspoon ground allspice

1/4 teaspoon baking soda

3/4 cup prune butter

3/4 cup sugar

1/2 cup canola oil

2 large eggs

1/2 teaspoon salt

1/2 teaspoon vanilla extract

3/4 cup milk

1/2 cup chopped pecans

1. Preheat the oven to 350°F. Grease an 8 1/2 × 4 1/2-inch loaf pan or a 9 × 5-inch loaf pan.

2. Sift the flour, baking powder, cinnamon, nutmeg, allspice, and baking soda together into a medium-size bowl and set aside.

3. Combine the prune butter and sugar in a large mixing bowl. Cream with an electric mixer at medium-low speed until smoothly blended. Add the oil, eggs, and salt and mix until well blended. Reduce the speed to low. Add the flour mixture, blending well. Add the vanilla to the milk and slowly pour the combination into the batter. Add the pecans and mix until thoroughly blended.

4. Pour the batter into the prepared loaf pan. Bake for about 1 hour, until a cake tester comes out clean. Cool in the pan on a wire rack for 10 minutes, then unmold the loaf onto the rack to cool completely.

Yield: 10 servings

*T*racy City, nestled in the mountains of the Cumberland Plateau, is home to Tennessee's oldest family-owned bakery, the Dutch Maid. The ninety-five-year-old establishment is still run by various members of the founding Baggenstoss family, who once lived above the bakery and delivered their goods in wicker baskets and by wheelbarrow. (Albert baked here for forty-two years, while his brother Herman didn't come into the bakery until he was eighty-seven.)

The 5,000-square-foot bakery has operated pretty much the same way for decades, with the same recipes and equipment. During World War II, when the Dutch Maid was producing bread for much of the state, four shifts of female bakers turned out 12,000 loaves each day because "no one told them they couldn't."

Today, tourists and mail orders keep the bakery busy, with up to 10,000 applesauce fruitcakes alone sold each year, according to Lynn Craig, a nephew of Herman Baggenstoss. Mr. Craig doesn't care much for fruitcake personally, but says "These applesauce ones are pretty good—real moist without citrus or soaking. Just gets better as it sits." The Dutch Maid is also known for sugar plum cakes made with plum butter. Craig explained that "none of our cakes have preservatives and the plum cake needs to be eaten in a few days, but if you don't eat a cake in five days, what did you buy it for?"

Rosh Hashanah Honey Cake

Wish family and friends a sweet New Year with this honey cake, a treasured recipe from the owners of a fondly remembered bakery on Chicago's North Shore, Purwin's Cake Box. I adapted Seymour Seltzer's recipe from a seventy-seven-pound batch yield to a single loaf cake for the home baker. The cake is stunning in its simplicity, sweet but not too sweet, with a fine, delicate texture. Enjoy it with Seymour and Violet Purwin Seltzer's compliments!

Rind of 1 lemon

1 cup water

1 scant cup orange blossom honey

1/2 cup packed dark brown sugar

2 teaspoons baking soda

1/3 cup vegetable oil

2 large eggs

2 cups baker's patent flour (see Mail Order Source Guide) or unbleached all-purpose flour

1. Preheat the oven to 325°F. Grease a 9 × 5-inch loaf pan.

2. Combine the lemon rind and water in a small saucepan. Bring to a boil over medium heat and boil for 1 minute. Remove the pan from the heat, cover, and set aside to steep.

3. Combine the honey, brown sugar, baking soda, and oil in a large mixing bowl. Begin to mix with an electric mixer at low speed. When the mixture is well blended, add the eggs and mix until smooth.

4. Strain the lemon rind from the steeped water and add 1/3 cup of the hot lemon water to the mixer bowl. Blend at low speed for 2 minutes. Gradually spoon in the flour. When the flour is completely incorporated, slowly add 1/3 cup more of the hot lemon water. (Reheat, if necessary.) When the batter is completely blended and smooth, pour it into the prepared loaf pan. (This batter is very fluid.)

5. Place the pan onto a baking sheet and bake for about 1 hour, until it springs back when very gently touched in the center (the delicate cake can collapse if touched too firmly) or a cake tester gently inserted comes out clean.

6. Cool the cake in the pan on a wire rack for 15 minutes, then unmold the cake onto the rack to cool completely. Serve at room temperature.

Yield: 10 servings

Opened in 1929, Purwin's Cake Box was in operation in Evanston, Illinois, for fifty years. It was the first kosher bakery in the Midwest to make fancy pastries and petit fours for sweet tables and special occasions. The Cake Box became famous for its elaborately decorated cakes, one of which looked like a basket of blooming flowers, as well as for its sponge cakes and honey cakes. The bakery shipped its cakes nationwide—including an annual birthday cake to the late Jackie Gleason in Florida—and actually made deliveries from its suburban Chicago locale to Wisconsin and Indiana.

Butter Rum Cake

The butter rum Bundt cake from Scialo Bros. in Providence is enough to make a grown woman weep. It's an incredibly buttery, tender cake soaked in a syrup heady with rum and simply garnished with a crown of sliced almonds. I flew home with the memory of that cake still fresh in mind to inspire my own creation. If you are not satisfied with unadorned ecstacy, serve it with softly whipped cream to which you've added a splash of rum.

Cake

3 cups all-purpose flour

2 teaspoons baking powder

1 teaspoon baking soda

1 teaspoon salt

1 pound (4 sticks) unsalted butter, at room temperature

2 cups sugar

6 large eggs, at room temperature

1 tablespoon vanilla extract

1 cup buttermilk, at room temperature

Hot Rum Syrup

¾ cup sugar

¾ cup water

1 cinnamon stick, broken in half

4 whole cloves

Freshly grated nutmeg to taste

¾ cup dark rum

1. Preheat the oven to 350°F. Grease a 12-cup Bundt pan.

2. Sift the flour, baking powder, baking soda, and salt together into a medium-size bowl and set aside.

3. Cream the butter and sugar in a large bowl with an electric mixer at medium speed until fluffy, about 2 minutes. At medium-low speed, add the eggs, one at a time, mixing until incorporated between additions. Beat in the vanilla. Reduce the speed to low and spoon in the flour mixture, alternating with the buttermilk, beating until smoothly blended. Pour the batter evenly into the prepared pan.

4. Bake for about 1 hour, until a cake tester comes out clean. Cool in the pan on a wire rack for 20 minutes, then unmold the cake onto a rack set over a baking sheet and allow to cool completely.

5. Meanwhile, prepare the rum syrup by combining the sugar, water, and spices in a small saucepan. Bring to a boil over medium heat, stirring until the sugar dissolves. Boil for 3 minutes and remove the pan from the heat. Immediately stir in the rum, then set aside to cool to room temperature.

6. Once cooled, strain out the cinnamon stick and cloves and bring the syrup back to a boil. Remove from the heat, pour a little of the syrup over the cake, and paint the sides of the cake with a brush. Continue to pour and paint on the syrup, a little at a time, until all of the syrup has been absorbed. Set the cake aside at room temperature for at least 1 hour before serving.

Yield: 12 to 16 servings

The ornately decorated cakes and picture-perfect pastries lining two windows of the tiny shop on Atwells Avenue is the first thing to stop pedestrians in their tracks. At the door, sweet and savory aromas beckon to the passerby. Now *this* is a bakery, as Rhode Islanders have long known. For the better part of this century, Scialo Bros. has been the standout among the many Italian bakeries dotting "the hill," as Providence's Federal Hill neighborhood is called. Now, it's the last. Scialo's three brick ovens, one dating back to 1916, are still used for baking. The recipes haven't changed much either—with everything still made from scratch on the premises.

Lemon Chiffon Cake

Chiffon cakes are winners in every category in my book. They're extremely easy to prepare and have a fabulously soft, moist texture and excellent flavor if prepared with freshly squeezed juice. Top this cake with the optional glaze if you want to dress it up a bit for company; it tastes equally delicious simply dusted with a little confectioners' sugar.

Cake

1½ cups granulated sugar

1 tablespoon grated lemon zest (about 2 lemons)

1½ cups cake flour

½ teaspoon baking soda

½ teaspoon salt

7 large eggs, separated, at room temperature

½ cup canola oil

⅔ cup water

2 tablespoons fresh lemon juice

1 teaspoon vanilla extract

½ teaspoon cream of tartar

Confectioners' sugar, for dusting

Glaze (optional)

4 tablespoons (½ stick) unsalted butter, at room temperature

1½ cups confectioners' sugar

2½ tablespoons fresh lemon juice

1. Preheat the oven to 325°F.

2. Combine 2 tablespoons of the granulated sugar and the lemon zest in a small dish. Mix and set aside.

3. Sift the cake flour, baking soda, salt, and remaining granulated sugar together into a large mixing bowl. Add the egg yolks, oil, water, lemon juice, and vanilla, whisking until the batter is smoothly blended.

4. Beat the egg whites in a large bowl with an electric mixer at medium-low speed until foamy. Add the cream of tartar and beat at medium speed until soft peaks form. Slowly add the sugar and lemon zest mixture, then increase the speed to medium-high. Beat to form stiff and shiny peaks. Fold into the batter with a large whisk until completely incorporated. Pour evenly into an ungreased 10-inch tube pan. Bake for about 55 minutes, until a cake tester comes out clean.

5. Immediately invert the cake pan and elevate by at least 2 inches above a countertop to allow air circulation. (Prop the pan up by setting a can or jar under the center tube to raise the pan.) Let the cake cool completely in this position, about 2 hours.

6. Loosen the cake from the outer and inner edges of the pan, then unmold it onto a serving plate. (Bang on the bottom and shake the pan gently to dislodge the cake.) Dust the top of the cake with confectioners' sugar through a sieve, or glaze the cake, if desired.

7. For the glaze, cream the butter and confectioners' sugar in a medium-size bowl until smoothly blended. Stir in the lemon juice and spoon evenly over the top of the cake, letting it drip down the sides slightly.

Yield: 12 servings

Through the 1950s and 1960s, towering chiffon cakes commanded prime shelf space in most urban bakeries, particularly in New York City. Unfortunately, it's rare to find a first-rate one in a bakery these days. I can't imagine why chiffon cakes are no longer in demand, other than the fact that they look a little plain by comparison to some other bakery cakes—an appearance I prefer to think of as refreshingly unfussy.

Lemon Poppy Seed Bundt Cake

Instead of just idly wishing that Suzanne's was still around to keep me supplied with a steady fix of Lemon Poppy Seed Bundt Cake, I set out to replicate it. After I had served my husband a single slice, he asked me not to make it again because he could easily eat it every day. I guess I succeeded.

Cake

2¹/₂ cups cake flour

¹/₂ tablespoon baking powder

³/₄ teaspoon salt

¹/₂ teaspoon baking soda

¹/₃ cup poppy seeds

1 tablespoon grated lemon zest
    (about 2 lemons)

1¹/₂ cups (3 sticks) unsalted butter, at
    room temperature

1¹/₂ cups sugar

5 large eggs, at room temperature

2 teaspoons vanilla extract

³/₄ cup sour cream, at room temperature

Lemon Glaze

¹/₂ cup sugar

¹/₂ cup fresh lemon juice (about 2 large
    lemons)

1. Preheat the oven to 350°F. Grease a 12-cup Bundt pan or a 10-cup tube cake pan.

2. To make the cake, sift the flour, baking powder, salt, and soda together into a medium bowl. Add the poppy seeds and lemon zest, stirring to combine thoroughly. Set aside.

3. Cream the butter and sugar in a large bowl with an electric mixer at medium speed until fluffy, about 2 minutes. At medium-low speed, add the eggs, one at a time, beating until incorporated between additions. Beat in the vanilla. Reduce the speed to low and spoon in the flour mixture, alternating with the sour cream and mixing until smoothly blended.

4. Pour the batter evenly into the pan. Bake for about 1 hour, until a cake tester comes out clean. Cool in the pan on a wire rack for 20 minutes.

5. Meanwhile, prepare the glaze. Combine the sugar and lemon juice in a small saucepan. Heat, stirring to dissolve the sugar, until the mixture comes to a boil, then remove from the heat.

6. Unmold the cake onto a rack set over a baking sheet. Pour half of the boiling syrup evenly over the top of the cake while still hot. Brush the remaining syrup onto the sides of the cake. Allow the cake to cool completely on the rack. Serve at room temperature.

Yield: 12 servings

Suzanne's was a little storefront bakery nestled in a crowded street of boutiques in Chicago's north side Lakeview community. During the late 1970s and early 1980s, it was the best place in the neighborhood to go for classic, homestyle Bundt and loaf cakes. They were the kind of cakes you just knew you could make yourself, even while realizing that Suzanne made them better. Her lemon poppy seed Bundt was a winner. Suzanne finished the rich pound cake with a fresh lemon glaze and didn't stint on the poppy seeds—in short, the kind of cake I could eat every day.

Marble Pound Cake Drizzled with Chocolate

This is my attempt to re-create the two-tone, chocolate-glazed pound cake of Edie Soldinger's recollections. It's an easy-to-prepare Bundt cake with a striking appearance. The cake slices beautifully and tastes superb.

Vanilla Cake

1¹/₂ cups all-purpose flour

³/₄ teaspoon baking powder

¹/₄ teaspoon salt

³/₄ cup (1¹/₂ sticks) unsalted butter, at room temperature

³/₄ cup sugar

3 large eggs, at room temperature

¹/₂ cup sour cream, at room temperature

1 tablespoon vanilla extract

Chocolate Cake

¹/₄ cup unsweetened cocoa powder

¹/₄ cup boiling water

¹/₂ tablespoon vanilla extract

1¹/₄ cups all-purpose flour

³/₄ teaspoon baking powder

¹/₄ teaspoon salt

³/₄ cup (1¹/₂ sticks) unsalted butter, at room temperature

1 cup sugar

4 large eggs, at room temperature

Toppings

4 ounces semisweet chocolate or semisweet coating chocolate (see box)

4 ounces white chocolate or white coating chocolate (see box)

1. Preheat the oven to 350°F. Grease a 12-cup Bundt pan.

2. To make the vanilla cake, sift the flour, baking powder, and salt together into a medium-size bowl and set aside.

3. Cream the butter and sugar in a large bowl with an electric mixer at medium speed until fluffy, about 2 minutes. At medium-low speed, add the eggs, one at a time, beating until incorporated between additions. Beat to blend thoroughly. Reduce the speed to low and spoon in the flour mixture, alternating with the sour cream and vanilla, mixing until the batter is smoothly blended.

4. For the chocolate cake, combine the cocoa and boiling water in a small bowl. Stir in the vanilla and set aside to cool to room temperature. Sift the flour, baking powder, and salt together in a medium-size bowl.

5. In a large mixing bowl, cream the butter and sugar at medium speed until fluffy, about 2 minutes. At medium-low speed, add the eggs, one at a time, blending thoroughly after each addition. (Don't worry about the curdled look.) Reduce the speed to low and spoon in the flour mixture, alternating with the cocoa mixture, until the batter is smoothly blended.

6. Spoon half of the vanilla batter evenly into the Bundt pan. Pour the chocolate batter over the vanilla batter. Spoon the remaining vanilla batter over the chocolate. Using a table knife, swirl the batters together in big strokes until marbleized.

7. Bake for 50 to 55 minutes, until a cake tester comes out clean. Cool in the pan on a wire rack for 20 minutes, then unmold the cake onto the rack to cool completely.

8. To prepare the toppings, melt the semi-sweet chocolate in a bowl over simmering water or in a microwave oven at 50 percent power for 1 to 4 minutes, checking every 30 seconds. Stir until smooth. Drizzle the chocolate all over the cake in a back-and-forth zigzag motion. Melt the white chocolate and stir until smooth. Drizzle over the cake in the same manner. Let the cake stand until the chocolates harden. Serve at room temperature.

Yield: 12 servings

In this recipe, I prefer to use coating chocolates which dry to a hard finish without melting at warm room temperature. They can be purchased from specialty stores (see Mail Order Source Guide).

---

*E*die Soldinger, an editor of restaurant guidebooks and a connoisseur of desserts made by the nation's best pastry chefs, fondly remembers a marble cake made by a local bakery when she was growing up in Harrison, New York. She describes it as a swirl of vanilla and chocolate cakes, dense and moist but not crumbly. Draped over the top was a combination of dark and white chocolates that crunched in your mouth as you ate.

Tennessee Jam Cake

Traditional jam cake, usually made with blackberry jam, is fruity, moist, and yummy to the last crumb. Now imagine it with three jams! Perfect for the holidays, this cake has pecans and a perfume of aromatic spices to boot. I use fruit juice–sweetened preserves or spreadable fruit, but this may be just the dessert you were looking for to showcase your own homemade preserves.

2¾ cups all-purpose flour

½ tablespoon baking soda

2 teaspoons ground cinnamon

1 teaspoon ground nutmeg

½ teaspoon ground cloves

½ teaspoon ground ginger

½ teaspoon salt

1 cup (2 sticks) unsalted butter, at room temperature

½ cup granulated sugar

½ cup packed light brown sugar

5 large eggs, at room temperature

1 cup buttermilk, at room temperature

1 teaspoon vanilla extract

½ cup each of 3 flavors of preserves or spreadable fruit (such as blackberry, strawberry, and plum)

1 cup coarsely chopped pecans

Confectioners' sugar, for dusting

1. Preheat the oven to 300°F. Grease a 12-cup Bundt pan.

2. Sift the flour, baking soda, spices, and salt together into a medium-size bowl and set aside.

3. Cream the butter, granulated sugar, and brown sugar in a large bowl with an electric mixer at medium speed until fluffy, about 2 minutes. At medium-low speed, add the eggs, one at a time, beating until incorporated between additions. (Don't worry that the batter looks curdled.)

4. Combine the buttermilk and vanilla. Reduce the mixer speed to low and spoon in the flour mixture, alternating with the buttermilk mixture, mixing until smoothly blended. Using a large rubber spatula, quickly fold in the preserves until the batter is marbleized, then fold in the pecans and pour the batter evenly into the prepared pan.

5. Set the pan onto a baking sheet and bake for 15 minutes. Raise the oven temperature to 350°F and continue to bake for about 45 minutes more, until the cake is well browned and a cake tester comes out clean. Cool in the pan on a wire rack for 20 minutes, then unmold the cake onto the rack to cool completely. Dust the cake with confectioners' sugar through a sieve before serving. Serve at room temperature.

Yield: 12 servings

ecker's, in Nashville, Tennessee, is a family-owned bakery run by a mother and daughter. It's well known for old-fashioned cakes and cookies and for a regional Southern specialty called "jam cake." A friendly neighborhood place, Becker's sits on a corner in the Green Hills community, seemingly unchanged since the 1940s. It has a kitchen not much bigger than those of its residential neighbors. One customer told me she still remembers "Miss Mary," who worked behind the counter at Becker's for years and made sure that no neighborhood child went home without his own special sweet.

Blueberry Sour Cream Coffee Cake

For my blueberry coffee cake, I use plump, fresh Michigan blueberries from a farmer's market in Chicago. It's very rich, thanks to a goodly portion of sour cream. A crunchy, nutty topping caps the tender cake.

Topping

½ cup packed dark brown sugar

2 teaspoons ground cinnamon

1 cup coarsely chopped walnuts

4 tablespoons (½ stick) unsalted butter, softened slightly

Coffee Cake

2 cups all-purpose flour

1 teaspoon baking powder

½ teaspoon baking soda

½ teaspoon salt

½ cup (1 stick) unsalted butter, at room temperature

1 cup sugar

2 large eggs

1 cup sour cream

2 teaspoons vanilla extract

1 pint fresh blueberries, picked over

1. Preheat the oven to 350°F. Grease a 9-inch springform pan.

2. To make the topping, combine the brown sugar and cinnamon in a medium-size bowl and mix. Add the walnuts and stir to combine. Add the butter and mix with your fingers until the mixture has a moist, crumbly texture. Set aside.

3. Prepare the cake by sifting the flour, baking powder, baking soda, and salt together into another medium-size bowl.

4. Cream the butter and sugar in a large bowl with an electric mixer at medium-high speed until light in color and fluffy, about 2 minutes. Reduce the speed to low and add the eggs, one at a time, beating well after the first addition. While beating, add half of the sour cream, followed by half of the flour mixture, the remaining sour cream and the vanilla, and then the rest of the flour mixture. Blend thoroughly. Remove the bowl from the mixer stand and gently fold in the blueberries. Stir sparingly so as not to turn the batter blue from the berries.

5. Spread the batter evenly in the prepared pan. Distribute the topping over the batter. Place the pan on a baking sheet and bake for about 55 minutes, until a cake tester comes out clean. Cool in the pan on a wire rack, then release the sides of the pan.

6. Cut the coffee cake into wedges and serve warm or at room temperature.

Yield: 1 coffee cake; 10 to 12 servings

The welcoming smells of cinnamon and brown sugar greet the crowd waiting in line on Saturday mornings to enter the Honey Bear Bakery in Seattle's Green Lake neighborhood. Something of a local hangout, the bakery doubles as a self-service breakfast café. Regulars settle in with newspapers, a steaming cup of coffee, and their favorite coffee cake, bun, scone, or muffin.

Savvy Seattle consumers know a thing or two about the region's abundance of fresh fruit, and the coffee cake I sampled at the Honey Bear was representative of local standards. It was brimming with ripe, juicy blueberries from the neighboring farmer's market.

Irish Soda Bread

Irish Soda Bread is a rustic, hearty loaf that can be prepared in scarcely more time than it takes to read the recipe, since baking soda and buttermilk replace yeast for leavening in most renditions. Sliced thick, it's the perfect bread to accompany soups and stews. Try thinly sliced soda bread as the base for incomparable Irish smoked salmon or for open-faced tea sandwiches.

2½ cups stone-ground whole wheat flour

2½ cups unbleached all-purpose flour

½ cup old-fashioned rolled oats

1 teaspoon baking soda

1 teaspoon salt

2¼ cups plus 2 tablespoons buttermilk

1. Preheat the oven to 425°F. Grease a baking sheet.

2. Combine the flours, oats, baking soda, and salt in a large mixing bowl. Stir to mix. Add 2¼ cups of the buttermilk and stir just to moisten the mixture completely.

3. Turn the dough out onto a work surface and knead 2 or 3 times. If the dough feels dry, add 1 to 2 more tablespoons of buttermilk, kneading with a light touch until the dough begins to stiffen, 1 to 2 minutes.

4. Shape the dough, which should feel moist but not sticky, into a round loaf about 7½ inches in diameter, slightly flattened. Transfer the round to the baking sheet and cut a crisscross slash into the top with a sharp knife. Bake for 30 to 35 minutes, until browned and crusty. Cool the loaf on a wire rack.

Yield: 1 large loaf; 8 to 10 servings

Soda bread, the national loaf of Ireland and once a tradition in Irish-American bakeries, is in danger of extinction on this side of the Atlantic. In most places other than Boston, one tends to see signs that read "Irish Soda Bread Available Today" in bakery windows only once a year—for St. Patrick's Day.

There are many variations of soda bread. The Avenue Bakery on Dorchester, in business in Boston since 1908, makes Irish loaves and rolls using a mix of whole wheat flour and white flour. Diane's Bakery in nearby Roslindale puts a spin on their soda bread by adding yeast, caraway seeds, and raisins.

Irish Soda
Bread

Jammer

Scone

Country Cornmeal Loaf

The critical ingredient in this simple, fabulous loaf is the cornmeal, which should be stone ground. Most health food markets carry at least one brand. The Nauvoo Mill & Bakery will also ship it to you (see Mail Order Source Guide).

2 cups stone-ground yellow cornmeal

1 cup unbleached all-purpose flour

$^1\!/_4$ cup sugar

1 teaspoon baking powder

1 teaspoon baking soda

$^1\!/_2$ teaspoon salt

3 tablespoons unsalted butter, melted

2 cups buttermilk

1. Combine the cornmeal, flour, sugar, baking powder, baking soda, and salt in a large mixing bowl. Stir to mix. Add the melted butter and buttermilk. Stir with a wooden spoon until well blended. Pour the batter into a greased 9 × 5-inch loaf pan.

2. Preheat the oven to 350°F. Allow the batter to sit in the pan for 15 to 20 minutes while the oven is heating.

3. Bake for about 50 minutes, until browned and firm in the center.

4. Unmold the bread and cool on a wire rack. Serve slightly warm, at room temperature, or toasted the next day.

Yield: 1 loaf; 8 servings

A visit to the Nauvoo Mill & Bakery in Nauvoo, Illinois, is a journey into the rural past. One of the few remaining operational grist mills in Illinois, it is also the home of a small, intriguing bakery. The bakery's breads are all made with the mill's own whole wheat flours and grains. The stone-ground cornmeal produced here is exceptional. It is made of meal flakes, not fine flour, with an intense golden color and the robust flavor of fresh corn. I buy several bags at a time to store in my freezer.

Flaky Biscuits

Warm from the oven, flaky and buttery, biscuits are one of life's simplest and greatest pleasures. Southern bakers have been making them for so long that the process is part of daily household routine. I use dried buttermilk in these biscuits for convenience. If you prefer to use fresh, omit the cultured buttermilk powder and substitute liquid buttermilk for the water.

2 cups pastry flour or White Lily all-purpose flour (see box)

2¹/₂ tablespoons cultured buttermilk powder

2¹/₂ teaspoons baking powder

¹/₂ teaspoon salt

¹/₂ teaspoon baking soda

¹/₂ cup (1 stick) unsalted butter or shortening, chilled, cut into small pieces, plus 1 additional tablespoon butter, melted

²/₃ cup cold water

1. Preheat the oven to 450°F. Grease a large cookie sheet.

2. Sift the flour, buttermilk powder, baking powder, salt, and baking soda together into a medium-size bowl. Cut in the butter with a pastry blender or transfer the mixture to a food processor, add the butter, and pulse until finely crumbled. Add the cold water and stir or pulse just until a dough begins to form.

3. Turn the dough out onto a floured work surface and gather it into a ball. Push the dough out into a round, ¹/₂ to ³/₄ inch thick, adding extra flour to the work surface if necessary. Cut out biscuits with a floured 2-inch round cutter and transfer with a spatula to the prepared cookie sheet, spacing ¹/₂ inch apart. Reshape dough scraps into a round for additional biscuits, handling the dough as little as possible.

4. Brush the tops of the biscuits lightly with the melted butter and bake for about 12 minutes, until lightly browned. Transfer the biscuits to wire racks to cool only slightly.

Yield: 16 to 18 biscuits

There are a few tips to keep in mind to ensure flaky biscuit baking success:

- *Use a soft wheat flour. In the South, White Lily brand flour is what every biscuit baker uses; in other parts of the country, use pastry flour.*

- *Make sure your butter or shortening is chilled and has been cut into small cubes.*

- *Pre–measure all liquid ingredients and keep them refrigerated until ready to use.*

- *Resist the temptation to add extra flour to the dough to make it more manageable— just push it out to a uniform thickness on a well-floured surface, handling as little as possible.*

- *Dip your biscuit cutter into flour before each cut, and cut by pushing the cutter straight down and pulling it straight up without twisting.*

- *Brush the tops with melted butter before baking for a beautiful golden crust.*

Biscuit aficionados in Richmond, Virginia, know of only one variety—the perfectly proportioned, flaky biscuit from Sally Bell's, often to be found cradling thin slices of Smithfield ham. Everything has been made daily from scratch since 1926 at Sally Bell's, and the heavenly biscuits are no exception. One of my friends still remembers the box lunches her family bought from Sally Bell's for years, containing fried chicken, deviled eggs, a devil's food cupcake for dessert, and, of course, Sally Bell's flaky biscuits.

Glazed Sweet Potato Biscuits

I liked Marsee Baking's concept of a flaky, vanilla-glazed breakfast biscuit so much that I headed straight for the kitchen upon my arrival home to work on an easy baking powder biscuit version for the home baker. I added sweet potato for a novel twist. These make a nice breakfast treat all by themselves, but they also pair well with a brunch plate of spicy sausage or smoked ham.

Vanilla Glaze

1/4 cup sugar

1/4 cup water

1 scant teaspoon vanilla extract

Biscuits

2 cups all-purpose or pastry flour (see Mail Order Source Guide)

2 teaspoons baking powder

1 teaspoon salt

5 tablespoons unsalted butter, chilled, cut into small pieces

1 cup mashed, cooked sweet potato

1/3 cup sugar

2 large eggs

1. To make the vanilla glaze, combine the sugar and water in a small saucepan. Bring to a boil over medium heat, stirring to dissolve the sugar. Boil for 1 minute and remove from the heat. Stir in the vanilla and let the syrup cool to room temperature before using.

2. Preheat the oven to 400°F. Grease a 12-well muffin tin.

3. To prepare the biscuits, combine the flour, baking powder, and salt in a medium-size mixing bowl. Stir to mix and cut in the butter with a pastry blender until the mixture is finely crumbled.

4. In a separate bowl, combine the sweet potato, sugar, and eggs and stir until smoothly blended. Add to the flour mixture and stir until a moist dough forms.

5. Turn the dough out onto a floured work surface. Sprinkle the dough with flour and push it into a rectangle about 12 inches long and 1/4 inch thick. Using a floured knife, cut the rectangle into roughly 1 1/2-inch squares of dough. Stack 4 to 5 dough squares upright, arranged side by side like dominoes, in each well of the prepared muffin tin.

6. Bake for 15 to 17 minutes, until lightly golden and firm to the touch. Brush the biscuits with the vanilla glaze while they are still hot. Serve warm.

Yield: 12 biscuits

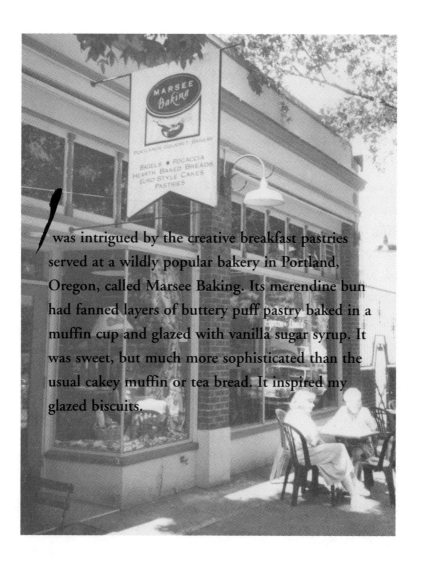

I was intrigued by the creative breakfast pastries served at a wildly popular bakery in Portland, Oregon, called Marsee Baking. Its merendine bun had fanned layers of buttery puff pastry baked in a muffin cup and glazed with vanilla sugar syrup. It was sweet, but much more sophisticated than the usual cakey muffin or tea bread. It inspired my glazed biscuits.

Oatmeal Raisin Scones

It's not hard to understand the popularity of these Oatmeal Raisin Scones. If you've somehow never sampled one before, you will probably sense a familiar taste with the first bite. Take another flavorful bite and concentrate—rather like an oatmeal raisin cookie, only less sweet, no?

The crystal sugar used to top the scones is a particularly coarse variety of granulated sugar, sometimes called sparkling sugar. It's available from specialty vendors (see Mail Order Source Guide).

2 cups quick-cooking oats

1 cup unbleached all-purpose flour

$1/3$ cup packed dark brown sugar

2 teaspoons baking powder

$1/2$ teaspoon baking soda

$1/2$ teaspoon salt

$1/4$ teaspoon ground cinnamon

$1/2$ cup (1 stick) unsalted butter, chilled, cut into small pieces

$3/4$ cup buttermilk, chilled

$1/2$ cup seedless raisins

1 egg yolk, beaten with 1 tablespoon water

White crystal sugar, for sprinkling

1. Preheat the oven to 425°F. Grease 2 cookie sheets.

2. Combine the oats and flour in a stationary electric mixer fitted with the flat paddle attachment. Add the brown sugar, baking powder, baking soda, salt, and cinnamon. Mix thoroughly. Add the butter and mix until it is evenly dispersed and the mixture has the texture of coarse crumbs. Add the buttermilk and mix briefly to form a dough. Add the raisins, mixing for about 30 seconds more to disperse.

3. Turn the dough out onto a lightly floured work surface. Sprinkle the dough with flour and pat it out into a round $1/2$ to $3/4$ inch thick. Using a $2\frac{1}{2}$-inch round biscuit cutter dipped in flour, cut a scone by pushing straight down on the cutter and pulling it straight up without twisting. Continue the process, dipping the cutter into flour before each cut. Transfer the scones to the prepared cookie sheets with a metal spatula, spacing them 1 inch apart. Push the dough scraps together for additional scones.

4. Brush the top of each scone with the egg and water wash and sprinkle with crystal sugar. Bake for about 12 minutes, until golden and firm. Remove the scones to wire racks to cool. Serve warm or at room temperature.

Yield: 12 scones

ortland, Oregon, is a city that takes both its coffee and the ubiquitous accompanying nosh very seriously. Most mornings, residents can be seen scurrying along the city's sidewalks with a cup of coffee to go in one hand and a tissue-wrapped pastry in the other. For close to twenty years, the Three Lions Bakery has been one of the most popular providers of this ritual morning repast. Scone lovers stream into the bakery's two storefront locations for their offerings, which are available in a wide selection of flavors.

Terry's Cornmeal Cranberry Scones

My friend Terry was my companion on a recent bakery binge. As we ate our way around town, she sampled variations of cornmeal scones, her favorite bakery treat, wherever she could find them. Terry loves the crunchy texture of cornmeal, which she has concluded is best set off by a cranberry and orange flavor combination. This is my recipe for Terry's ideal scone. I vary the amount of sugar by using 1/4 cup when making them for breakfast and 1/3 cup when making them for dessert. Try pairing the scones with ice cream or baked custard when serving them as a dessert.

3/4 **cup all-purpose flour**

1/2 **cup stone-ground yellow cornmeal**

1/4 **to** 1/3 **cup sugar, to taste**

1/2 **tablespoon baking powder**

1/4 **teaspoon salt**

4 **tablespoons (**1/2 **stick) unsalted butter, chilled, cut into small pieces**

1/2 **cup heavy (whipping) cream, chilled**

Zest of 1 small orange

1/2 **cup dried cranberries**

1. Preheat the oven to 375°F.

2. Combine the flour, cornmeal, sugar, baking powder, and salt in a medium-size mixing bowl. Stir to mix thoroughly. Cut in the butter with a pastry blender or fork until the mixture is evenly crumbly. Add the cream and orange zest, stirring until moistened. Add the cranberries and mix to form a ball of dough.

3. Turn the dough out onto a lightly floured work surface and divide it in half. Pat one piece out into a 5-inch round, 1/2 to 3/4 inch thick. Cut the round into 6 wedges and place them 1/2 inch apart on an ungreased cookie sheet. Repeat the process with the second piece of dough.

4. Bake the scones in the upper third of the oven for about 15 minutes, until lightly browned and firm. Remove the scones to wire racks to cool slightly. Serve warm.

Yield: 12 scones

Morning Glory Muffins

Increasingly the breakfast-on-the-run choice for so many busy folks, muffins have become big business for bakeries in recent years. In general, the biggest selling varieties are those that contain the most fruit, vegetables, whole grains, seeds, or nuts—those ingredients seen as tipping the balance in the direction of nutrition.

This is a real kitchen-sink muffin, loaded with carrot, apple, coconut, and candied pineapple. The batter can be mixed ahead and refrigerated for morning baking. (That's how the pros do it.) You will have sufficient batter for sixteen muffins; bake them all at once or as desired over the next two to three days, storing the batter in the refrigerator.

2 cups all-purpose flour

³/₄ cup sugar

2 teaspoons ground cinnamon

1 teaspoon baking soda

¹/₂ teaspoon salt

¹/₄ teaspoon ground nutmeg

2 cups shredded carrots (6 medium carrots)

1 tart apple, peeled, cored, and shredded

¹/₂ cup unsweetened flaked coconut (or sweetened coconut rinsed thoroughly and patted dry)

¹/₂ cup chopped candied pineapple

3 large eggs

²/₃ cup canola oil

2 teaspoons vanilla extract

¹/₂ tablespoon grated orange zest

1. Preheat the oven to 375°F. Grease or line 16 wells of muffin tins with paper cups.

2. Sift the flour, sugar, cinnamon, baking soda, salt, and nutmeg together into a large mixing bowl. Stir to mix. Add the carrots, apple, coconut, and pineapple.

3. In a medium-size bowl, combine the eggs, oil, vanilla, and orange zest and beat until blended. Add the mixture to the dry ingredients, stirring until thoroughly mixed and evenly moistened.

4. Fill the wells of the muffin tins three-fourths full with the batter. Bake for about 25 minutes, until the muffins have browned and a cake tester comes out clean. Unmold the muffins onto wire racks. Serve warm or at room temperature.

Yield: 16 muffins

Pumpkin-Banana Muffins with Lemon Icing

Especially popular in the fall and winter, pumpkin breads and muffins are pleasantly moist. Pumpkin puree can lend a somewhat startlingly orange hue that is tempered by the addition of flavorful banana to the baked good. Lemon icing adds a nice finishing touch to this pumpkin and banana combination.

1³/₄ cups all-purpose flour

²/₃ cup packed light brown sugar

1 teaspoon baking powder

¹/₂ teaspoon baking soda

¹/₂ teaspoon salt

1 teaspoon ground cinnamon

¹/₂ teaspoon ground allspice

¹/₄ teaspoon ground cloves

2 large eggs

¹/₂ cup canola oil

¹/₄ cup sour cream

¹/₂ cup mashed ripe banana
    (about 1 large banana)

¹/₂ cup pumpkin puree

¹/₂ teaspoon vanilla extract

¹/₂ cup coarsely chopped walnuts

Lemon Icing

2 cups confectioners' sugar

4 tablespoons (¹/₂ stick) unsalted butter,
    melted

1 teaspoon grated lemon zest

3 to 4 tablespoons fresh lemon juice

1. Preheat the oven to 375°F. Grease or line a 12-well muffin tin with paper cups.

2. Sift the flour, brown sugar, baking powder, baking soda, salt, cinnamon, allspice, and cloves together into a large mixing bowl. Stir to mix.

3. In a medium-size bowl, combine the eggs, oil, sour cream, banana, pumpkin, and vanilla. Beat until well blended. Add the mixture to the dry ingredients, along with the chopped nuts and stir until thoroughly mixed and evenly moistened.

4. Fill the wells of the muffin tin three-fourths full with the batter. Bake for about 25 minutes, until the muffins have browned and a cake tester comes out clean. Unmold the muffins onto wire racks to cool.

5. Prepare the icing while the muffins cool. Combine the confectioners' sugar, butter, and lemon zest in a small bowl. Stir in the lemon juice, a little at a time, until the mixture is smoothly blended and has a thick but spreadable consistency. Frost the muffins when they have cooled. Serve at room temperature.

Yield: 12 muffins

The Jampot Bakery is situated amid the towering pines of Michigan's scenic, sparsely populated upper peninsula. Operated by monks of the Society of St. John, the bakery is housed in a cottage by the side of a rushing waterfall in the little town of Eagle Harbor. From March through October, four of the monks are busy baking abbey cakes (fruit, nut, and bourbon cakes) and specialty cookies, breads, and muffins, including a popular pumpkin muffin topped with lemon icing.

Across the Midwest plains in Hutchinson, Kansas, you will find the Helmuth Country Bakery, which does a booming business in honey-wheat breads, cinnamon rolls, and a wonderful banana-pumpkin bread.

In developing the Pumpkin-Banana Muffins recipe, I combined my favorite elements of each of the bakery's offerings into one muffin.

Cinnamon Sugar Doughnuts

Doughnuts have long been a favorite sweet. My husband's mother, Elizabeth, remembers a time when Freihofer Bakery in Schenectady, New York, delivered them door-to-door by a horse-drawn wagon.

They are a bit of an indulgence in today's health-conscious world, since deep-fat frying is the only successful method of cooking doughnut batter. I've tried baking, but the result simply was not a proper doughnut. The payoff for frying is in the taste. These doughnuts are best served very fresh, but finishing them off in their prime just never seems to be a problem.

4 cups all-purpose flour

2 teaspoons baking powder

1 teaspoon baking soda

1 teaspoon salt

½ teaspoon ground cinnamon

2 large eggs

1 cup granulated sugar

4 tablespoons (½ stick) unsalted butter, melted

1 cup buttermilk

Canola oil, for deep-frying

About ½ cup cinnamon-sugar for coating

1. Sift the flour, baking powder, baking soda, salt, and cinnamon together into a medium-size bowl and set aside.

2. Beat the eggs in a large bowl. Add the sugar and blend well. Beat in the butter, then half of the flour mixture. Beat in the butter-milk, then the remainder of the flour mixture, blending to form a soft dough.

3. Transfer the dough to a lightly floured work surface and divide it in half. Push or roll one piece out into a ½ inch thick round. Cut with a floured doughnut cutter (2¾-inch diameter with a 1-inch hole) into rings and holes, placing them onto a pan lined with waxed paper. Gather dough scraps and reroll for additional doughnuts. Repeat the process with the second piece of dough. Cover the pan with a towel while heating the oil.

4. Pour 2 to 2½ inches of oil into a skillet and heat to 365°F. Fry the doughnut rings and holes, a few at a time, until well browned on both sides. Drain on paper toweling. Dredge the doughnuts in the cinnamon-sugar to coat all over while still hot. Serve warm or at room temperature.

Yield: About 12 doughnut rings and 12 holes

*L*ocated in an uptown Chicago neighborhood, Dinkel's Bakery is a classic German bakeshop with an equally classic history. It was founded in 1922 by Joseph Dinkel, the son of a family of master bakers from the town of Dinkelsbuhl in Bavaria. The family first set up shop across the street from the Lincoln Avenue building that the bakery occupies today.

Son Norman Sr. and grandson Norman Jr. now run the business, still using the same recipes to make such items as Joseph's original stollen, nut strudels, 1922 crunch cake, chocolate walnut brandy cake, pecan pie, and the best doughnuts in town, which are made from scratch and are as tender as cake. When we started carrying Dinkel's doughnuts in our dessert bakery, they would literally fly out the door, sold out by mid-morning.

FIVE

Cookies

Cookies are entwined with our bakery memories. Just ask anyone what a visit to the bakery of his or her childhood would have been like without receiving a favorite cookie. Cookies run the gamut from big, soft, and chewy to thin, crisp, and elegant, but we love them in all their guises—particularly at holidays. Christmas is the holiday most celebrated by cookie bakers, who produce goodies ranging from Alsatian anise cookies to German pfeffernusse to Viennese nut linzers. Why not enjoy them year-round to preserve a bit of holiday joy?

Tips and Techniques

Equipment

- I prefer to use shiny aluminum cookie sheets with cushioned bottoms. Avoid dark metal sheets, which tend to overheat and could cause the cookies to burn on the bottom. Nonstick sheets can be substituted when greased or parchment-lined sheets are called for and are terrific for baking sticky cookies, such as florentines. However, if a recipe calls for using ungreased cookie sheets, avoid the nonstick variety. To grease, I spray cookie sheets with vegetable oil cooking spray and then wipe lightly with a paper towel to remove any excess.

Scoops of different sizes are particularly helpful for measuring and dropping uniform amounts of dough.

Preparation and Baking

- Chill cookie doughs for easier handling. For rolled cookies, transfer the chilled dough to a lightly floured work surface and cover with a sheet of waxed paper before rolling. If you roll the dough out too thin at first, gather and roll it out again.

- Take care not to overbake cookies. Check early for visual doneness cues and remember that the cookies will continue to set out of the oven if left on the sheet for a minute or two before removal to racks.

Storage

- Use the cookie jar for stashing grocery lists or receipts—with the exception of biscotti, cookies are best eaten within one to two days of baking. Store in cookie tins or cover with aluminum foil. Most freeze well for up to three months. Place the cookies into a freezer storage bag in a single layer, remove as much air as possible, seal tightly, and set on a level surface in the freezer. Thaw at room temperature before unwrapping.

Danoise

This miniature Danish pastry is a kissing cousin of the more widely known Polish kolachy. Either cookie is very simple to prepare and consists of a flaky pastry filled with fruit spread. The Danish-style Danoise dough is made with cottage cheese, whereas kolachy dough is made with either cream cheese or sour cream. You could also fill the cookies with poppy seed or prune filling.

Danoise or kolachy are very popular bakery additions to holiday cookie trays or gift tins, in which a variety of textures and tastes is desirable. Subtly sweet Danoise contrast perfectly with sugary or chocolaty cookies. Variously filled with apricot, cherry, and prune, Danoise add color to an arrangement of cookies.

½ cup small-curd cottage cheese, drained

1 cup all-purpose flour

½ cup (1 stick) unsalted butter, chilled, cut into small pieces

⅓ to ½ cup apricot or plum preserves or spreadable fruit

1 large egg white, beaten with 1 tablespoon water

Confectioners' sugar, for dusting

1. Mash the cottage cheese with a potato masher or a large fork until it looks finely chopped. Set aside.

2. Place the flour in a medium-size mixing bowl. Cut in the butter with a pastry blender until the mixture is crumbly. Add the cottage cheese and stir until evenly moistened. Turn the mixture out onto a work surface and knead into a ball of dough. Wrap in waxed paper and refrigerate for at least 1 hour to firm.

3. Preheat the oven to 375°F.

4. Turn the dough out onto a floured work surface. Place a sheet of waxed paper over the dough and roll it out into a 12 × 10-inch rectangle. Cut the rectangle into thirty 2-inch squares.

5. Spoon ½ teaspoon of the preserves or spreadable fruit onto the center of a square. Fold one corner over the filling to the center of the square. Brush the opposite corner lightly with the egg white and water wash and fold it into the center, overlapping the first flap of dough slightly to seal the pastry closed. Repeat the process for all the squares, placing them 1 inch apart on a large ungreased cookie sheet.

6. Bake for about 15 minutes, until lightly golden. Remove the cookies to wire racks to cool to room temperature, then dust lightly with confectioners' sugar through a sieve.

Yield: 30 cookies

Anise Caps

The dough for this cookie is left out overnight on lined cookie sheets to dry and harden. Baking is done in a low oven to maintain its pure white color, and the cookies emerge perched on little "feet" below their crisp, mushroom-like caps.

I recommend starting out with the minimum amount of robust anise oil and testing the batter before adding more. Be sure to beat the eggs in a stationary electric mixer. Even with the aid of this heavy-duty appliance, the process takes fifteen minutes. Yvonne Tschirhart of Haby's Alsatian Bakery in Texas told me the original Alsatian recipe calls for beating by hand for one hour.

3 large eggs, at room temperature

1 cup sugar

1½ cups all-purpose flour

¼ to ½ teaspoon anise oil, to taste

¼ teaspoon anise seed, finely crushed

1. Crack the eggs into the bowl of a stationary electric mixer fitted with the wire whip and begin to mix at medium speed. When the eggs are smooth and thickened, about 5 minutes, add the sugar. Continue to beat the mixture, which will look shiny and very thick, for 10 minutes more.

2. Reduce the mixer speed to low. Add the flour, ½ cup at a time, and blend until smooth between additions. Thoroughly mix the anise oil (start with ¼ teaspoon) and the crushed anise seed into the batter.

3. Line 3 cookie sheets with waxed paper. Using a ¼-ounce (½ tablespoon) scoop, drop cookies 1½ inches apart onto the waxed paper. Set the sheets aside uncovered, and at room temperature, overnight.

4. Preheat the oven to 275°F.

5. Bake the cookies on the lined sheets for 20 minutes. Let the cookies cool to room temperature before peeling them off the waxed paper.

Yield: About 5 dozen cookies

"Little Alsace" can be found along an unlikely stretch of rural Texas highway. Most of the residents of Castroville, Texas, have roots in Alsace, France, or nearby Germany, including Yvonne Tschirhart, the owner since 1974 of Haby's Alsatian Bakery. The bakery itself, like many of the other buildings in town, was built in Alsatian architectural style.

Haby's offers a full range of baked goods, from country-style breads to apple fritters, along with such Alsatian specialties as anise cookies. Mrs. Tschirhart warns, "You have to like licorice to like them," a sentiment I can appreciate after tasting her intensely flavored cookies. Haby's used to offer anise cookies only during the Christmas season, but they are now available year-round owing to customer demand. When last visiting Alsace, Mrs. Tschirhart compared her recipe with that of a local baker. "They were identical, exactly the same formula," she notes proudly.

Chocolate Leaves

Made with almond paste, these leaf cookies have a subtle nutty taste. They are crisp, not overly sweet, and finished with a contrasting yet highly complementary coating of bittersweet chocolate. I use real leaves to create my stencils for the cookie cutouts. If you do as well, select leaves without sharp or pointy edges.

1½ cups all-purpose flour

¼ teaspoon baking soda

⅛ teaspoon salt

½ cup (1 stick) unsalted butter, at room temperature

½ cup sugar

½ cup almond paste

2 large egg whites

8 ounces bittersweet chocolate or dark coating chocolate (see page 157), chopped

1. Combine the flour, baking soda, and salt in a small bowl and stir to mix.

2. Cream the butter and sugar in a medium-size mixing bowl until smooth. Add the almond paste and cream the mixture until well blended. Beat in the egg whites. Stir in the flour mixture to form a soft dough. Cover with plastic wrap and refrigerate at least 3 hours or overnight.

3. Preheat the oven to 350°F. Lightly grease 2 large cookie sheets.

4. Transfer the dough to a floured work surface and divide it in half. Cover one piece again and return it to the refrigerator until ready to use. Cover the other piece with a sheet of waxed paper and roll it out to a thickness of ⅛ to ¼ inch. Using 3-inch leaf stencils, cut leaves into the dough. Transfer the leaves to the prepared cookie sheets with a metal spatula, spacing 1 inch apart. Reroll dough scraps for additional cookies. Repeat the process with the second piece of dough.

5. Bake for about 15 minutes, until lightly browned and firm to the touch. Remove the cookies to wire racks to cool.

6. Melt the chocolate in a bowl over simmering water or in a microwave oven at 50 percent power for 1 to 4 minutes, checking every 30 seconds. Stir until smooth. Place the cookies on an icing rack set over a tray to catch drips. Brush melted chocolate onto the top of each cookie to coat it completely. Allow the chocolate to set at cool room temperature before serving the cookies.

Yield: About 20 cookies

Ramberg's Bakery and Ericann Candy Company are two operations under one tiny roof in the small town of Union Pier, Michigan, where many Chicagoans summer. Their business is basically seasonal, focused on the summer residents and a brisk holiday mail order trade.

For forty years, baker-confectioner Erich Hamburger of Ericann's served holiday customers only his three specialty sweets: German gingerbread rounds the size of small plates, a praline loaf covered with milk chocolate, and chocolate-dipped leaf cookies. When he retired in 1989, Hamburger selected Ramberg's, in business in Union Pier for three decades, to buy him out, knowing his holiday traditions would be carried on with the same recipes, methods, and standards.

Ramberg's and Ericann's chocolate dipping process is an amazing example of small-town ingenuity. A large floor-model mixing bowl filled with melted chocolate is heated and stirred electronically as a pump forces chocolate from the bowl up through pipes and onto a narrow conveyor tray. An employee places almond leaf cookies, one by one, onto the conveyer, which carries the cookies along in their chocolate bath to the next station. Here, the chocolate is drained and the cookies are brushed of excess chocolate by a swinging plastic dough scraper. A little farther along, a second employee removes each leaf to a paper-lined sheet pan to dry.

Linzer Dainties

My linzer cookies consist of two almond shortbreads sandwiching a raspberry filling that oozes up through a center hole, dusted with confectioners' sugar and cut out with fluted cutters for a decorative touch. The same dough, rolled into little horseshoe-shaped cookies and dredged in confectioners' sugar, become crescents. In either incarnation, this delicate, crumbly cookie is a delight.

I prefer the classic addition of ground blanched almonds to the shortbread dough, but hazelnuts or walnuts could easily be substituted for the almonds. This produces a slightly darker but equally delicious cookie.

6 tablespoons unsalted butter, at room temperature

1/4 cup granulated sugar

1/2 cup ground blanched almonds

1 teaspoon vanilla extract

1/2 teaspoon grated lemon zest

1/8 teaspoon salt

3/4 cup all-purpose flour

1/3 cup Raspberry Filling (see page 117) or seedless raspberry jam

1 teaspoon kirsch brandy (optional)

Confectioners' sugar, for dusting

1. Cream the butter and granulated sugar in a medium-size mixing bowl until light and fluffy. Stir in the almonds, blending well. Stir in the vanilla, lemon zest, and salt. Add the flour, 1/4 cup at a time, to form a soft dough. Shape the dough into a disk, wrap in plastic wrap, and refrigerate for at least 1 hour to firm.

2. Preheat the oven to 325°F. Lightly grease a large cookie sheet.

3. Transfer the dough to a lightly floured work surface and divide it in half. Cover one piece with a sheet of waxed paper and roll it out into a circle, 1/8 to 1/4 inch thick. Using a 1 1/2-inch fluted cutter, cut out rounds. Transfer half to the prepared sheet with a small metal spatula, spacing 1/2 inch apart. Using a 1/2-inch fluted cutter, cut holes out of the center of each remaining round and transfer to the cookie sheet. Reroll dough scraps for additional cookies. Repeat the process with the second piece of dough.

4. Bake for 12 to 14 minutes, until firm to the touch and pale in color. Let the cookies cool on the sheet.

5. Combine the raspberry filling and kirsch in a small saucepan over medium-low heat. Cook and stir until the mixture is melted and heated. Remove from the heat and allow to cool until barely warm before using. Brush a thin layer of filling over each of the solid rounds and cover with the donut-cut rounds. Dust the tops with confectioners' sugar through a sieve. Fill the center hole in each sandwich with ¼ teaspoon of the remaining raspberry filling.

Yield: About 2 dozen sandwich cookies

To make Almond Crescents from the same dough, follow recipe directions for Linzer Dainties through the chilling of the dough. Break off 2-teaspoon chunks from the disk of dough. Shape into balls and roll each with your fingertips into a 2½-inch strip about ½ inch in diameter. Bend each strip into a horseshoe shape and place on a lightly greased cookie sheet. Bake as you would the linzer cookies. After the cookies have cooled to room temperature, dredge in sifted confectioners' sugar to coat all over; omit the raspberry filling. Makes about 1½ dozen cookies.

Linzer cookies, a variety of classic nut shortbread, are always holiday favorites. They are usually associated with Viennese-style bakeries, but their popularity has spread well beyond their ethnic origin. The Villa Italia Pasticceria in Rotterdam, New York, offers a similar cookie named bucati, while the version sold by the Golden Grains Mediterranean Bakery in Redondo Beach, California, goes by the name of pasta flora.

Snickerdoodles

This old-fashioned cinnamon and sugar-coated cookie is still found in bakeries in every part of the country, mostly baked into big 3- to 4-inch rounds. The best pair a tender but crunchy cookie with a generous coating of sugar and spice. You can nibble away at a single cookie for days and it will only get better!

$^{1}/_{2}$ cup (1 stick) unsalted butter, at room temperature

$^{3}/_{4}$ cup sugar

1 large egg

2 tablespoons milk or half-and-half

$^{1}/_{2}$ teaspoon vanilla extract

$1^{1}/_{2}$ cups all-purpose flour

$^{3}/_{4}$ teaspoon cream of tartar

$^{1}/_{2}$ teaspoon baking soda

$^{1}/_{4}$ teaspoon salt

Topping

1 tablespoon sugar

1 tablespoon ground cinnamon

1. Cream the butter and sugar until smooth in a medium-size mixing bowl. Add the egg, milk or half-and-half, and vanilla, beating until well blended. Sift the flour, cream of tartar, baking soda, and salt together into the bowl and blend the mixture into a dough. Wrap in waxed paper or plastic wrap and refrigerate for at least 1 hour to firm.

2. Preheat the oven to 375°F.

3. Combine the sugar and cinnamon for the topping on a flat plate and mix thoroughly.

4. Shape the dough into a log about 12 inches long and 2 inches in diameter. Cut into 1-inch-thick rounds and press into the topping to coat on one side only. Place them 2 inches apart, topping side up, on ungreased cookie sheets.

5. Bake, one sheet at a time, for 12 to 15 minutes, until the edges are lightly browned. Remove the cookies to wire racks to cool.

Yield: 1 dozen cookies

Snickerdoodles are always a special treat, but I've never had another quite as good as the snickerdoodles from the Black Diamond Bakery in Black Diamond, Washington. An old coal-mining town, Black Diamond is surrounded by lush green mountains and logging forests.

The tiny bakery has been in business since the early 1900s, as the faded black-and-white photographs hanging on the walls will attest. Only recently has the Black Diamond expanded to include a restaurant, ice cream parlor, and candy shop in response to the area's growing tourist trade.

Entering the bakery, one is immediately captivated by the aromas wafting from nearby ovens, enough to weaken the strongest will. A display case of fresh-baked, double-crusted pies filled with local, seasonal fruit stands in front of a wall of breads with names like miner's loaf. Cinnamon rolls, apple buns, turnovers, and brownies share shelf space with an assortment of big, round cookies, including the delightful snickerdoodles.

Florentines

Lacy Florentines are made with a cooked nut batter that spreads as it bakes into crisp, porous wafers. Nonstick cookie sheets, which facilitate spreading, are ideal for these cookies. After cooling, Florentines are decorated with melted chocolate. In this recipe, which makes a Florentine sandwich, I add a vanilla filling between the wafers. Try ground pecans or walnuts instead of almonds for variety.

Lace Cookies

¹/₂ cup granulated sugar

¹/₄ teaspoon salt

6 tablespoons unsalted butter

2 tablespoons honey

2 tablespoons water

³/₄ cup ground almonds

¹/₄ cup all-purpose flour

Vanilla Filling

6 tablespoons unsalted butter, melted

1¹/₂ cups confectioners' sugar

¹/₂ tablespoon vanilla extract

Chocolate Topping

6 to 8 ounces semisweet chocolate or dark coating chocolate (see page 157), melted

1. Combine the granulated sugar, salt, butter, and honey in a heavy-bottomed medium-size saucepan over medium-low heat. Bring the mixture to a boil, stirring constantly. Add the water and bring back to a boil. Add the nuts and flour, and return to a boil again, stirring constantly. Remove the pan from the heat and let batter cool to warm before using, 20 to 30 minutes.

2. Preheat the oven to 350°F. Grease cookie sheets if you are not using nonstick sheets.

3. Drop the batter by teaspoonfuls onto the nonstick or prepared cookie sheets, spacing 4 inches apart to allow for spreading. Bake for 8 to 9 minutes, until golden brown. Cool the cookies on the sheets for 5 minutes, then remove them with a metal spatula to wire racks to cool.

4. For the filling, combine the melted butter and confectioners' sugar in a medium-size bowl. Stir until thick and smooth. Add the vanilla and blend well. Carefully spoon 1 to 1¹/₂ teaspoons of the filling onto the center of half of the cookies, then sandwich the filling by carefully pressing a second cookie on top of each.

5. Pipe the melted chocolate onto the sandwiches in stripes or drizzles using a small pastry bag, or transfer the melted chocolate to a bowl and half dip each cookie into the chocolate. Let the chocolate set at cool room temperature before serving.

Yield: About 20 sandwich cookies

I have a friend who has pleaded for years with the staff of Tag's Pastry in Evanston, Illinois, for the bakery's famous florentine recipe. She swears there is none better than Tag's almond lace cookie with chocolate coating one side. But as is often the case when a bakery develops a loyal following for a house specialty, the recipe has remained shrouded in mystery.

My own favorite florentine can be found a few miles to the south on Chicago's North Clark Street, home of the Swedish Bakery, which has been offering traditional Old World favorites since 1928. If nuts had nationalities, almonds would certainly be Swedish. As toasted nuggets, ground into paste or creamed in fillings, almonds are used by the Swedes in an amazing variety of cookies, tarts, pastries, and cakes.

Black and Whites

Black and Whites are classic two-tone frosted cookies that are a favorite on the Eastern seaboard. The Black and Whites in this recipe bake into 3¹/₂-inch rounds, which is a big cookie by most people's standards, but still manageable. I have seen them up to twice this size in some bakeries. Beneath its namesake frosting, the cookie is soft and flavored with just a hint of lemon; most of the sweetness comes from the frosting.

Cookies

1 cup all-purpose flour

1 cup cake flour

¹/₂ teaspoon baking powder

¹/₄ teaspoon salt

1 teaspoon grated lemon zest

2 large eggs

³/₄ cup granulated sugar

¹/₂ cup milk

6 tablespoons unsalted butter, melted and cooled

¹/₂ teaspoon vanilla extract

Frostings

2 cups confectioners' sugar

At least 3 tablespoons boiling water

1 ounce unsweetened chocolate, chopped

At least 1 tablespoon light corn syrup

1. Preheat the oven to 350°F. Grease 2 cookie sheets.

2. Combine the flours, baking powder, salt, and lemon zest in a small bowl and set aside.

3. Beat the eggs and granulated sugar in a medium-size mixing bowl until smoothly blended. Mix in the milk, melted butter, and vanilla. Slowly add the flour mixture, blending into a soft dough.

4. Using a 2-ounce (¹/₄-cup) scoop, drop cookies 2¹/₂ inches apart onto the prepared sheets. Bake for about 15 minutes, until the tops feel firm to the touch. Remove the cookies to wire racks and allow to cool to room temperature before frosting.

5. For the frostings, place the confectioners' sugar in a bowl. Add 3 tablespoons boiling water and whisk to a thick, smooth, and spreadable consistency. Remove and reserve ¹/₃ cup of the frosting; use the remainder to frost half of each cookie. If the frosting becomes too thick, add drops of boiling water until it is again spreadable.

6. Melt the chocolate in a small bowl over simmering water or in a microwave oven at

50 percent power for 1 to 4 minutes, checking every 30 seconds. Stir in 1 tablespoon corn syrup. Add the reserved ⅓ cup white frosting and stir to a spreadable consistency. Spread the bare half of each cookie with the chocolate frosting. If it becomes too thick, thin the frosting with additional drops of corn syrup. Set the cookies aside until the frostings set.

Yield: 10 cookies

Big round cookies with two-tone frosting, called black and whites, have been bakeshop staples for years in New York City. These monster cookies are really little cakes, half coated with white sugar icing, the other half painted with chocolate icing.

One friend, a born and bred New Yorker now living in Chicago, recalls from childhood that whenever black and whites were toted home from the local bakery, his brother devoured all of the chocolate-frosted sides within a matter of minutes. My friend just can't get enough now that he's able to eat the whole cookie. Visitors from New York are instructed to arrive bearing black and whites.

Apricot–White Chocolate Chunk Cookies

This is a buttery "cookie jar" cookie, loaded with chunks of dried apricots and white chocolate. It's very easy to make and fast to bake. A touch of caramel complements the tart apricot and sweet white chocolate—a single cookie will almost never do.

½ cup (1 stick) unsalted butter, at room temperature

½ cup packed light brown sugar

1 large egg

½ teaspoon vanilla extract

1 cup all-purpose flour

½ teaspoon baking soda

¼ teaspoon salt

¾ cup dried apricots, cut into ½-inch cubes

4 ounces white chocolate, cut into ½-inch chunks

1. Preheat the oven to 350°F.

2. Cream the butter and brown sugar in a medium-size mixing bowl until smoothly blended. Beat in the egg and vanilla. Add the flour, baking soda, and salt, stirring the mixture into a smooth dough. Add the apricots and white chocolate, stirring until the pieces are thoroughly dispersed.

3. Drop the batter by tablespoonfuls onto ungreased cookie sheets, spacing 2 inches apart. Bake for about 10 minutes, until the edges are lightly browned. Let the cookies set on the sheet for 1 to 2 minutes before transferring them with a spatula to wire racks to cool.

Yield: About 26 cookies

*F*or nearly a century, Eilenberger's Bakeshop has been serving customers homey baked goods using family recipes that came to Palestine, Texas, by way of Leipzig, Germany. It was fruitcake that launched Eilenberger's in 1898, but the bakery produces a range of cakes and cookies, including something called an apricot angel, the inspiration for my apricot and white chocolate creation. Their methods have hardly changed at all over the decades—mixing of batters, moving of cakes in and out of the oven, and all decorating are still done by hand.

The operation is now run by Fred Eilenberger, the founder's grandson, who has been a part of the family baking tradition for fifty years. Fred admits that his father, also a baker, wanted him to become a lawyer rather than follow in his footsteps, given the grueling physical nature of the work. But Fred told his father that he had to work with his hands; besides, he loves to see the smiles on customers' faces when they sample an Eilenberger treat. As Fred acknowledges, baking has always been more than a job for him—it's a tradition.

Toasted Almond Shortbread

Buttery shortbread cookies are plain and not too sweet, a perfect canvas to showcase toasted almonds. They're normally made with the addition of a little cornstarch to the flour. Using a trick picked up from bakers in North Carolina, I use rice flour along with the all-purpose flour instead of adding cornstarch. This produces a fine, crumbly-textured cookie that instantly melts in the mouth.

½ **cup (1 stick) unsalted butter, at room temperature**

¼ **cup sugar**

¼ **teaspoon almond extract**

1 **cup all-purpose flour**

3 **tablespoons rice flour**

Rounded ¼ **cup slivered almonds, toasted**

1. Lightly grease a large cookie sheet.

2. Cream the butter and sugar in a medium-size bowl until smoothly blended. Stir in the almond extract. Sift the flours into the mixture and blend well. Add the toasted almonds, stirring to mix in thoroughly.

3. Shape the dough into a ball and knead 2 or 3 times on a work surface. Sprinkle the surface with flour. Cover the dough ball with a sheet of waxed paper and roll it out into a ¼-inch-thick circle. Cut into 12 pie-shaped wedges and arrange the wedges 1 inch apart on the cookie sheet. Refrigerate for 30 minutes.

4. Preheat the oven to 300°F.

5. Bake for about 30 minutes, until firm to the touch and the color of sand. (Shortbread cookies should not brown.)

Yield: 1 dozen cookies

The Boulangerie, located in Seattle's Wallingford neighborhood, has the air of an authentic Parisian bakery. Customers stand two deep at a stand-up bar near the window to nibble and sip. Stacks of baguettes, *petit pains,* and croissant line walls behind a marble-topped counter. Fine pastries are daintily arranged on white doilies in baskets and displayed behind glass-fronted cases. The day I visited, almonds—one of my favorite nuts—were celebrated in a selection of offerings that included honeyed nut tarts and shortbread cookies.

Opened in 1979, the Boulangerie was purchased by a supermarket giant a few years later. Its days as an intimate independent catering to a neighborhood trade seemed to be numbered, but one employee, a Vietnamese baker named Xon Luong, worked his way up and eventually bought the bakery back from the superstore.

Chocolate Globs

If you like chocolate, you probably like a lot of it—and that is what this cookie is all about. My globs are triple chocolate treats that have a familial resemblance to fudgy brownies. Chunks of crunchy walnuts make these bittersweet bits of sin even better.

1½ cups all-purpose flour

1 teaspoon baking powder

¼ teaspoon salt

4 ounces semisweet chocolate, coarsely chopped

4 ounces unsweetened chocolate, coarsely chopped

½ cup (1 stick) unsalted butter, at room temperature

1 cup sugar

2 large eggs

1 teaspoon vanilla extract

½ cup semisweet chocolate chips

½ cup coarsely chopped walnuts

1. Preheat the oven to 350°F. Grease 2 large cookie sheets.

2. Combine the flour, baking powder, and salt in a small bowl. Stir to mix and set aside.

3. Combine the chopped chocolates and butter in a medium-size mixing bowl. Set the bowl in the oven for about 3 minutes, until the chocolate and butter have melted. Stir until smooth and let cool to room temperature.

4. Combine the sugar and eggs in a large mixing bowl and beat until lightened and smoothly blended. Add the vanilla, then pour in the melted chocolate mixture. Blend well. Add the flour mixture, ½ cup at a time. Blend into a smooth dough. Stir in the chocolate chips and walnuts until evenly dispersed.

5. Drop the dough by the rounded tablespoonfuls onto the prepared cookie sheets, spacing 1 inch apart. Bake for about 10 minutes, until the cookies look puffed and set. Let the cookies rest on the sheets for 2 minutes before removing them to wire racks to cool.

Yield: About 34 cookies

eep, dark chocolaty cookies attract bakery customers unfailingly; and a good formula can spell success.

Ina Pinkney, former owner of the Dessert Kitchen in Chicago, says the secret to a wildly popular chocolate cookie that she made was her method of melting the chocolate. Ina would place a bowl filled with pieces of chocolate in her gas oven before closing up shop every evening. Overnight, the warmth of the pilot light would ever so slowly and gently melt the chocolate while retaining its temper, or smooth consistency and gloss. By morning, the chocolate was barely warm. In the time it took Ina to assemble the ingredients for her dough, the chocolate was at the perfect room temperature to add to her beaten eggs.

Then there is the baker I talked to who claims his bakery achieved its signature cookie's fudgy texture by accident. One day, an employee added hot, melted chocolate to the cookie batter instead of cooling it first. The bakers thought they liked the cookie more when prepared this way, and the customers loved it too.

Raisin Sandwich Cookies

The recipe for the raisin-filled cookies that are such a hit at Weaver's in Maryland is a family secret, but these have to be at least second best, since I made them based on Penny Pittman's description of her cookies. It's a sandwich of two deliciously tender buttermilk sugar cookies, with a sweet raisin filling.

Raisin Filling

1/4 cup packed light brown sugar

3/4 cup seedless raisins

1 tablespoon all-purpose flour

1/4 cup water

1 teaspoon grated orange zest

Sugar Cookies

2 1/4 cups all-purpose flour

3/4 teaspoon baking soda

3/4 teaspoon cream of tartar

1/2 teaspoon salt

1/4 teaspoon ground nutmeg

3/4 cup (1 1/2 sticks) unsalted butter,
    at room temperature

3/4 cup granulated sugar

1 large egg

1/3 cup buttermilk

3/4 teaspoon vanilla extract

1. To make the filling, sprinkle 1 tablespoon of the brown sugar over the raisins on a cutting board. Chop finely and scrape the mixture into a saucepan. Add the remaining 3 tablespoons brown sugar, the flour, and water. Cook over medium heat, stirring occasionally, until thick, about 5 minutes. Remove the pan from the heat and stir in the orange zest. Set the filling aside to cool before using.

2. For the cookie dough, sift the flour, baking soda, cream of tartar, salt, and nutmeg together into a medium-size bowl.

3. Cream the butter and granulated sugar until smooth in a mixing bowl. Beat in the egg, buttermilk, and vanilla. Add the flour mixture and blend into a dough. Cover with plastic wrap and refrigerate for at least 1 hour to firm.

4. Preheat the oven to 375°F. Lightly grease 2 cookie sheets.

5. On a work surface sprinkled with flour, roll the dough out into a 1/4-inch-thick round. Cut out 2 1/2-inch circles with a biscuit cutter. Place 1 rounded teaspoon of the raisin filling in the center of half of the circles. Top each with another circle of dough and press together. Seal the edges by pressing all around with a fork. Place 2 inches apart on the prepared cookie sheets.

6. Bake for 12 to 15 minutes, until lightly golden and firm to the touch. Remove the cookies to wire racks to cool.

Yield: About 1¹/₂ dozen sandwich cookies

*T*ravelers stopping for a bite to eat on Main Street in Hancock, Maryland, are likely to find themselves in a family-owned bakery restaurant called Weaver's. Gertie Weaver launched the business as a bar with light meal service during World War II. Shortly afterward, Gertie's daughter, Hazel, started baking the treats that Weaver's still serves, more than fifty years later, from the original recipes: homemade cream pies piled high with meringue topping, honey-glazed doughnuts, and best of all, raisin-filled cookies.

According to current owner Penny Pittman, customers from as far away as Ohio have begged her to ship the coveted cookies, but she refuses. "They have a shelf life of two days and would be two days old by the time someone received them in the mail. I don't want anyone tasting an old cookie of mine in the bakery or anywhere else."

Lemon Wafers

These cookie wafers are simplicity itself—crisp, light, and supremely satisfying. They're really straightforward sugar cookies, in which fresh lemon juice and zest add just the right degree of tartness, transforming the cookie from the realm of the ordinary to that of the extraordinary. I made these in the style of a baker friend, Nicole Bergere, who creates the most extraordinary wafers. Lemon Wafers are an ideal accompaniment to ice cream or sorbet, baked or stirred custard, or just plain coffee or tea.

½ cup (1 stick) unsalted butter

2½ cups pastry flour

½ teaspoon baking soda

⅛ teaspoon salt

2 tablespoons fresh lemon juice

1 cup sugar

2 teaspoons grated lemon zest

1 large egg

1. Melt the butter and set it aside to cool to room temperature.

2. Meanwhile, combine the flour, baking soda, and salt in a medium-size bowl. Stir to mix.

3. Pour the melted butter into a large mixing bowl. Stir in the lemon juice, sugar, lemon zest, and egg, blending thoroughly after each addition. Stir in the flour mixture to form a soft dough. Cover the bowl and refrigerate the dough for at least 3 hours to firm.

4. Preheat the oven to 375°F. Grease or line 3 large cookie sheets with parchment paper. Cut an extra 5-inch square of parchment or waxed paper and set aside.

5. Using a ¼-ounce (½-tablespoon) scoop, drop the dough onto the prepared sheets, spacing 2 inches apart. Flatten each by covering the cookie with the square of parchment or waxed paper and pressing it into a 2-inch round with the flat bottom of a glass or cup.

6. Bake for about 10 minutes, until the edges are barely golden. Cool the cookies on the sheets for 3 minutes before removing them to wire racks to cool.

Yield: 60 cookies

Hazelnut Biscotti

Biscotti, the traditional twice-baked Italian bakery cookies that look like thin slices of toast, are immensely popular in the boutique coffee shops cropping up in cities across the country. This crisp cookie, brimming with luscious hazelnuts, seems destined to be dipped into a double espresso, although some may prefer to dunk theirs in a glass of sweet Tuscan dessert wine. Stored in an airtight container, biscotti have a shelf life of up to one month.

½ **cup hazelnuts**

1¼ **cups all-purpose flour**

½ **tablespoon baking powder**

¼ **teaspoon salt**

⅛ **teaspoon ground ginger**

4 **tablespoons (½ stick) unsalted butter, at room temperature**

⅓ **cup sugar**

1 **large egg**

1 **tablespoon Frangelico liqueur**

½ **tablespoon grated orange zest**

1. Preheat the oven to 350°F. Line a cookie sheet with parchment paper.

2. Place the hazelnuts on a baking sheet in a single layer and bake for about 10 minutes, until browned. Remove from the oven, leaving the oven on. Allow the hazelnuts to cool, then rub the skins off with your fingers or by rolling the nuts back and forth inside a cloth towel. Finely chop and set aside.

3. Sift the flour, baking powder, salt, and ginger together into a medium-size bowl.

4. Cream the butter and sugar in a medium-size mixing bowl until lightened in color and fluffy. Beat in the egg and blend well. Stir in the liqueur and orange zest. Add the flour mixture and blend to form a dough. Stir in the hazelnuts.

5. Turn the dough out onto a work surface and shape it into a log about 12 inches long and 3 inches wide, mounded slightly in the center with gradual down-sloping sides. Transfer the log to the prepared cookie sheet. Bake for 20 to 25 minutes, until the log is pale gold in color and the top is cracked and firm to the touch. Remove from the oven and lower the oven temperature to 300°F.

6. Cool the log on the sheet for 10 minutes, then remove it to a wire rack for 10 minutes more, until warm but no longer hot. Transfer the log to a cutting board and cut on a diagonal into ½-inch-thick slices. Lay the slices flat on the cookie sheet. Bake for 10 minutes, turn the cookies over, and bake for about 10 minutes more, until lightly toasted. Remove to wire racks to cool.

Yield: About 1½ dozen cookies

Blackberry Cobbler Bars

With its shortbread crust and crumbled cobbler topping, this bar cookie is particularly good with a robust blackberry filling, but it could be made with other fruit as well. The flavor of the preserves used is a less important factor than their quality. Sugary preserves are too sweet for this cookie. Instead, use spreadable fruit sweetened only with fruit juice, called spoon fruit, according to one specialty purveyor.

Shortbread Crust

¹/₂ cup (1 stick) unsalted butter, at room temperature

¹/₃ cup confectioners' sugar

1 cup all-purpose flour

Cobbler Topping

¹/₂ cup all-purpose flour

2 tablespoons packed light brown sugar

¹/₄ teaspoon baking powder

4 tablespoons (¹/₂ stick) unsalted butter, chilled, cut into small pieces

1 large egg yolk, lightly beaten

³/₄ cup blackberry spreadable fruit

1. Preheat the oven to 350°F.

2. To make the crust, cream the butter and confectioners' sugar in a medium-size bowl until smoothly blended. Add the flour and stir until crumbly. With floured fingers, press the crumbs firmly into the bottom of an ungreased 8-inch square baking pan. Bake for about 12 minutes, until the crust has set but not yet browned. Remove from the oven, leaving the oven on. Set the crust aside to cool.

3. For the topping, combine the flour, brown sugar, and baking powder in a medium-size bowl. Cut in the butter with a pastry blender or fork until the mixture is evenly crumbled. Add the egg yolk and stir or mix with your fingers to incorporate.

4. Stir the fruit and spread it evenly over the crust. Sprinkle on the topping in an even layer. Bake for about 30 minutes, until the topping is lightly golden. Cool in the pan on a wire rack.

5. Cut into 4 × 3-inch bars.

Yield: 1 dozen cookies

I first tasted this type of crumbly, berry-filled cookie in a West Seattle establishment called Frombach's Old Home Bakery. Walking into this storefront shop, its walls adorned with kitchenware, utensils, and potholders gathered from flea markets, felt like walking into a 1950s home kitchen. Frombach's baked goods are likewise reminiscent of a bygone era that included specialties such as glazed doughnuts, pastry twists, cinnamon bread, apple loaves—and, of course, all manner of cookies to go with owner Kathy Stokesberry's collection of cookie jars.

Ginger Saucers

The mellow taste of sorghum is a perfect foil for the ginger in these spiced saucers. I use a locally produced Midwestern variety (see Mail Order Source Guide). If you substitute molasses for the sorghum syrup in this recipe, be sure to use a mild one.

2¼ cups all-purpose flour

½ tablespoon baking soda

1 teaspoon ground ginger

1 teaspoon ground cinnamon

½ teaspoon ground cloves

¼ teaspoon salt

¾ cup (1½ sticks) unsalted butter, at room temperature

¾ cup packed light brown sugar

¼ cup sorghum syrup

1 large egg

¼ cup granulated sugar

1. Sift the flour, baking soda, spices, and salt together into a medium-size bowl and set aside.

2. In a large bowl, cream the butter and brown sugar until smooth. Add the sorghum and egg, blending well. Add the flour mixture and blend into a dough. Cover with plastic wrap and refrigerate for at least 1 hour to firm.

3. Preheat the oven to 375°F.

4. Using 3 to 4 tablespoons of dough for each cookie, shape into 2-inch balls and roll to coat in sugar on a flat plate. Place 2 inches apart on ungreased cookie sheets, flattening each slightly by hand into a 2½-inch round.

5. Bake for 12 to 15 minutes, until golden brown and slightly cracked on top. Let the cookies set on the sheet for 1 to 2 minutes before removing them to wire racks to cool.

Yield: About 1 dozen cookies

*S*hipshewana is an Amish and Mennonite community nestled in the rich farm countryside of northeastern Indiana. Chicagoans make the three-hour drive east to Shipshewana to visit Amish furniture makers, shop the seasonal flea market, watch cheese and butter being made, and stop at Yoder's Meats for locally raised beef. Most important, they can carry home a load of baked goods from the Bread Box Bakeshop.

Who could pass up a bakery with "Grandma's famous saucer-sized cookies" displayed in its window, to say nothing of the apple cinnamon bread and the half-moon pies? The Bread Box is owned by a retired Mennonite minister, but the baking is done by a team of Amish women who obviously know only one way to do things—and that's the right way.

The cookies, available in a variety of flavors, come packaged in a stack of twelve in clear cellophane, with a slice of fresh white bread sitting on top of the stack. "The cookies will absorb the moisture from the bread and stay fresh longer," a saleswoman explained.

Peppernuts

There are as many varieties of this traditional German-Swiss Christmas cookie, called pfeffernusse, *as there are bakeries that sell them. They vary in the type of flour and amount of spice used. Some have a crunchy icing, others are dredged in sugar. Sometimes, the cookies are aged in tins until rock-hard. This recipe makes cookies that have a wonderful Old World taste. The firm—but not too firm—whole wheat nuggets have a slight pepper kick and a simple coating of confectioners' sugar that covers the cookies like new-fallen snow.*

6 tablespoons unsalted butter, at room temperature

³⁄₄ cup granulated sugar

¹⁄₄ cup packed dark brown sugar

1 large egg

¹⁄₄ cup sour cream

1 cup all-purpose flour

1 cup whole wheat flour

¹⁄₂ teaspoon baking soda

¹⁄₄ teaspoon salt

¹⁄₄ teaspoon ground allspice

¹⁄₄ teaspoon ground nutmeg

¹⁄₄ teaspoon ground cloves

¹⁄₄ teaspoon ground ginger

¹⁄₄ teaspoon ground cardamom

¹⁄₈ teaspoon ground black pepper

Sifted confectioners' sugar, for coating

1. Combine the butter and the sugars in a large mixing bowl and cream until smooth. Add the egg and sour cream, mixing until well blended.

2. Sift the flours, baking soda, salt, spices, and pepper together into a medium-size bowl. Gradually stir the mixture into the wet ingredients to form a stiff dough. Divide the dough in half. Gather each piece into a ball, wrap each ball in plastic wrap, and refrigerate overnight.

3. Preheat the oven to 350°F. Grease a large cookie sheet.

4. On a work surface, roll each ball of dough back and forth to shape it into a log about 12 inches long and 1 inch wide. Cut ¹⁄₂-inch-thick rounds from the logs and arrange 1 inch apart on the cookie sheet.

5. Bake for about 15 minutes, until lightly browned and firm to the touch. Remove the cookies to wire racks to cool, then dredge them in sifted confectioners' sugar to coat evenly on all sides.

Yield: About 4 dozen cookies

*A*t Christmastime, I imagine the bakeries in Munich, Germany, to be a fantasyland of elaborately decorated *lebkuchen* (gingerbread) houses and cookie cut-outs of Hansel and Gretel. For those who can't get to Bavaria, the German Home Bakery in Costa Mesa, California, replicates this fantasy every year. For the month of December, the bakery is transformed into a storybook store of Christmas decorations complete with gingerbread houses covered in assorted candies and dangling icicle frosting, anise-flavored springerle cookies stamped with designs from imported German molds, decorated Yule logs, and holiday rum cakes.

The owner, Oskar Streit, learned his trade through classical training in the old country before acquiring the then-twenty-five-year-old German Home Bakery in 1976. Streit continued the bakery's signature line of Bavarian breads while expanding the shop's repertoire to include the traditional cakes, pastries, and cookies of his homeland.

According to German custom, each of the four Sundays prior to Christmas is celebrated with visits to relatives and friends. On these Sundays, hosts serve their guests holiday cookies presented on a festively decorated plate called a *kuchenteller*, or cookie teller. At the German Home Bakery, you can buy a teller, along with an assortment of cookies.

SIX

Pies and Pastries

*S*ome bakeries have built their reputation on a single specialty item that they do better than anyone else—and more often than not, that item is a pie or pastry. Pies and pastries of all sorts are immensely popular just about everywhere, bridging the differences in regional taste buds although often sporting a local accent.

Mention pie to most people and the first words uttered, besides "Ooh, I love pie," are "I can't make a crust." No one ever says "I can't make a filling." However, making a crust is not difficult once you've mastered a few tricks. A perfect pie crust is flaky and flavorful, and depends on the right equation of flour, fat, and water combined at the proper temperature. Most of the crusts in this chapter are variations of a basic formula.

Tips and Techniques

Ingredients and Equipment

- I call for all-purpose flour in my recipes, but you can substitute pastry flour for an even more delicate crumb. Also, you need a little salt for flavor enhancement, but sugar is optional.

- I like using some butter in my crusts for flavor, but combine the butter with lard or shortening for a flakier crust. Make sure that the fat is cold.

- Some recipes require using pans of depths differing from that of standard-size pie pans. I specify the depth of pan to be used when this factor will significantly affect the outcome.

Preparation and Baking

The water used to make crusts must be thoroughly chilled. I measure out cold tap water and refrigerate it for at least 15 minutes before I begin to prepare the crust.

Once the cold pieces of fat have been added to the flour, quickly cut it in with a hand-held pastry blender until the mixture is crumbly. (The crumbs don't need to be tiny; the size of corn kernels is fine.) You can also mix the dough in a food processor, using short pulses and stopping at the crumbly stage.

The trickiest part of making a crust is just after you add the water. Pour it in all at once, briefly stir, then push everything into a ball of dough—all in less than a minute. Handle the dough as little as possible with your bare hands, as the heat will begin to soften the solid fat.

Chill the dough well before rolling it out.

Bake pies and pastries in the middle of the oven.

Storage

Pies and cream- or fruit-filled pastries can be stored in the refrigerator for two to three days, covered with plastic wrap.

Doughs freeze well for two to three months. Form the dough into a disk, wrap in plastic wrap, and place in a plastic freezer bag. With the exception of the recipes made from Quick Puff Pastry Dough, most should not be frozen once baked.

Easter Pie

This holiday pie has an Old World taste: a cookielike pastry crust encasing ricotta custard, with tongue-tingling candied orange and a slight tapioca consistency lent by cooked barley. Originally served at Easter, the dessert is now associated with other holidays as well.

2 tablespoons pearled or hulled barley

Crust

1¹/₂ cups all-purpose flour

¹/₄ cup granulated sugar

Pinch of salt

¹/₂ cup (1 stick) unsalted butter, chilled, and cut into small pieces

1 large egg

1¹/₂ tablespoons cold water

Filling

1 cup water

1 tablespoon plus ¹/₂ cup granulated sugar

¹/₄ teaspoon ground cinnamon

1¹/₂ cups (12 ounces) part-skim ricotta cheese

2 large eggs

1 teaspoon vanilla extract

1 teaspoon grated lemon zest

¹/₃ cup finely chopped candied orange peel

¹/₃ cup heavy (whipping) cream

Confectioners' sugar, for dusting

1. Place the barley in a small bowl, cover with cold water, and set aside for at least 8 hours. (The barley can soak overnight.)

2. To make the crust, combine the flour, granulated sugar, and salt in a medium-size mixing bowl. Cut in the butter with a pastry blender until the mixture is finely crumbled. Add the egg and water, stirring to mix. On a work surface, knead the mixture to form a compact ball of dough. Cover with plastic wrap and refrigerate for at least 1 hour, or overnight.

3. For the filling, drain the barley through a sieve to remove excess water. You should have ¹/₃ cup swollen barley after draining. Bring the water to a simmer in a medium-size saucepan. Stir in 1 tablespoon of the granulated sugar and the cinnamon. Add the barley, cover, and simmer over low heat for 20 minutes. Uncover the pan and continue to simmer until the liquid is absorbed and the barley is tender, 25 to 30 minutes more. Set aside to cool.

4. Preheat the oven to 350°F.

5. In a large bowl, beat the ricotta and the remaining ¹/₂ cup sugar with an electric mixer at medium speed until smoothly blended.
continued

Add the eggs and beat until fluffy. Remove the bowl from the mixer stand and stir in the barley, the vanilla, lemon zest, candied orange peel, and cream. Mix thoroughly.

6. Roll out two-thirds of the pastry dough on a lightly floured work surface into a 12-inch round. Line a 9-inch pie pan that is 1½ inches deep with the pastry. Roll out the remaining dough into a 10 × 6-inch rectangle and cut it into six 10-inch strips.

7. Pour the filling into the bottom crust. Arrange the strips of dough in a lattice pattern over the filling. Roll up excess overhanging dough to the inside of the rim and crimp all around to seal.

8. Place the pan on a baking sheet. Bake for 45 to 50 minutes, until the filling is set and the crust is lightly browned. Transfer the pan to a wire rack to cool.

9. Dust with confectioners' sugar through a sieve and serve at room temperature.

Yield: 8 servings

*P*hilip Ansalone's grandfather hailed from Naples, Italy, where Easter pie originated. When Philip was growing up in the New York City neighborhood known as Hell's Kitchen, his grandmother made the traditional cheese-filled wheat pie every year. Philip's father carried on the custom after his grandmother passed away. However, the family never wrote the recipe down. When Philip's father was gone, so was the pie.

After a lengthy bakery odyssey, the surviving Ansalones discovered a pie called *sfogliatella* at Veniero's, a century-old *pasticceria* on the Lower East Side—the only commercial offering to closely resemble the lost but never forgotten family recipe. Years later, friends found a very similar pie at Allegretti's, a neighborhood Chicago bakery that has been serving traditional Italian specialties since 1962.

Mostly Rhubarb Pie

Double-crust fruit pies are one of the most universally loved desserts. In spring, the first of the fresh fruit pies to appear in bakery windows is rhubarb, a harbinger of summer's bountiful fruits. Fresh rhubarb has a bitter edge, so I use slightly more sugar in this classic than I would in other fruit pies. The addition of strawberries enhances the taste and lends a bit of natural sweetness to counter the bite of the rhubarb.

Crust

2 cups all-purpose flour

¹/₂ teaspoon salt

6 tablespoons unsalted butter, chilled, cut into small pieces

6 tablespoons lard, chilled, cut into small pieces

¹/₃ cup cold water

Filling

1¹/₄ pounds fresh rhubarb stalks, trimmed and cut into ¹/₂-inch thick slices

1 pint ripe strawberries, hulled and cut into thick slices

¹/₂ cup granulated sugar

¹/₄ cup packed dark brown sugar

1 tablespoon grated orange zest (about 1 orange)

¹/₄ cup cornstarch

¹/₄ teaspoon ground ginger

1 tablespoon unsalted butter, cut into pieces

Milk, for painting

Additional granulated sugar, for sprinkling

1. To make the crust, combine the flour and salt in a medium-size mixing bowl. Add the butter and lard, stirring briefly to coat with flour. Cut the fat into the flour with a pastry blender until the mixture is evenly crumbled. Add the cold water and stir briefly, just until moist. Turn the mixture out onto a work surface and knead gently and quickly into a ball of dough. Flatten the ball into a disk, wrap in plastic wrap or waxed paper, and refrigerate for at least 30 minutes.

2. Preheat the oven to 400°F.

3. For the filling, combine the rhubarb and strawberries in a large bowl. (You should have about 6 cups of fruit.) Stir in the sugars, orange zest, cornstarch, and ginger. Mix thoroughly.

4. To assemble, roll out two-thirds of the dough on a floured work surface into a 13-inch round. Fit the dough into a 9-inch pie pan with 1¹/₂-inch sides. Roll out the remaining piece of dough into a 10-inch round.

5. Pour the filling into the bottom crust and dot with the butter. Brush milk on the edges of the pastry to moisten. Fit the top crust over the fruit and trim away excess bottom-crust dough hanging over the rim of the pan. Press the top and bottom together and roll inward while crimping to finish the edge.

6. Place the pie on a baking sheet. Cut slits in the top, brush the exposed dough with milk, and sprinkle with granulated sugar. Bake for 55 to 60 minutes, until the crust is golden brown and the fruit is bubbly.

7. Transfer the pan to a wire rack to cool. Serve warm or at room temperature.

Yield: 8 servings

Indiana Sugar Cream Pie

This could also be called Indiana State Pie, since it has been so popular in the state over the years and is not, to the best of my knowledge, found in bakeries anywhere else.

Cate Erickson, a Midwestern colleague, recalls it fondly from her days at Indiana's Purdue University. The student cafeteria would serve the pie once a month. Much to her delight, she managed to obtain the recipe before graduating, only to misplace it later. I hope this replaces Cate's lost treasure.

Sugar cream pie is really unique—much like a custard, only made without eggs. I've got to tell you that I tried a lot of recipes without success before relentless tinkering finally produced a winning formula. True to Midwestern pie tradition, it's baked in a lard pastry crust. As an added treat, serve with fresh raspberries spooned over each slice.

Crust

1 cup all-purpose flour

¹/₂ tablespoon sugar

¹/₄ teaspoon salt

4 tablespoons lard, chilled, cut into small pieces

2 tablespoons margarine, chilled, cut into small pieces

3 tablespoons cold water

Filling

³/₄ cup sugar

¹/₃ cup unbleached all-purpose flour

¹/₄ teaspoon salt

¹/₈ teaspoon ground nutmeg

1¹/₂ cups heavy (whipping) cream

2 tablespoons unsalted butter, at room temperature

1 teaspoon vanilla extract

1. To make the crust, combine the flour, sugar, and salt in a medium-size mixing bowl. Add the lard and margarine, stirring briefly until coated with flour. Cut the fat into the flour with a pastry blender until the mixture is evenly crumbled. Add the cold water and stir briefly, just to moisten. Turn the mixture out onto a work surface and knead gently and quickly into a ball of dough. Flatten the ball into a disk, wrap in plastic wrap or waxed paper, and refrigerate for at least 30 minutes.

2. On a lightly floured work surface, roll the dough out into a 12-inch round. Fit the round into a 9-inch pie pan. Trim uneven edges of dough, then roll inward while crimping around the rim. Chill for at least 30 minutes.

3. Preheat the oven to 425°F.

4. For the filling, combine the sugar, flour, salt, and nutmeg in a medium-size bowl and whisk until thoroughly mixed.

5. Heat the cream to a simmer on top of the stove or in a microwave oven for 3 to 5 minutes at full power. Pour the hot cream over the sugar mixture while whisking. Continue to whisk until smoothly blended. Beat in the butter, whisking until melted, then the vanilla.

6. Place the pie pan on a baking sheet. Pour the cream mixture into the crust and bake for 15 minutes. Reduce the oven temperature to 350°F and bake for about 15 minutes more, until the filling is set but still jiggles slightly.

7. Transfer the pan to a wire rack to cool. Serve at room temperature.

Yield: 8 servings

The year 1944 was when Mr. and Mrs. Wickersham started baking sugar cream pies, along with nineteen other varieties, on a quiet street in Winchester, Indiana. The pies were all made by hand and delivered to customers in the family's 1934 Buick sedan. The small company had a simple philosophy that persists to this day: "To make the very best pie so that repeat customers will bring new customers."

Today, seventy employees turn out 12,000 pies during every eight-hour shift in Wick's modernized, block-long bakery production facility, and the family also operates a café that's a short walk away.

An interesting twist to the bakery's history is that Wick's sugar cream recipe was the first pie recipe ever to be patented. Needless to say, both formula and method of baking are top secret. Why all the fuss? Beneath the golden skin that thinly blankets Wick's sugar cream pie lies a creamy, almost translucent filling with a consistency slightly looser than that of a baked custard and a sweet, almost caramel taste—all achieved without a single egg. Adding to the pie's mystique is the fact that, unlike a true custard pie, it does not spoil at room temperature and it freezes beautifully.

Sweet Potato Pie

The allure of Sweet Potato Pie, a traditional Southern delicacy, is its very creamy, almost feathery, texture. It has a depth of flavor not equaled in its pumpkin cousin, and a beautiful autumnal deep red-brown hue. This pie is delicious plain or garnished with whipped cream.

Crust

1 cup all-purpose flour

1/4 teaspoon salt

3 tablespoons unsalted butter, chilled, cut into small pieces

3 tablespoons lard or shortening, chilled, cut into small pieces

3 tablespoons cold water

Filling

1 to 1 1/4 pounds (1 large) sweet potato

4 tablespoons (1/2 stick) unsalted butter, at room temperature

1/2 cup packed light brown sugar

2 large eggs

3/4 cup half-and-half

1 tablespoon blackstrap molasses

1/2 tablespoon grated orange zest

1 teaspoon ground cinnamon

1/2 teaspoon ground ginger

1/4 teaspoon ground nutmeg

1/4 teaspoon salt

1. To make the crust, combine the flour and salt in a medium-size mixing bowl. Add the butter and lard or shortening, stirring briefly to coat with flour. Cut the fat into the flour with a pastry blender until the mixture is evenly crumbled. Add the cold water and stir briefly, just to moisten. Turn the mixture out onto a work surface and knead gently and quickly into a ball of dough. Flatten the ball into a disk, wrap in plastic wrap or waxed paper, and refrigerate for at least 30 minutes.

2. Preheat the oven to 400°F.

3. For the filling, bake the sweet potato for about 1 hour, until very tender. Remove the potato from the oven and set aside to cool, leaving the oven on.

4. When the potato has cooled enough to handle but is still hot, peel it and mash the pulp to a smooth puree. (You should have about 1 1/2 cups puree.)

5. Combine the warm puree and the butter in a medium-size mixing bowl. Stir until the butter melts. Whisk in the brown sugar, eggs, half-and-half, molasses, orange zest, spices, and salt. Mix thoroughly and set aside.

continued

6. On a floured work surface, roll the dough out into a 12-inch round. Fit the round into a 9-inch pie pan. Trim excess dough and crimp the edge around the rim. Line the crust with aluminum foil and fill the foil with dried beans or pie weights. Bake for 15 minutes. Remove the pan from the oven and lift out the foil liner and its contents. Return the crust to the oven for 5 minutes more. Remove and set aside to cool to room temperature, once again leaving the oven on.

7. Pour the filling into the crust. Place the pie pan on a baking sheet and bake for 15 minutes. Reduce the oven temperature to 350°F and bake for about 35 minutes more, until the pie is browned and the center is set.

8. Transfer the pan to a wire rack to cool. Serve warm or at room temperature.

Yield: 8 servings

*T*he ovens in bakeries elsewhere may be roaring in a frantic effort to keep up with the demand for pumpkin pie, but the bakers at the 27th Street Bakery in the South Central neighborhood of Los Angeles crimp the crusts of well over 1,000 sweet potato pies every year on the day before Thanksgiving. Outside, hundreds of people from all over the area crowd the bakery, many obsessed with the notion of obtaining a sweet potato pie for the holiday from the day's last bake.

The oldest African-American–owned business in South Central, the 27th Street Bakery was founded in the 1930s by Harry L. Patterson. Grandson Gregory Spann started in the family baking business at the tender age of nine and still hasn't found a way to improve on his grandfather's recipes.

Pineapple Meringue Pie

We called him the "pineapple man." An older gentleman, he would walk into our bakeshop periodically, always alone, to ask the same question: "Do you have that pineapple pie yet?" He regaled us with descriptions of the pineapple pies offered by all of the neighborhood bakeries when he was growing up—made with fresh fruit, nothing canned. "You should really try making a pineapple pie," he always advised in a stern, fatherly sort of way.

Well, I finally made the pie; and the pineapple man was right. It's a truly memorable pie with a rich sour cream crust, chunky fresh fruit filling, and a golden meringue top.

Crust

1 cup all-purpose flour

¼ teaspoon salt

4 tablespoons (½ stick) unsalted butter, chilled, cut into small pieces

½ cup sour cream, chilled

Filling

1 ripe pineapple, peeled and cored (1¼ pounds fruit)

½ cup sugar

½ cup fresh orange juice

2 tablespoons cornstarch

3 large egg yolks

1 tablespoon unsalted butter

Grated zest of 1 lemon

Topping

3 large egg whites, at room temperature

¼ teaspoon cream of tartar

⅛ teaspoon salt

½ teaspoon vanilla extract

⅓ cup sugar

1. To make the crust, combine the flour and salt in a medium-size mixing bowl. Add the butter pieces and stir briefly to coat with flour. Cut the fat into the flour with a pastry blender until the mixture is evenly crumbled. Add the sour cream and stir briefly, just to moisten. Turn the mixture out onto a work surface and knead gently and quickly into a ball of dough. Flatten the ball into a disk, wrap in plastic wrap or waxed paper, and refrigerate for at least 30 minutes.

2. On a floured work surface, roll the dough out into a 12-inch round. Fit the round into a 9-inch pie pan with 1½-inch sides. Trim the excess dough and crimp the edge around the rim. Line the crust with aluminum foil and fill the foil with dried beans or pie weights. Refrigerate for at least 30 minutes.

3. Preheat the oven to 375°F.

continued

4. Bake for 20 minutes. Remove the pan from the oven and lift out the foil liner and its contents. Prick the bottom of the crust with a fork and bake for about 15 minutes more, until lightly golden. Remove from the oven and set aside to cool. Reduce the oven temperature to 350°F.

5. For the filling, chop the pineapple and scrape the fruit and any juice that collects on the cutting board into a saucepan. (You should have between 2½ and 3 cups of fruit.) Add the sugar, orange juice, and cornstarch. Stirring, bring to a boil over medium heat. Boil for 1 minute to thicken slightly.

6. Beat the egg yolks in a medium mixing bowl and pour the hot fruit mixture over the yolks, stirring to blend. Return the combination to the saucepan. Stirring constantly, bring back to a boil over medium heat and boil for 1 minute. Remove the pan from the heat and add the butter and lemon zest, stirring until the butter melts.

7. To prepare the topping, combine the egg whites, cream of tartar, salt, and vanilla in the bowl of a stationary electric mixer fitted with the wire whip. Beat at medium speed until soft peaks form. Raise the speed to medium-high and slowly add the sugar, a spoonful at a time, beating to stiff and shiny peaks, about 4 minutes total.

8. Pour the hot pineapple filling into the crust and spread the meringue evenly on top to cover completely. Bake for about 15 minutes, until the meringue is golden.

9. Remove the pan to a wire rack to cool. Serve at room temperature or chilled.

Yield: 8 servings

Apple Custard Pie with Almond Topping

One of the biggest sellers at our dessert bakery was a freshly baked, loaded-with-fruit apple pie. Another popular item was a creamy apple bread pudding. Experimenting at home one day, I combined the best of both desserts into one really delicious pie—with soft slices of cooked apple suspended in custard and a crunchy toasted almond topping. This creation satisfied my craving for something different, while my mother instantly claimed it as her new favorite pie.

Crust

1¼ cups all-purpose flour

2 tablespoons sugar

¼ teaspoon salt

3 tablespoons unsalted butter, chilled, cut into small pieces

3 tablespoons vegetable shortening, chilled, cut into small pieces

3 tablespoons cold water

Filling

2 tablespoons unsalted butter

3 Granny Smith apples (about 1½ pounds), peeled, cored, and cut into 16 wedges per apple

¼ cup sugar

1 tablespoon apple brandy or dark rum

2 large eggs, plus 1 egg yolk

⅔ cup heavy (whipping) cream

1 teaspoon vanilla extract

Topping

1 cup sliced almonds (about 4 ounces)

¼ cup sugar

2 tablespoons unsalted butter, at room temperature

1. To make the crust, combine the flour, sugar, and salt in a medium-size mixing bowl. Add the butter and shortening, stirring briefly to coat with flour. Cut the fat into the flour with a pastry blender until the mixture is evenly crumbled. Add the cold water and stir briefly, just until moist. Turn the mixture out onto a work surface and knead gently and quickly into a ball of dough. Flatten the dough into a disk, wrap in plastic wrap or waxed paper, and refrigerate for at least 30 minutes.

2. On a lightly floured work surface, roll the dough out into a 12-inch round. Fit the round into a 9-inch pie pan with 1½-inch sides. Trim away uneven edges of dough, then roll inward while crimping around the rim. Chill for at least 30 minutes.

3. Preheat the oven to 400°F.

4. Line the crust with aluminum foil and fill the foil with dried beans or pie weights. Bake for 10 minutes. Remove the pan from the oven and lift out the foil liner and its contents. Return the crust to the oven and bake for 5 to 7 minutes more, until the edges are lightly colored. Remove from the oven and set aside to cool. Reduce the oven temperature to 350°F.

5. For the filling, melt the butter in a large skillet over medium heat. Add the apples, 1 tablespoon of the sugar, and the brandy or rum. Stir and cook until the apples soften, 5 to 8 minutes.

6. Meanwhile, combine the eggs and the additional yolk, the remaining 3 tablespoons sugar, the cream, and vanilla in a medium-size mixing bowl. Beat until smoothly blended.

7. Transfer the apples and their cooking juices to the crust. Pour the egg mixture over the apples. Place the pie on a baking sheet and bake for 20 minutes, until the custard is almost set.

8. While the pie is baking, prepare the topping. Combine the almonds, sugar, and butter in a medium-size bowl. Using both hands, mix until the butter is evenly distributed.

9. Remove the pie from the oven, sprinkle evenly with the topping, and immediately return the pie to the oven to bake for 15 to 20 minutes, until the topping is golden brown and the custard completely set.

10. Transfer the pan to a wire rack to cool. Serve warm or at room temperature.

Yield: 8 servings

Banana Cream Pie

David SooHoo fondly remembers the banana cream pies of his youth. He recalls a flaky lard crust, layers of sliced ripe bananas interspersed with creamy vanilla pudding, and a topping of mounded hand-whipped fresh cream. With that description in mind, I created this extraordinary pie.

Crust

1 cup all-purpose flour

1/2 tablespoon granulated sugar

1/4 teaspoon salt

4 tablespoons lard, chilled, cut into small pieces

2 tablespoons butter or margarine, chilled, cut into small pieces

3 tablespoons cold water

Filling

2 cups milk

1/3 cup granulated sugar

1/4 teaspoon salt

3 large egg yolks, plus 1 whole egg

1/4 cup cornstarch

2 tablespoons unsalted butter

1/2 tablespoon vanilla extract

3 ripe medium-size bananas, sliced

1 cup heavy (whipping) cream

3 tablespoons confectioners' sugar

1. To make the crust, combine the flour, granulated sugar, and salt in a medium-size mixing bowl. Add the lard and butter or margarine and stir briefly to coat with flour. Cut the fat into the flour with a pastry blender until the mixture is evenly crumbled. Add the cold water and stir briefly, just to moisten. Turn the mixture out onto a work surface and knead gently and quickly into a ball of dough. Flatten the ball into a disk, wrap in plastic wrap or waxed paper, and refrigerate for at least 30 minutes.

2. Prepare the custard filling by combining the milk, granulated sugar, and salt in a heavy-bottomed medium-size saucepan. Bring to a bare simmer over medium-low heat.

3. Meanwhile, combine the egg yolks, whole egg, and cornstarch in a mixing bowl. Whisk to blend smoothly. Pour the heated milk mixture over the egg mixture, stirring constantly, then return the combination to the saucepan. Return the pan to the heat, whisking until the mixture thickens and begins to boil, about 2 minutes. Stirring constantly, boil for 1 minute and remove from the heat. Add the butter and vanilla, stirring until the butter melts. Transfer the custard to a bowl, place a piece of waxed paper directly on top to prevent a crust from forming, and refrigerate until cold.

continued

4. Preheat the oven to 375°F.

5. On a floured work surface, roll the dough out into a 12-inch round. Fit the round into a 9-inch pie pan. Trim excess dough and crimp the edge around the rim of the pan. Line the crust with aluminum foil and fill the foil with dried beans or pie weights. Bake for 20 minutes. Remove the pan from the oven and lift out the foil liner and its contents. Return the crust to the oven and bake for about 15 minutes more, until lightly golden. Set aside to cool.

6. To assemble, spread about one-third of the custard in the crust and arrange a layer of sliced bananas over the custard. Add a second layer of custard and cover with the remaining bananas. Top with the rest of the custard. Chill for at least 1 hour.

7. Whip the cream and confectioners' sugar until stiff peaks form. Spread the topping over the pie. Serve chilled.

Yield: 8 servings

*O*ver a century ago, immigrants from Canton settled in California, bringing their culinary skills and baking techniques with them. Touring Sacramento bakeries with David SooHoo, a restaurateur and specialist on California Chinese-American food traditions, I learned that rich formulas are favored by Cantonese bakers, egg-thickened custards being a traditional filling for everything from pies to tarts to sponge cakes. Contrast is also an important element in their baking, such as pairing a crispy crust with a creamy filling.

Holiday Cranberry Pie

In November and December, cranberries burst onto the market, ripe for a prime place on the holiday table. These scarlet red jewels deserve the best treatment. I serve them in this tasty and not overly filling pie. It's my answer to the perennial problem of providing a refreshing finale to the usually all-too-abundant holiday meal that is followed by an overly rich dessert. This pie features fresh tart cranberries cooked with golden raisins, citrus, brown sugar, and rum, then baked inside a crumbly nut crust.

Pastry

1½ cups pastry flour

½ cup ground walnuts, toasted

¼ cup granulated sugar

¼ teaspoon salt

¼ teaspoon ground cinnamon

½ cup (1 stick) unsalted butter, chilled, cut into small pieces

2 large egg yolks

2 tablespoons cold water

Filling

2 cups fresh cranberries

½ cup golden raisins

½ cup fresh orange juice

1 tablespoon grated orange zest

½ cup packed dark brown sugar

¼ cup granulated sugar

1 teaspoon grated lemon zest

1 teaspoon fresh lemon juice

2 tablespoons dark rum

2 tablespoons unsalted butter

1 egg white, beaten with 1 tablespoon water

White crystal sugar, for sprinkling (see Mail Order Source Guide)

1. To make the pastry, combine the flour, toasted walnuts, granulated sugar, salt, and cinnamon in a medium-size mixing bowl. Stir to mix thoroughly. Cut the butter in with a pastry blender until the mixture is evenly crumbled.

2. In a small dish, beat the egg yolks and cold water. Add to the flour mixture and stir to moisten. Gather the dough into a ball. Flatten the ball into a disk, wrap in plastic wrap, and refrigerate for at least 30 minutes.

3. For the filling, combine the cranberries, raisins, orange juice, orange zest, brown sugar, granulated sugar, and lemon zest in a saucepan. Bring to a boil over medium heat, stirring constantly. Reduce the heat to low and cook until the cranberries have mostly popped, about 8 minutes. Stir in the lemon juice and rum. Simmer for 1 minute more. Remove the pan from the heat and add the butter, stirring until melted. Set the filling aside to cool.

4. Preheat the oven to 350°F.

5. On a well-floured work surface, roll out two-thirds of the dough into an 11-inch round. Fit the round into a 9-inch fluted quiche pan. (If the dough breaks or splits, patch in the pan with extra dough.) Trim the edge flush with the rim. Roll out the remaining piece of dough into a 10-inch round and cut into 1/2-inch-wide strips.

6. Pour the cranberry filling into the crust. Weave the strips of dough into a lattice pattern on top of the filling. Trim excess dough and crimp around the edge of the pan. Brush the lattice top with the egg white and water wash, and sprinkle with white crystal sugar. Place the quiche pan on a baking sheet and bake for 40 to 45 minutes, until the crust is browned and the filling bubbly.

7. Remove the pan to a wire rack to cool. Serve at room temperature.

Yield: 8 servings

Wisconsin Sour Cherry Pie

In June, Wisconsin farm stands are ablaze with bright red sour cherries, a regional favorite of Midwestern pie bakers, displayed in wooden baskets. The demand is such that some Door County growers freeze pitted sour cherries in buckets and ship them year-round.

Not surprisingly, there are many variations of sour cherry pie. My friend Grace, who operates a wholesale bakery in Chicago, is convinced that the secret of the wonderful cherry pies she has so enjoyed since childhood is the chicken fat in the crust. Combined with a little butter, rendered chicken fat produces an exceptionally flaky, crisp golden crust.

This sour cherry pie is my personal favorite. I take it on picnics and to patio parties whenever possible, and it never fails to win a round of compliments.

Crust

2 cups all-purpose flour

1 tablespoon granulated sugar

1/2 teaspoon salt

6 tablespoons rendered chicken fat, chilled or frozen, or lard, chilled, cut into small pieces

6 tablespoons unsalted butter, chilled, cut into small pieces

1/3 cup cold water

Filling

1 quart sour cherries (thawed, if frozen), pitted

1/2 cup granulated sugar

1/4 cup packed dark brown sugar

2 teaspoons grated orange zest

1/4 teaspoon ground cinnamon

1/8 teaspoon ground allspice

1/4 cup cornstarch

1/2 tablespoon rum (optional)

1 tablespoon unsalted butter, cut into pieces

Milk, for painting

Additional granulated sugar, for sprinkling

1. To make the crust, combine the flour, granulated sugar, and salt in a medium-size mixing bowl. Add the chicken fat or lard and the butter, stirring briefly to coat with flour. Cut the fat into the flour with a pastry blender until the mixture is evenly crumbled. Add the cold water and stir briefly, just until moist. Turn the mixture out onto a work surface and knead gently and quickly into a ball of dough. Flatten the ball into a disk, wrap in plastic wrap or waxed paper, and refrigerate for at least 30 minutes.

2. Meanwhile, prepare the filling. Combine the cherries, the sugars, orange zest, spices, cornstarch, and rum (if desired) in a saucepan. Bring to a boil over medium-high heat, stirring constantly. Boil until thickened, about 45 seconds more, and remove the pan from the heat. Transfer the mixture to a bowl and allow to cool completely. (The filling can be made ahead and stored in the refrigerator.)

3. Preheat the oven to 400°F.

4. To assemble, roll out two-thirds of the dough on a floured work surface into a 13-inch round. Fit the round into a 9-inch pie pan. Roll out the remaining piece of dough into a 10-inch round. (Cut this piece of dough into strips if a lattice top is desired.)

5. Pour the filling into the bottom crust and dot with the butter. Brush milk on the edges of the pastry to moisten. Fit the top crust over the filling, or weave the strips of dough into a lattice pattern on top. Trim excess dough hanging over the rim of the pan. Press the top and bottom together and roll inward while crimping to finish the edge.

6. Place the pie pan on a baking sheet. Cut slits into the top if using a solid crust. Brush the exposed dough with milk and sprinkle with granulated sugar. Bake for 50 to 55 minutes, until the crust is golden brown and the filling is bubbly.

7. Transfer the pan to a wire rack to cool. Serve warm or at room temperature.

Yield: 8 servings

Guava-Strawberry Pie

Guavas can be hard to find in many regions, but they are an exotic taste treat that is well worth seeking out. For this pie, I use a combination of feijoa, or pineapple guavas, along with strawberries. Feijoa is a small, egg-shaped fruit that is fragrantly perfumed and tastes somewhat like pineapple. When ripe, it is still green and yields to the touch, like a pear or peach.

Crust

2 cups all-purpose flour

1 tablespoon granulated sugar

1/2 teaspoon salt

9 tablespoons lard, chilled, cut into small pieces

3 tablespoons unsalted butter, chilled, cut into small pieces

1/3 cup cold water

Filling

12 ripe pineapple guavas (about 1 pound), peeled and halved

8 ounces ripe strawberries, hulled and cut into thick slices

1/2 cup packed light brown sugar

1 tablespoon fresh lime juice

1 teaspoon grated lime zest (about 1 lime)

1/4 teaspoon ground allspice

2 tablespoons cornstarch

1 tablespoon unsalted butter, cut into pieces

Milk, for painting

Additional granulated sugar, for dusting

1. To make the crust, combine the flour, granulated sugar, and salt in a medium-size mixing bowl. Add the lard and butter, and stir briefly to coat with flour. Cut the fat into the flour with a pastry blender until the mixture is evenly crumbled. Add the cold water and stir briefly, just until moist. Turn the mixture out onto a work surface and knead gently and quickly into a ball of dough. Flatten the ball into a disk, wrap in plastic wrap or waxed paper, and refrigerate for at least 30 minutes.

2. Preheat the oven to 400°F.

3. For the filling, puree the pineapple guava pulp in a food processor. (You should have about 1 1/3 cups puree.) Combine the puree and strawberries in a large bowl. Stir in the brown sugar, lime juice, lime zest, allspice, and cornstarch. Mix thoroughly.

4. To assemble, roll out two-thirds of the dough on a floured work surface into a 13-inch round. Fit the round into a 9-inch pie pan. Roll the remaining piece of dough out into a 10-inch round.

continued

5. Pour the filling into the bottom crust and dot with the butter. Brush milk on the edges of the pastry to moisten. Fit the top crust over the fruit. Trim away the excess bottom-crust dough hanging over the rim of the pan. Press the top and bottom together and roll inward while crimping to finish the edge.

6. Place the pie on a baking sheet. Cut slits into the top, brush the exposed dough with milk, and sprinkle with granulated sugar. Bake for 15 minutes. Reduce the oven temperature to 350°F and bake for 30 to 35 minutes more, until the crust is browned and the fruit is bubbly.

7. Transfer the pan to a wire rack to cool. Serve warm or at room temperature.

Yield: 8 servings

When Gilbert Arriaza arrived in Miami's Little Havana neighborhood in 1962, he began his new American life the way many poor immigrants do—washing dishes in a restaurant. Today he owns Gilbert's, Miami's foremost Cuban bakery, as well as a wedding cake gallery in a second location. One of the most popular bakeries in the city, Gilbert's specializes in such Cuban delicacies as guava, pineapple, and coconut pies, custard flans, and tropical fruit-filled cakes.

Baker's Custard
(For Custard-Filled Baba and Cream Puffs)

This all-purpose custard, a replica of the soft custards used by bakeries everywhere, is creamy and not overly sweet. Use it in Custard-Filled Baba (page 236) and Cream Puffs (page 238). The custard also makes a tasty pudding served alone or with fruit. I sometimes replace the vanilla with almond extract, reducing the amount of the stronger almond flavoring to ¹/₄ teaspoon.

1²/₃ cups milk

¹/₂ cup sugar

Pinch of salt

¹/₄ cup cornstarch

¹/₂ cup water

3 large eggs

3 tablespoons unsalted butter, at room temperature

1 teaspoon vanilla extract

1. Combine the milk, sugar, and salt in a saucepan over medium heat. Stirring to dissolve the sugar, heat to a bare simmer.

2. In a medium-size mixing bowl, whisk the cornstarch and water until blended. Add the eggs and whisk thoroughly. Pour in the hot milk mixture, whisking constantly, then return the combination to the saucepan. Cook over medium heat, stirring, until the custard thickens and comes to a boil. Boil for 30 seconds, remove the pan from the heat, and stir in the butter and vanilla.

3. Immediately transfer the custard to a bowl. Cover the top of the custard with waxed paper and refrigerate until cold, about 2 hours. Stir the custard well before using.

Yield: 3 cups

Custard-Filled Baba

I pipe dough for this luscious dessert into a free-form rectangle on a baking sheet, soak the baba in hot rum syrup after baking, and fill with creamy custard. The filling can be made well ahead of time, but the pastry should be prepared the same day it is to be served.

Glacé cherries can be found in King Arthur Flour Baker's Catalogue (see Mail Order Source Guide).

Pastry

²/₃ cup lukewarm milk (95° to 110°F)

2¹/₂ teaspoons (1 envelope) active dry yeast

2²/₃ cups unbleached all-purpose flour

¹/₄ cup granulated sugar

1 teaspoon salt

1 teaspoon vanilla extract

1 teaspoon grated orange zest

5 large eggs

6 tablespoons unsalted butter, melted and cooled to lukewarm (95° to 110°F)

Rum Syrup

1¹/₄ cups water

2 cups granulated sugar

¹/₃ cup light corn syrup

¹/₃ cup rum (light or dark)

3 cups Baker's Custard (page 235)

Confectioners' sugar (optional, for dusting)

12 glacé cherries (optional, for garnish)

1. To make the pastry, prepare the sponge starter. Combine the milk and yeast in the bowl of a stationary electric mixer fitted with the flat paddle attachment. Add 1 cup of the flour and mix until smoothly blended. Cover the bowl tightly with plastic wrap and let stand at room temperature until well risen and bubbly, 45 minutes to 1 hour.

2. Add the granulated sugar, salt, vanilla, and orange zest to the starter. Begin mixing at low speed using the flat paddle attachment. Add the eggs, one at a time, allowing each to be completely incorporated into the dough before the next addition. Add the remaining 1²/₃ cups flour, a little at a time. Pour in 5 tablespoons of the melted butter and mix until the dough is smooth and soft, about 2 minutes.

3. Fill a pastry bag, fitted with a large (¹/₂-inch) open tip, with the dough. Pipe twelve ¹/₂-inch-thick rectangles measuring 3¹/₂ × 2 inches onto a greased baking sheet. Space 1¹/₂ inches apart to allow for spreading. (You may need to pipe each rectangle twice to achieve a thickness of $1/2$ inch, as the dough will spread a little.) Lightly brush the dough with the remaining 1 tablespoon melted butter and set aside for 30 minutes.

4. Preheat the oven to 350°F.

5. Bake for 15 to 20 minutes, until golden brown and firm to the touch. Remove the pastries to wire racks to cool.

6. For the rum syrup, combine the water, granulated sugar, and corn syrup in a high-sided 12-inch skillet. Bring to a boil over medium-high heat, stirring to dissolve the sugar, and boil for 2 minutes. Remove from the heat and stir in the rum.

7. Immerse as many baba in the hot syrup as fit in a single layer, soak for about 2 minutes on each side, and remove to a baking sheet to cool. Continue the soaking process for the remaining baba, reheating the syrup between batches.

8. Return the remaining syrup to the heat and bring to a simmer. Brush generously over the baba to glaze. Repeat the glazing process until all of the syrup has been used. Set aside at room temperature until ready to fill and serve.

9. Make a slit down the center of each baba without cutting all the way through the pastry. Fill a pastry bag, fitted with a large star tip, with custard. Pipe into the center of each pastry, mounding the custard. Garnish with a dusting of confectioners' sugar and a glacé cherry, if desired.

Yield: 12 pastries

I n a French bakery, this yeast-raised and egg-enriched pastry is called *baba au rhum* for the rum syrup with which it is glazed. In an Italian bakery, such as Scialo Bros. Bakery in Providence, Rhode Island, it's simply called baba. At Scialo's, each baba is filled with custard and garnished with a bright red cherry, a finishing touch that transforms a relatively plain pastry into a celebratory dessert for one. The Scialo family has been making baba for eighty-plus years, and their devoted customers still eat it up. The bakery's Italian pastries remain the legacy of Luigi Scialo, the founder. Luigi's daughters own the bakery now, although "Bros." remains in the name.

Cream Puffs

From the pristine French bakeries of Manhattan's Upper East Side to the scruffy Italian bakeries of San Francisco's North Beach, Cream Puffs have long been a popular choice. The key to perfect Cream Puffs is airy pastry; the rounds of dough should rise in the oven to quadruple their original size and emerge as shells with cavelike interiors just waiting to be filled.

In addition to custard, you could use ice cream or whipped cream as a filling. If you wish, top these with a fruit sauce or chocolate sauce. Once baked, the shells freeze well, so this versatile dessert can be prepared almost spontaneously!

1 cup all-purpose flour

1 cup plus 1 tablespoon water

¹/₂ teaspoon salt

¹/₂ cup (1 stick) unsalted butter

5 large eggs

3 cups Baker's Custard (page 235)

1. Sift the flour and set aside.

2. Combine 1 cup of the water, the salt, and butter in a medium-size saucepan. Bring to a boil over medium-high heat. Remove from the heat and add the flour all at once, beating with a wooden spoon until the mixture forms a ball of dough around the spoon. Return the pan to medium-high heat for just 30 seconds, stirring the dough with the spoon, then remove from the heat.

3. Immediately transfer the dough from the pan to the bowl of a stationary electric mixer fitted with the flat paddle attachment. Begin mixing at low speed. Beat in 4 of the eggs, one at a time, allowing each egg to be completely incorporated before the next addition.

4. In a small dish, mix the remaining egg and the 1 tablespoon water.

5. Preheat the oven to 400°F. Line a cookie sheet with parchment paper. With a pencil, trace nine 3-inch rounds onto the paper at least 2 inches apart.

6. Using a pastry bag fitted with an open-hole tip, pipe the dough onto the rounds to fill, beginning at the outer border of each and working toward the center in a continuous spiral motion. Each round of dough should be about ¹/₂ inch thick, with the highest point at the center.

7. Brush the rounds of dough with the egg and water wash. Bake for about 30 minutes, until golden brown and puffed. Remove the shells to wire racks to cool.

8. Just before serving, fill shells with the custard. The easiest method is to simply split the shells in half horizontally and sandwich the filling between the halves. The professional method is to make a small hole in the bottom of each and fill by piping into the hole, using a pastry bag fitted with an open-holed tip.

Yield: 9 pastries

From the 1940s through the mid-1970s in Venice Beach, California, the Helm's Bakery truck would make its afternoon rounds throughout the neighborhood. Venice Beach children weren't impressed by the three-block-long Helm's bakery facility. It was the trademark blue-and-yellow truck, built to resemble a ship, that made a lasting impression. The Helm's logo was that of a ship's captain at the helm of a large wooden wheel, and the "captain" steered the truck through Venice Beach daily at about three o'clock P.M., just as children were emerging from school.

Inside the truck, the walls were made of cherry paneling and lined with wide drawers that pulled open to reveal fresh-baked pastries. One daily visitor still longingly recalls his standing order: a 50-cent cream puff, the size of two hands held together, filled with soft whipped cream.

Dutch Letters

This recipe for Dutch Letters comes from Ralph Jaarsma of Jaarsma Bakery in Pella, Iowa. It consists of three steps: making the flaky puff pastry, making the sweet almond filling, and putting the two together for an irresistible treat.

Pastry

2¼ cups all-purpose flour

½ teaspoon salt

1 cup (2 sticks) unsalted butter, chilled, cut into ½-inch cubes

1 large egg

½ cup cold water

Filling

4 ounces (½ cup) almond paste

¼ cup granulated sugar

¼ cup packed dark brown sugar

1 large egg white

Milk, for painting

Additional granulated sugar, for sprinkling

1. To make the pastry, combine the flour and salt in a large mixing bowl. Add the butter and stir to coat with flour. Combine the whole egg and the cold water in a small dish, stirring to mix. Add to the flour mixture and stir briefly to form a moist, lumpy dough.

2. Turn the dough out onto a lightly floured work surface. Knead about 10 times, until the dough forms a ball. Working quickly, roll the dough out on a well-floured work surface into a 15 × 10-inch rectangle. Fold the 2 short ends in to the center to meet, then fold in half lengthwise to form 4 layers. Sprinkle the work surface liberally with flour and roll the dough out again into a 15 × 10-inch rectangle. Again fold the short ends in to the middle and then in half. Wrap in plastic wrap and refrigerate for at least 30 minutes. (If butter oozes out of the dough after the first set of folds, refrigerate for 30 minutes before the second roll-and-fold sequence.)

3. On a lightly floured work surface, roll out the chilled dough once more into a 15 × 10-inch rectangle and fold up as before. For a final time, roll the dough again into a 15 × 10-inch rectangle and repeat the folding process into 4 layers. The dough should be easier to handle, requiring less flour, by this last roll-and-fold series. Wrap the dough in plastic wrap and refrigerate for at least 20 minutes.

4. Meanwhile, prepare the filling. In a small mixing bowl, combine the almond paste, the sugars, and the egg white. Stir the mixture until smoothly blended.

5. Preheat the oven to 375°F.

6. Cut the dough in half crosswise and return one piece to the refrigerator. Roll the other half out into a 10 × 13-inch rectangle. Cut the rectangle into five 10 × 2½-inch strips. Spread 1 tablespoon of the almond filling down the center third of each strip. Brush one long edge and both ends of each strip with milk. Starting with the unmoistened edge, fold up each strip lengthwise to enclose the filling, pinching the seams to seal closed.

Place seam side down on an ungreased baking sheet, twisting each strip into an *S*. Repeat the cutting, filling, and shaping process with the second piece of dough.

7. Brush with milk and sprinkle lightly with granulated sugar. Bake for about 25 minutes, until lightly golden. Remove the letters to wire racks to cool to room temperature.

Yield: 10 large pastries

Every day Jaarsma Bakery in Pella, Iowa, bakes nearly 1,000 Dutch letters, or *sinterklaas,* as the traditional Christmas pastries are known in Holland. *Sinterklaas* is the Dutch name for Santa Claus.

A rather small bakery considering its volume of business, Jaarsma is situated in the middle of Iowa livestock country. The bakery's product line is extensive and of high quality, but it is the Dutch letters that lure both the locals and the tour buses.

Dutch letters were made completely by hand for much of the nearly hundred years Jaarsma has been in business. Today, third-generation owner Ralph Jaarsma proudly shows off his letter-making machine in the back of the bakery. In modern production fashion, the machine rolls and seals a sixty-four-layer strip of dough around a line of deposited almond filling, then quickly twists the dough into an S shape—for *sinterklaas* or Santa Claus—and sprays the pastry with sugar water in preparation for baking.

Quick Puff Pastry Dough

(For Big Apple Turnovers, Chocolate Twists, and Cheese Sticks)

There are two ways to make puff pastry. One is the classic French "roll-in" method, whereby butter is conditioned and rolled into the dough between numerous folds. The other is the Scottish method, often called "quick" because it significantly reduces the amount of rolling and folding. It also eliminates the necessity of kneading the butter with flour to a malleable consistency, which is called conditioning the butter. This is not much different from making pie crust dough, except that more folding of the rolled dough is necessary to produce flaky layers.

The two methods do not produce identical results. Master bakers with classic French training prefer the roll-in method because it results in hundreds of paper-thin layers of buttery, tender pastry leaves. For home baking, however, I can't honestly say that the roll-in method is worth the trouble. This recipe, following the Scottish method, produces a very tender, flavorful, and flaky pastry. I use it for my Big Apple Turnovers (page 244), Chocolate Twists (page 246), and Cheese Sticks (page 248). Note that unlike most baking recipes, salted butter is called for in this case.

1^1/$_2$ to 1^3/$_4$ **cups bread flour**

^{1}/$_2$ **teaspoon cream of tartar**

1 cup (2 sticks) salted butter, chilled, cut into ^{1}/$_2$-inch cubes

^{1}/$_2$ **cup cold water**

1. Combine 1^1/$_2$ cups of the flour and the cream of tartar in a medium-size mixing bowl. Add the butter and stir briefly to coat with flour. Cut the butter into the flour mixture with a pastry blender until crumbs the size of corn kernels form. (You can also cut the butter in by pulsing until crumbly in a food processor.) Add the cold water and stir until a dough forms.

2. Turn the dough out onto a work surface sprinkled with 1 tablespoon flour. Flatten into a disk and sprinkle with another 1 tablespoon flour. Roll the dough out into a rectangle ^{1}/$_4$ to ^{1}/$_2$ inch thick, sprinkling with additional flour only as necessary to keep it from sticking.

3. Brush excess flour from the rectangle of dough. Fold the short ends in to meet at the center, then fold in half, lengthwise, to form 4 layers of dough. Roll the dough out again into a rectangle, sprinkling the work surface with flour as necessary. Fold up as before, first with the short ends to the middle, then in half. Wrap the dough in plastic wrap and refrigerate for 20 minutes.

4. Repeat the same roll-and-fold sequence twice more, each time rolling the dough out into a rectangle, folding the short ends in to the center, and then folding in half, using only a sprinkle of flour on the work surface this time. Wrap in plastic wrap and refrigerate for 20 minutes more.

5. The dough may be stored in the refrigerator for up to 2 days.

Yield: 1¼ pounds

Big Apple Turnovers

Not many people can resist turnovers—oversized triangles of golden, gossamer puff pastry filled with a sweetened seasonal fruit filling, such as apples spiked with rum-soaked raisins and imbued with just a hint of lemon. Long the province of French bakeries, turnovers can be made at home using Quick Puff Pastry Dough. Both the dough and the filling can be made ahead of time to accommodate a busy schedule.

3 tablespoons golden raisins

2 tablespoons dark rum

1¼ pounds firm, tart apples, peeled, cored, and cut into ½-inch-thick slices

1 tablespoon unsalted butter

3 tablespoons granulated sugar

½ teaspoon ground cinnamon

½ to ¾ teaspoon grated lemon zest

1 recipe Quick Puff Pastry Dough (page 242), chilled

1 tablespoon ground nuts (almonds, pecans, or walnuts)

1 large egg, beaten with 1 tablespoon water

Superfine sugar (optional, for sprinkling)

1. Combine the raisins and rum in a small dish and set aside to soak for at least 20 minutes.

2. Combine the apples and butter in a skillet over medium heat. Add the granulated sugar and cinnamon. Cook, stirring occasionally, until the apples are soft but not mushy, 12 to 15 minutes. Drain the raisins well and add to the cooked apples along with the lemon zest. Set aside to cool completely. (If making in advance, cover and refrigerate the filling until ready to use.)

3. On a lightly floured work surface, roll out the dough into a 18 × 12-inch rectangle and cut into six 6-inch squares. Fill each square with ⅓ cup of the apple filling and sprinkle with ½ teaspoon of the nuts. Brush the edges of each pastry square with the egg and water wash. Grasp one corner of each square and fold it over the filling to the opposite corner, making a triangle. Press the edges together with a fork to seal and transfer the triangles to a baking sheet lined with parchment paper. Brush exposed dough with the wash and set aside for 30 minutes.

4. Preheat the oven to 400°F.

5. Brush the turnovers again with the wash. Sprinkle evenly with superfine sugar, if desired. Poke 3 holes in the top of each with a fork. Bake for about 25 minutes, until golden and crisp.

6. Remove the turnovers to wire racks to cool. Serve warm or at room temperature.

Yield: 6 pastries

Lafayette, deep in the heart of Louisiana bayou country, is home to Poupart's, one of the finest French bakeries in the country. It is here on Pinhook Street that master baker François Poupart and his wife, Louise, have been dazzling the Cajun community—which spends a goodly amount of time preparing, eating, or just talking about food—with their nationally acclaimed baking expertise for over thirty years.

I asked Eula Mae Dore, chef at the McIlhenny company's Marsh House, on Avery Island, to recommend good bakeries in southern Louisiana. "Oh, you want to go to Poupart's," she replied. "Now, there's a bakery!" Eula Mae has even brought François wet seeds and skins, the ground fermented seeds of Tabasco peppers, to add to his dough for hot and spicy French baguettes.

The Pouparts started their business with fifty dollars in the cash register and not speaking a word of English. François bought three sacks of flour each day and made everything without the aid of any special equipment. Louise made deliveries out of the couple's station wagon.

Today, François has twenty bakers working for him, including his son Patrick, and Louise has ten salespeople to assist their customers. The Pouparts' daily routine hasn't really changed that much, however. François and Patrick begin pastry preparations at 5:00 A.M. each morning, break at midday for three hours, and return to the bakery to complete their twelve-hour work shift. "This is the way French bakers live," François explains.

Chocolate Twists

This singularly delicious pastry delivers a double treat. Chocolate twists are a combination of two doughs—flaky puff pastry and bittersweet chocolate pastry—rolled together into a spiral. Although the sticks are sugared before baking, the result is not really sweet. I think of it as a French twist to complement an Italian espresso.

2 ounces unsweetened chocolate

¼ cup water

1¼ cups all-purpose flour

⅓ cup sugar

½ cup (1 stick) unsalted butter, chilled, cut into small pieces

1 recipe Quick Puff Pastry Dough (page 242), chilled

Additional sugar, for coating

1. Cut the chocolate into coarse pieces and combine in a small bowl with the water. Melt the mixture over a pan of simmering water or in a microwave oven at 50 percent power for 1 to 4 minutes, checking every 30 seconds. Set aside to cool.

2. Combine the flour and sugar in a medium-size mixing bowl. Add the butter and mix with a pastry blender until crumbly. Add the chocolate and water mixture and stir just until a dough begins to form. Turn the mixture out onto a work surface and knead briefly to form a smooth dough. Flatten into a disk, wrap in plastic wrap, and refrigerate for at least 30 minutes.

3. On a lightly floured work surface, roll the puff pastry dough out into a 15 × 10-inch rectangle. On a separate lightly floured work surface, roll the chocolate dough out into a 15 × 5-inch strip. Carefully roll up the chocolate strip onto the rolling pin and then unroll it to cover half the puff pastry dough lengthwise. Fold the uncovered half of puff pastry dough over to cover the chocolate dough completely. Cut crosswise into ½-inch-wide strips. (You should have about 24 strips.)

4. Twist each strip tightly into a striped spiral, pushing on each end to flatten slightly. Dredge the twists in sugar to coat all over and place 1 inch apart on a baking sheet lined with parchment paper. Set aside for 30 minutes.

5. Preheat the oven to 375°F.

6. Bake for about 25 minutes, until golden and crisp. Remove the twists to wire racks to cool. Serve warm or at room temperature.

Yield: About 24 pastries

The Italian French Baking Company of San Francisco is aptly named. It sits on the top of a hill in North Beach, the city's most prominent Italian neighborhood, and displays French puff pastries and baguettes baked in its original 1911 brick oven side by side with biscotti. It was here that I first tasted heavenly spirals of puff pastry and chocolate dough.

Cheese Sticks

Peter Rathjen and Kelly Bennett of the Palo Alto Baking Company sent me the recipe for their wonderful cheese pastry. I combined it with my own puff pastry to create these crisp, savory sticks. They're heaven when eaten fresh from the oven and perfect with cocktails. For entertaining, it's easiest to prepare the doughs one day in advance.

1¾ cups cake flour

1 cup grated Swiss cheese

¾ cup plus ⅓ cup grated Parmesan cheese

¾ cup (1½ sticks) unsalted butter, chilled, cut into small pieces

1 cup heavy (whipping) cream, chilled

1 recipe Quick Puff Pastry Dough (page 242), chilled

1. Combine the flour, Swiss cheese, and ¾ cup of the Parmesan cheese in a large mixing bowl and stir to mix thoroughly. Cut in the butter with a pastry blender until the mixture is crumbly. Add the cream and stir to form a moist dough. Wrap completely in waxed paper and refrigerate for at least 1 hour to firm. (The dough can be made a day in advance and refrigerated overnight.)

2. On a lightly floured work surface, roll out the puff pastry dough into a 10 × 15-inch rectangle. On a separate lightly floured work surface, roll out the cheese pastry dough into a 10-inch square. Position the cheese square to cover two-thirds of the puff pastry dough. Fold the uncovered flap of puff pastry over onto the cheese, then fold the opposite end

over to cover completely. Wrap in plastic wrap and refrigerate for at least 30 minutes.

3. Return the dough to a lightly floured work surface and roll it out again into a 10 × 15-inch rectangle. Fold a short end over to cover one-third of the rectangle, then fold the opposite end over to cover completely. Wrap in plastic wrap and refrigerate for at least 30 minutes more.

4. Return the dough to a lightly floured work surface and roll it out into a 10 × 18-inch rectangle about ¼ inch thick. Cut crosswise into ½-inch-wide strips. Twist each strip tightly into a spiral, pushing on each end to flatten slightly. Place 1 inch apart on parchment-lined baking sheets and sprinkle with the remaining ⅓ cup Parmesan cheese. Set aside or refrigerate until ready to bake.

5. Preheat the oven to 350°F.

6. Bake for 25 minutes, until lightly golden, and reduce the oven temperature to 300°F. Bake for about 15 minutes more, until golden and crisp.

7. Remove the sticks to wire racks to cool. Serve warm or at room temperature.

Yield: 32 to 36 pastries

In 1980, Peter Rathjen and Kelly Bennett bought a thirty-four-year-old California bakery located in an upscale neighborhood near Stanford University. One month later, the bakery burned down. It took extraordinary effort, but the owners rebuilt the bakery facility and their fledgling business, the Palo Alto Baking Company. They opened a café that brought in lunchtime regulars who raved about their bakery products throughout the neighborhood. Today, the bakery serves as something of a local social club, where families and friends gather to savor treats such as cheese sticks.

Caramel Pecan Tart

Pecan pastries of any sort almost always score a big hit with bakery customers. I'm partial to pairing pecans with caramel, a match made in heaven. In this recipe, I toast the pecans to boost the tart's nutty flavor. Also, I bake sweetened condensed milk for the filling, a step that turns the sometimes tricky procedure of making caramel sauce into child's play.

1 recipe Tart Pastry Dough (page 252)

14 ounces sweetened condensed milk

2 tablespoons butter, at room temperature

1 teaspoon vanilla extract

2 large eggs

2 cups (8 ounces) pecan halves, toasted

1. On a lightly floured work surface, roll out the dough into a 13-inch round. Fit the round into a 10 × ¾-inch tart pan and trim the edge so it is even with the rim. Chill for at least 30 minutes.

2. Preheat the oven to 425°F.

3. Line the crust with aluminum foil and fill the foil with dried beans or pie weights. Bake for 15 minutes. Remove the pan from the oven and lift out the foil liner and its contents, leaving the oven on. Set aside to cool.

4. Pour the condensed milk into a shallow baking pan. Cover the pan with foil and place it inside a larger pan. Pour hot water into the larger pan to come halfway up the sides of the smaller. Bake the nested pans for 1½ hours, until the condensed milk has caramelized into a thick sauce. Remove from the oven, and lower the oven temperature to 350°F.

5. Pour the hot caramel into a medium-size mixing bowl. Whisk in the butter and vanilla. Let the mixture cool to warm. Beat in the eggs, then stir in the pecans. Pour the filling evenly into the crust.

6. Place the tart pan on a baking sheet and bake for about 30 minutes, until golden brown and puffed.

7. Transfer the pan to a wire rack to cool. Serve slightly warm or at room temperature.

Yield: 12 servings

*I*n tasting nut tarts from coast to coast, two stood out. One is made at the Pink Rose, a bakery in Philadelphia. It is housed in a vintage three-story building with a pressed-tin ceiling and charming white lace curtains on the windows. This full-service bakery makes elegant versions of homespun baked goods, including one of the best pecan tarts I've ever tasted. Its tart has a pretty scallop-edged, flaky pastry crust that is loaded with big pieces of pecans in a filling spiked with dark rum.

Across the continent, Fran's occupies a tiny storefront on East Madison Street in Seattle. The exquisite chocolate and dessert shop serves up a simple mixed nut tartlet that is close to perfection. The nuts are suspended in Fran's wildly popular caramel sauce atop a delicate buttery tart crust.

Tart Pastry Dough

(For Caramel Pecan Tart and Plum and Almond Cream Tart)

You can use this superb dough to make an all-purpose pastry for almost any kind of dessert tart. I use it in my recipes for Caramel Pecan Tart (page 250) and Plum and Almond Cream Tart (page 253).

1 cup all-purpose flour

½ cup cake flour

2 tablespoons sugar

½ teaspoon salt

½ cup (1 stick) unsalted butter, chilled, cut into small pieces

¼ cup cold water

1. Combine the flours, sugar, and salt in a medium-size mixing bowl. Add the butter, stirring briefly to coat with flour. Cut the fat into the flour with a pastry blender until the mixture is evenly crumbled. Add the cold water and stir briefly, just until moist.

2. Turn the mixture out onto a work surface and knead gently and quickly into a ball of dough. Flatten the ball into a disk, wrap in plastic wrap or waxed paper, and refrigerate for at least 30 minutes.

Yield: Enough dough for one 10 × ¾-inch tart

Plum and Almond Cream Tart

I adore this type of rustic regional French tart. French bakers excel in the art of pastry making. They take their craft seriously and devote the same care to simple fruit tarts as to fancier presentations of puff pastries and pastry creams. This tart looks as though it could come from an old small-town bakery with stone flooring, barn wood shelving, and stained marble countertops.

Other soft-fleshed seasonal fruit, such as sliced pears, can be substituted for the prune plums. Do not substitute almond paste for the ground almonds and sugar.

1 recipe Tart Pastry Dough (page 252)

6 tablespoons unsalted butter, at room temperature

1/2 cup sugar

1 large egg

1/2 cup ground blanched almonds

2 tablespoons all-purpose flour

1 teaspoon grated lemon zest

1/4 teaspoon ground cardamom

1 to 1 1/4 pounds prune plums (about 1 dozen)

1/4 cup red currant jelly

1 teaspoon water

1. On a lightly floured work surface, roll the dough out into a 13-inch round. Fit the round into a 10-inch tart pan with a 3/4-inch side. Trim the edge so it is even with the rim and chill for at least 30 minutes.

2. Preheat the oven to 375°F.

3. Cream the butter and sugar in a medium-size mixing bowl until smoothly blended. Add the egg and beat until smooth. Add the almonds, flour, lemon zest, and cardamom, beating until well blended.

4. Halve and pit the prune plums. Cut each piece into 2 wedges. Spread the almond cream mixture evenly over the bottom of the crust. Arrange the plum wedges side by side over the filling in concentric circles, pushing lightly to half submerge them into the cream.

5. Place the tart pan on a baking sheet and bake for about 45 minutes, until browned and puffed. Remove the pan to a wire rack to cool to room temperature.

6. Combine the jelly and water in a small saucepan. Bring to a boil, let boil for 2 minutes, and remove from the heat. Brush the surface of the tart with the warm glaze. Serve at room temperature.

Yield: 10 to 12 servings

Blueberry Cheesecake Tarts

Modern times have seen a reduction in fat and sugar in our daily diet, but that doesn't mean we are about to give up such sinfully rich favorites as cheese-cake. We just eat smaller portions, such as these perfectly proportioned little cheesecake tarts. "Just a bite" was an oft-heard customer refrain in our bakery.

This recipe provides a triple treat—seasonal fresh fruit, creamy cheesecake, and a sweet cookie crust. I use wild Maine blueberries, which are smaller and more intensely flavored than cultivated berries.

Crust

6 tablespoons unsalted butter, at room temperature

¼ cup sugar

½ teaspoon vanilla extract

1 large egg yolk

1 cup all-purpose flour

Filling

8 ounces cream cheese, at room temperature

⅓ cup sugar

1 large egg

2 teaspoons all-purpose flour

½ teaspoon vanilla extract

½ teaspoon grated lemon zest

2 tablespoons heavy (whipping) cream

1 cup wild Maine blueberries, picked over

1. To make the crust, cream the butter, sugar, and vanilla together in a medium-size mixing bowl. Beat in the egg yolk. Add the flour and mix until a dough forms.

2. Gather the dough into a ball and divide it into 8 equal pieces. Lightly grease eight 3 × ¾-inch scalloped-edge tart pans. Press each piece of dough firmly and evenly into a tart pan to line the bottom and sides of the pan. Set the pans onto a baking sheet and refrigerate for at least 1 hour.

3. Preheat the oven to 375°F.

4. Prick the bottoms of the pastry shells in several places with a fork. Bake for 10 minutes until firm. Remove the baking sheet from the oven and allow the crusts to cool. Reduce the oven temperature to 325°F.

5. For the filling, beat the cream cheese and sugar in a bowl until fluffy and light. Add the egg and blend, then beat in the flour. Add the vanilla, lemon zest, and cream, blending until smooth. Gently fold in the blueberries, mixing thoroughly. Ladle the filling into the crusts.

6. Bake the tarts on the baking sheet for about 25 minutes, until the fillings are set. Cool the tart pans on wire racks to room temperature. Loosen the pastry from the sides of the pans with the tip of a sharp knife, then unmold the tarts. Serve at room temperature or chilled.

Yield: 8 pastries

Cheesecake is the number-one-selling dessert in restaurants and the signature product of Janet Rosing, owner of Cheesecakes by JR. This neighborhood bakeshop, located in Chicago, is also a supplier to restaurants, hotels, and grocery stores.

Janet started her business fifteen years ago in a space rented from a commercial test kitchen and worked evenings and weekends while holding down a full-time day job. Her mother and sisters pitched in to help bake and clean, and her father set up a bookkeeping system. Meanwhile, like all fledgling bakery entrepreneurs, young Janet devised recipes, ordered supplies, supervised baking, made sales calls, and packaged and delivered the cheesecakes in her own car.

What began as a thirty-cake-a-week business grew within ten years into an operation producing four tons of cheesecake alone each week, along with a growing assortment of cakes, pies, muffins, and cookies.

Janet now offers fifteen different flavors of cheesecake. Her tour de force is a stunning six-tiered wedding cake made entirely of cheesecake and decoratively frosted with pure fresh whipped cream.

Mail Order Source Guide

Ingredients and Equipment

American Spoon Foods
P.O. Box 566
Petoskey, Michigan 49770
(800) 222-5886
Fruit juice–sweetened spoon fruits, preserves, jellies, fruit butters, dried fruit, and berries; catalog available

King Arthur Flour Baker's Catalogue
P.O. Box 876
Norwich, Vermont 05055-0876
(800) 827-6836
Specialty flours including high-gluten, clear, pastry, baker's patent, white rye, and pumpernickel; specialty grains, sourdough starters, bulk yeast, malt syrup, almond paste, sparkling sugar and other baking supplies, along with equipment and tools including panettone molds: catalog available

Blommer Chocolate Co.
600 W. Kinzie
Chicago, Illinois 60610-3977
(312) 226-7700
Confectioners' coating chocolates, dark and white chocolates; product list in production; call with questions

Bob's Red Mill Natural Foods
5209 S.E. International Way
Milwaukie, Oregon 97222
(503) 654-3215
Natural stone-ground whole-grain flours, grains, cereals, meals, nuts, and seeds; product list available

Maasdam Sorghum Mills
Lynnville, Iowa 50153
(515) 594-4369
Sorghum syrup; no list, just call

Morgan's Mills
168 Payson Road
Union, Maine 04862
(207) 785-4900
Freshly milled organic whole-grain flours and baking supplies; product list available

The Nauvoo Mill and Bakery
1530 Mulholland / Highway 96
Nauvoo, Illinois 62354
(217) 453-6734
Stone-ground whole-grain wheat flours and whole-grain yellow cornmeal; no list, just call

Penzeys, Ltd.
P.O. Box 1448
Waukesha, Wisconsin 53187
(414) 574-0277
Spices and seeds; catalog available

Seaquist Orchards
11482 Highway 42
P.O. Box 204
Sister Bay, Wisconsin 54234
(800) SEA-8850
Frozen pitted sour cherries; no list, just call

Spiceland, Inc.
P.O. Box 34378
Chicago, Illinois 60634-0378
(773) 736-1000
Spices, extracts, and flavors; product list available

Sur La Table
410 Terry Avenue North
(catalog division)
Seattle, Washington 98109-5229
(800) 243-0852
Specialty equipment and gift items for cooks and bakers including pastry blenders, cake stands, baking stones, fluted cutters, and a variety of cookie cutters; catalog

Williams-Sonoma Catalog for Cooks
Mail Order Department
P.O. Box 7456
San Francisco, California 94120-7456
(800) 541-2233
Specialty cookware including a variety of baking equipment, tools, baking and cake pans, molds and some ingredient items; catalog

Wilton Enterprises
2240 W. 75th Street
Woodridge, Illinois 60517
(630) 963-7100
Specialty baking and cake-decorating supplies including pastry bags and tips; catalog sells for $6.99; allow 4–6 weeks for delivery

The Wooden Spoon
P.O. Box 931
Clinton, Connecticut 06413
(800) 431-2207
Specialty cookware including pie
pans, cake domes, cooling racks,
biscuit cutters, and parchment
paper; catalog

Bakeries

Cheesecakes by JR
2841 W. Howard Street
Chicago, Illinois 60645
(773) 465-6733
Cheesecakes, pecan squares, and
brownies

Dinkel's Bakery
3329 N. Lincoln Avenue
Chicago, Illinois 60657
(800) 822-8817
Cakes, strudels, stollens, and
brownies

Dutch Maid Bakery
Tracy City, Tennessee 37387
(615) 592-3171
Applesauce fruitcakes

Eastern Lamejun Bakers
145 Belmont Street
Belmont, Massachusetts 02178
(617) 484-5239
Middle Eastern breads and
pastries

Eilenberger's Bakeshop
512 N. John/P.O. Box 710
Palestine, Texas 75802
(800) 831-2544
Pecan pies and cakes, fruitcake,
pound cake

Ericann Candy Company
9811 Townline Road
P.O. Box 225
Union Pier, Michigan 49129
(616) 469-1010
Holiday cookies

Fran's Chocolates, Ltd.
1300 East Pike Street
Seattle, Washington 98122
(800) 422-3726
Specialty chocolates and desserts

German Home Bakery
2950 Grace Lane
Costa Mesa, California 92626
(714) 540-0281
German-style breads, coffee cakes,
and strudels

Hank's Cheesecakes
1063 South Big Bend
St. Louis, Missouri 63117
(800) 466-HANK
Cheesecakes

Jaarsma Bakery
727 Franklin
Pella, Iowa 50219
(515) 628-2940
Dutch letters, pastries, and cookies

Just Desserts
1970 Carroll Avenue
San Francisco, California 94124
(800) 253-4438
Cakes, cookies, and brownies

Lehmann's Bakery
2210 Sixteenth Street
Racine, Wisconsin 53405
(414) 632-4642 (kringle hotline)
Danish kringle

New Glarus Bakery
534 First Street
New Glarus, Wisconsin 53574
(608) 527-5799
Christmas stollen

Nicole's Bakeshop
1505 Kingsbury
Chicago, Illinois 60622
(312) 640-8883
Holiday gift baskets

O & H Danish Bakery
1841 Douglas Avenue
Racine, Wisconsin 53402
(800) 227-6665
Danish kringle

Old Salem/The Town Merchant
(Winkler Bakery Products)
P.O. Box 10516
Winston-Salem, North Carolina
27108
(800) 822-5151
Moravian cookies, sugar cake mix,
and gifts

Pink Rose Pastry Shop
630 South 4th Street
Philadelphia, Pennsylvania 19147
(800) ROSE-383
Gift cookie tins, gift baskets,
brownies, and tarts

Poupart's Bakery
1902 W. Pinhook Road
Lafayette, Louisiana 70508
(318) 232-7921
King cakes

The Sweetery
1814 E. Greenville Street
Anderson, South Carolina 29621
(800) 752-1188
Uggly Cake, pound cakes, layer
cakes, brownies, and cookies

Villa Italia Pasticceria
3028 Hamberg Street
Schenectady, New York 12303
(800) 631-1442
Panettone and cookies

Wick's Pies, Inc.
217 Greenville Avenue
Winchester, Indiana 47394
(317) 584-8401
Sugar creams and assorted pies
(6-pie minimum for shipping)

Bakeries by Region

Northeastern

Alba Bakery
Alter's Bakery
Avenue Bakery
Cushman's
Diane's Bakery
Eastern Lamejun Bakers
Ebinger's
Grossinger's Bakeshop
Kaufman's
Massis
Orwasher's
Richer's Bakery
Scialo Bros. Bakery
Sevan
Ursula's European Pastries
Veniero's
Villa Italia Pasticceria

Eastern

Pink Rose
Rindelaub's Bakery
Shupp's

Tomaro's Bakery
Weaver's

Southeastern

Dot's
Epicure Gourmet Market
Gilbert's
Flakowitz
Sally Bell's
Sweetery
Winkler Bakery

Southern

Becker's
Dutch Maid
Eilenberger's Bakeshop
Haby's Alsatian Bakery
Poupart's

Western

Diamond Bakery
Dick's Bakery
Downtown Bakery & Creamery

German Home Bakery
Helm's Bakery
Italian French Baking Company
Just Desserts
Larraburu Brothers Bakery
Model Bakery
New Roma Bakery
Palo Alto Baking Company
27th Street Bakery

Northwestern

Black Diamond Bakery
Blakes
Boulangerie
Fran's Chocolates
Frombach's Old Home Bakery
Home Fires Bakery
Honey Bear Bakery
La Panzanella
Marsee Baking
Three Lions Bakery

Midwestern

Allegretti's
Bread Box Bakeshop
Burny Brothers

Cheesecakes by JR
Dessert Kitchen
Dinkel's
Eagel Bakery
Hank's Cheesecakes
Helmuth Country Bakery
Jaarsma Bakery
Jampot Bakery
Kirschbaum's
Lehmann's
Lilac Pastry Shop
Nauvoo Mill & Bakery
New Glarus Bakery
Nicole's Bakeshop
O & H Danish Bakery
Pasieka Bakery
Purwin's Cake Box
Ramberg's Bakery and Ericann
    Candy Company
Reynens
Suzanne's
Swedish Bakery
Tag's Pastry
Vesecky's
Wautlet's
Wick's Pies, Inc.

Index

Lucia buns, 54–55
Mardi Gras king cake, 58–60
panettone, 49–51
Yulekage, 56–57
holiday cranberry pie, 229–230
honey:
    almond brittle, for burnt almond cake, 110–111
    cake, Rosh Hashanah, 148
hot cross buns, 61–63
Houska, 74–75

I

icing(s):
    for hot cross buns, 61–62
    for Judy's cinnamon buns, 68–69
    lemon, 172–173
    for pecan kringle, 84–85
    for pumpkin banana muffins, 172–173
    for seven sisters almond coffee cake, 82–83
Indiana sugar cream pie, 219–220
ingredients:
    for pies and pastries, 213–214
    for special occasion cakes, 97–98
    for yeast-raised breads and rolls, 3–4
Irish soda bread, 162
Italian baker's loaf, 6–7

J

jam cake, Tennessee, 158–159
Judy's cinnamon buns, 66, 68–69

K

kimelwick rolls, 10–11
king cake, Mardi Gras, 58–60
kuchen, fruit, 92–93

L

lace cookies, for florentines, 190–191
layer cake(s):
    Danish, 98, 117, 121, 122–123
    seven-, lemon, 134, 136–137
    two-in-one, 112–113
leaves, chocolate, 184–185
lemon:
    cake, seven-layer, 134, 136–137
    chiffon cake, 152–153
    cream frosting, for seven-layer lemon cake, 136–137
    curd filling, for seven-layer lemon cake, 136–137
    glaze, for lemon poppy seed Bundt cake, 154
    icing, for pumpkin banana muffins, 172–173
    poppy seed Bundt cake, 154–155
    syrup, for New York–style charlotte russe, 141–142
    wafers, 202
letters, Dutch, 240–241
linzer dainties, 179, 186–187
loaf:
    brioche, 60
    country cornmeal, 163
    Dutch apple nut bread, 76–77
    English muffin, 40–41
    French, 6
    Houska, 74–75
    Italian baker's, 6–7
    prune, 146
    Sicilian, 6
    Vienna, 10–11
    Yulekage, 56–57
Lucia buns, 54–55

M

mail order source guide, 257–261

maple bars, 78–79
    glaze for, 78–79
marble:
    pound cake drizzled with chocolate, 156–157
    rye, 14, 15, 20–21
Mardi Gras king cake, 58–60
meringue:
    hazelnut, 130–131
    pie, pineapple, 223–224
    torte, chocolate hazelnut, 98, 130–131
Moravian sugar bread, 72–73
morning glory muffins, 171
mostly rhubarb pie, 217–218
mousse:
    chocolate rum, for chocolate roll, 138–139
    filling, chocolate, for chocolate hazelnut meringue torte, 130–131
mud cake, *see* Brooklyn chocolate decadence
muffin(s):
    loaf, English, 40–41
    morning glory, 171
    pumpkin-banana, with lemon icing, 172–173
    Sally Lunn, 42–43

N

natural sourdough starter, 32–33
    for sourdough biscuits, 32–33, 36
    for sourdough French baguettes, 32–33, 34–35
New York rye, *see* corn rye
New York–style charlotte russe, 98, 117, 141–142
nuts:
    apple bread, Dutch, 76–77
    toasting of, 111

O

oatmeal raisin scones, 168
old-fashioned Southern dinner rolls, 37

sweet yeast bun dough, 66,
68–69, 70
for Judy's cinnamon buns,
66, 68–69
for pecan sticky buns, 66,
70
yeast for, 47
syrup(s):
for butter rum cake,
150–151
for cassata cake, 124–125
for custard-filled baba,
236–237
for hot cross buns, 61–62
hot rum, 150–151
lemon, 141–142
for New York–style charlotte
russe, 141–142
rum, 124–125, 236–237
simple, 61–62

T

tart(s):
blueberry cheesecake,
254–255
caramel pecan, 250, 252
plum and almond cream,
252, 253
tart pastry dough, 252
for caramel pecan tart, 250,
252
for plum and almond cream
tart, 252, 253
Tennessee jam cake, 158–159
Terry's cornmeal cranberry
scones, 170
timing, for sourdough French
baguettes, 35
tips and techniques:
for cookies, 179–180
for flaky biscuits, 165
for pies and pastries,
213–214

for quick breads, cakes, and
biscuits, 145
for special occasion cakes,
97–99
for yeast-raised breads and
rolls, 3–5
for yeast-raised holiday
breads, coffee cakes,
and sweet rolls, 47–48
toasted almond shortbread, 196
topping(s):
almond, 225–226
for apple custard pie,
225–226
for blackberry cobbler bars,
204–205
chocolate, 190–191
cobbler, 204–205
for florentines, 190–191
for marble pound cake
drizzled with chocolate,
156–157
for New York–style charlotte
russe, 141–142
for pineapple meringue pie,
223–224
for snickerdoodles, 188
whipped cream, 141–142
torte, chocolate hazelnut
meringue, 98
turnovers, big apple, 242,
244–245
twists, chocolate, 242, 246
two-in-one cake, 98, 112–113

U

upside-down cake, pineapple,
98, 114–115

V

vanilla:
cake, for marble pound,
156–157

filling, for florentines,
190–191
glaze, for sweet potato
biscuits, 166
Vienna bread, 10, 11

W

wafers, lemon, 202
wheat walnut bread, 24–
25
whipped cream:
filling, for chocolate roll,
140
frosting, chocolate, for
chocolate knockout
cake, 103–104
topping, for New York–style
charlotte russe,
141–142
white chocolate:
apricot–, chunk cookies,
194
cheesecake with raspberry
glaze, 98, 128–129
cream cheese–, filling, for
chocolate knockout
cake, 103–104
filling, for white chocolate
cheesecake with
raspberry glaze,
128–129
Wisconsin sour cherry pie,
231–232

Y

yeast:
for bread dough, 4
for sweet bun dough,
47
yeast-raised breads and rolls, *see*
breads and rolls, yeast-
raised
Yulekage, 56–57